PTSD

PTSD

Diagnosis and Identity in Post-empire America

Jerry Lembcke

LEXINGTON BOOKS
Lanham • Boulder • New York • Toronto • Plymouth, UK

Published by Lexington Books
A wholly owned subsidiary of Rowman & Littlefield
4501 Forbes Boulevard, Suite 200, Lanham, Maryland 20706
www.rowman.com

10 Thornbury Road, Plymouth PL6 7PP, United Kingdom

British Library Cataloguing in Publication Information Available

Library of Congress Cataloging-in-Publication Data

Lembcke, Jerry, 1943- author.
PTSD : diagnosis and identity in post-empire America / Jerry Lembcke.
pages cm.
Includes bibliographical references and index.
ISBN 978-0-7391-8624-4 (cloth : alk. paper) -- ISBN 978-0-7391-8625-1 (electronic)
1. Post-traumatic stress disorder--United States. 2. Veterans--Diseases--United States. 3. War--Psychological aspects. I. Title. II. Title: Post-traumatic stress disorder.
RC552.P67L398 2014
616.85'21--dc23
2013041560

Printed in the United States of America

Contents

Acknowledgements

I am grateful to my writers group, Tim Black, Chris Doucot, Mary Erdmans, Bill Major, and Jim Russell, for their critical reading of early drafts leading to this book. Conversations about veterans and PTSD with Lynn Barowski, Carolyn Howe, Laura Gross, Jeremy Kuzmarov, Linda Peterson, and Heather Walton were also helpful. Holy Cross College students Adair Bender, Mary Conner, and Carolyn Morrison read the entire manuscript and made good suggestions for changes. Kati Chorbanian helped with data searches, and Molly Del Howe-Lembcke prepared power-point presentations from the book material. Holy Cross librarians Eileen Cravedi, Gudrun Krueger, and Diana Antul were generous with their time and skills. Administrative Assistant Michele Latour solved many computer problems for me and just generally kept my work life better organized than it would otherwise have been. I am thankful for my long-standing friendships with Beverly and Levon Chorbajian, John and Lorraine Connelly, Corey Dolgon, Gib Fay, Mary Hobgood, Walter Landberg, Deborah Milbauer, and Bob Ross, and for the new friendships with Carol Austad, David Blitz, Larry Feldman and Kathryn Robertson that were forged during the course of this writing.

Preface

Post Traumatic Stress Disorder has traced a meteoric trajectory. Out of the early 1960s when diagnostic manuals had no page for war trauma, screenwriters molded a traumatized Vietnam War veteran out of stock WWI shell shock imagery and their own imaginations. The twitchy and emotionally damaged veteran "flashing-back" to jungle warfare in films like *Motor Psycho* (1965) provided the prototype into which journalists and mental health workers would fit the disaffection and angry political dissent that many soldiers were bringing home from Vietnam. This early pop-culture imagery shaped a first draft of new diagnostic nomenclature called Post-Vietnam Syndrome.

During the 1970s, PVS was honed into a medical alternative to the political discourse of the anti-war veterans' movement, achieving legitimacy as Post Traumatic Stress Disorder with its inclusion in the Diagnostic and Statistical Manual of the American Psychiatric Association in 1980.

Post Traumatic Stress Disorder encoded a victim-veteran identity that dovetailed during the 1980s with lost-war lore such as veterans spat on by protesters, and POWs left behind in Southeast Asia, to construct a betrayal narrative for the American defeat. By 1990, the memory of veterans marching arm-and-arm with pacifists to end the war was obscured by the mythology that the war had been lost on the home front, with the image of troops empowered and politicized by their wartime experience pushed off screen by figures of emotional and psychological casualties.

The political and affecting appeal of PTSD, enhanced in the social climate of the 1980s, underwrote analogies such as "like Vietnam veterans" upon which inquiries into distressed populations in the farm belt, workers displaced by layoffs in the rust belt, Judith Herman's study of sexual trauma, and Cathy Caruth's look into the very definition of trauma would be based.

The malleability of PTSD meanwhile, lent it to use in legal cases involving veterans for which it provided defense rationales for innocence. Massachusetts Governor William Weld pardoned Joseph Yandle, convicted in 1992 for second degree murder, after hearing Yandle's claim that trauma suffered in Vietnam accounted for his crime. Yandle was later rearrested after it was found that he had never been in Vietnam. By the end of the 1990s, the Veterans Administration and other health programs were swamped with disability claims based on PTSD, so many of them false that the concept of "factitious PTSD" gained a standing in the mental health literature.

The power of PTSD imagery in film—well into the 1990s, Hollywood portrayed almost all Vietnam veterans as physically and mentally damaged—and the allure of it as a sympathetic framing for veterans' coming home stories, meant that by the time soldiers returned from the Persian Gulf War of 1990-91 the home-from-war-and-hurt narrative dominated the expectations of storytellers and listeners alike. Thirteen years later when the first veterans of the 2003 invasion of Iraq began returning, PTSD had morphed into yet another mode of discourse, that of "the purple heart" as a badge of honor credentialing the combat bona fides of the awardees. Symptoms of psychic disorder were equated with physical impairments as validation for martial accomplishment; the absence of visible symptoms, in turn, a conjurer of the "unseen wounds" currently at work in manufacturing PTSD's latest permutation, Traumatic Brain Injury.

There is a vast literature on the origins of PTSD in America's post–Vietnam War experience, and its application as a diagnostic category to the needs of subsequent generations of war veterans and victims of other forms of trauma. This book, however, builds on a focused set of critical studies interested in the political and cultural properties of PTSD as a socially constructed category whose meaning is only partly derived from its medical context.

The best of the constructionist studies of PTSD are those by anthropologist Allan Young whose 1995 book *The Harmony of Illusion: Inventing Post-Traumatic Stress Disorder* set the standard for critical scholarship on the subject, and cultural studies professor Elaine Showalter whose 1997 book *Hystories* crossed sex and gender boundaries, pushing the study of hysteria into the realm of male post-war trauma. Their critical approach is enhanced by other historical scholarship that finds patterns in the formulation of war trauma going back to World War I, and the way cultural forces shaped what doctors looked for and found; notable among those are Anne Harrington's *The Cure Within: A History of Mind-Body Medicine*; Wilbur Scott's *The Politics of Readjustment: Vietnam Veterans Since the War*; and Ben Shepard's *A War of Nerves: Soldiers and Psychiatrists in the Twentieth Century*.

Of particular interest to my study is the way that art, photography, silent film, and later Hollywood film all played roles in their respective time periods to write and rewrite the tangled story of military experience, masculinity, medical practice, and political and popular culture. The titles alone of some of those studies suggest the kind of imaginative and critical insight their authors have brought to the subject: Georges Didi-Huberman's *Invention of Hysteria: Charcot and the Photographic Iconography of the Salpêtrière*; Sander Gilman's *Seeing the Insane*; and Anton Kaes,

Shell Shock Cinema: Weimar Culture and the Wounds of War. The story told by these authors continues into the present with the interventions of news media, theater, and entertainment venues, an extension of their work that I make in this book.

Constructionist writing about PTSD is inevitably met with the objection, "So, you think PTSD isn't real?" A casual reading of the following chapters might seem to confirm that that is my thinking. But the reality of the medical condition known as PTSD is not my concern here. Rather, my concern is with the labeling of that condition's symptoms as PTSD, and how that terminology gained acceptance. Indeed, I hope to show that the reality of PTSD is far greater than that given it by medical science. With historical perspective we can see the antecedents of PTSD spawned in previous wars having evolved a realness that now extends into political and cultural spheres with consequences for the entire society.

Among its other missions this book is an epistemological excursion along the soft boundary between subjective and objective notions for what is real, and an inquiry into the imperious nature of PTSD that has enabled its expansion from diagnostic category to a social trope.

The sociological calling for this book is, then, to suggest that the American post- and *lost*-war experiences in which trauma discourse became pervasive have also nourished sentiments of resentment and vengeance that are silently maturing into a reactionary, and dangerous, end-of-empire culture. The political hope inspiring the book is that the critical introduction of those lost-war themes to the wither-America conversation might also point to their apocalyptic consequences and, thereby, encourage a search for different directions in how we think, talk, and write about who and what we are.

Chapter One

Wound on the War Front, Alibi on the Home Front: Post Traumatic Stress Disorder in Medical and Legal Guise

With the Sunday *New York Times* tucked under my arm, I boarded the Metro North train in New Haven bound for Grand Central Station. Getting seated and unfolding the paper, my eyes were drawn to a montage of twenty-four men's faces that filled the top two-thirds of the front page. The caption beneath the photographs reading "Postscripts to Combat" led to an article by Deborah Sontag and Lizette Alvarez entitled "Across America, Deadly Echoes of Foreign Battles." Together, the collection of individual portraits with the accompanying words was evocative enough of my interest in post-war culture and the representations of veterans in news media, film, and literature to draw me into the story.

MATTHEW SEPI'S STORY

The hint of something familiar in this mid-January 2008 story turned quickly to affirmation as I began to read—and affirmation turned to silent conjecture: Could I write the ending of the article before reading it? Sontag and Alvarez were reporting the case of Matthew Sepi, a 20-year-old Iraq War veteran who headed out to a

7-Eleven one summer night in 2005. On his way, he bought two cans of beer from a stranger, alcohol being his self-prescribed medication for Post Traumatic Stress Disorder. He was in a seedy neighborhood, a part of the city that became "like Falluja" after dark, a local homicide detective told the reporters. Falluja was the city in Iraq that saw heavy fighting in 2003 and with that my mind leaped ahead of the words on the page: Sepi had been at Falluja and his path to the mini-mart two years later was reminiscent of that experience; now, he has a flashback that revives the kill-or-be-killed response drilled into him by military training; Sepi kills someone he imagines to be an enemy terrorist. But it's 2005 and he's in Las Vegas—who did he really kill?

Playing the investigator, my mind plied the algorithms that matched the details of this story with those I had become acquainted with while writing a 1999 article, "'The Right Stuff' Gone Wrong: Vietnam Veterans and the Social Construction of Post-Traumatic Stress Disorder." So far, the story resembled one reported by Jon Nordheimer in the *New York Times* in 1971. In that one, Dwight Johnson had gone berserk during a battle at Dak To four years earlier. After treatment for depression at a Veterans Administration center, he was killed during a late night hold-up at a Detroit liquor store.[1]

My thoughts drifted away from the page. Was the similarity between Sepi's and Johnson's stories just coincidental? Had Johnson's story gotten sifted into barracks lore over the years, becoming a kind of home-from-war war story, pieces of which found their way into post-service scenarios the current generation of veterans imagined for themselves? Flashbacks could be as much about imagination as memory, so where might the balance between them be in this case? If not Johnson's story, maybe one from a movie resembling it—lot's of choices there, I knew.[2]

Or, I wondered, were the reporters Sontag and Alvarez familiar enough with the writing of their older colleague Nordheimer to have used what he wrote as a template to arrange the details of Sepi's story into a form their editors and readers would recognize?

But Iraq War veteran Matthew Sepi hadn't killed someone at the 7-Eleven or been killed there himself. In fact, he never got to the store. On his way out of the house that evening, he had grabbed his AK-47 because he was scared of the neighborhood. Waylaid by some street thugs after purchasing his beer, Sepi "snapped" and turned his assault rifle on them, killing one and wounding another. Later arrested by police, he lapsed into combat jargon to explain his response: he had "taken fire" before "engaging the targets" and then "breaking contact" with the enemy.[3]

The divergence of Sepi's details from those of Johnson sent my mind back through its file of cases involving war veterans and violence. He hadn't been killed like Dwight Johnson so how does the story end? War veteran, military weapon, a flashback to the war triggered by familiar images, a crime committed, and the veteran arrested—what comes next? Is this like Joseph Yandle's case? Yandle was convicted of murder for his role in a 1972 robbery. Later, he plied the press with a story that PTSD from his service in Vietnam made him dependent on heroin, money for which led him to commit the robbery. His story caught the ear of Massachusetts governor William Weld who commuted his sentence. Sepi used PTSD as an alibi and gets off—is that where this goes? I thought it might be.

Reading deeper into the *Times* 5,600 word report that ran across three pages, I learned that police found an assortment of weapons and 180 rounds of ammunition in Sepi's car but sympathized with him nevertheless, a veteran victimized by street violence. His public defender told Alvarez and Sontag that when she asked him about PTSD, "he starts telling me about Iraq and all of a sudden his eyes well up with tears, and he cries out: 'We had the wrong house! We had the wrong house!' And he's practically hysterical." In a deal the reporters labeled "unusual," charges against Sepi were dropped in return for his successful completion of treatment for substance abuse and PTSD.[4]

The deal that ended Sepi's legal case may have been "unusual" but what bears greater scrutiny is how the authorities' empathy for him came to pass. Why, in a sense, did they deem a down-and-out veteran who killed a woman with a weapon associated with terrorists, the AK-47, more deserving of sympathy and legal privilege than his victims who by all appearances were at least as dispossessed and deserving of compassion as he? And what role did the power of suggestion play in Sepi's embrace of the PTSD defense? As reported, it seems the lawyer's question about PTSD caused him to remember something he had forgotten or repressed but Alvarez and Sontag don't explore for us how the legal context of his situation and the complexities of remembering and forgetting might be related. And where did the lawyer get her sense that PTSD might be appropriated for a legal strategy? Was she familiar with the Joseph Yandle case or cases like it?

THE VICTIMS: WOMEN AND CHILDREN

The report featuring Matthew Sepi was the first in the *Times* series about 121 veterans of the wars in Iraq and Afghanistan who had been charged with homicide for killings committed after their return home. About a third of the victims were spouses, girlfriends, and children; among them two-year-old Krisiauna Calaira Lewis who was slammed against a wall by her father, an Iraq War veteran, who then pled guilty to murder and confessed to having sexually abused her. The trauma and stress of combat were implicated in many of the cases, according to Alvarez and Sontag.

The emphasis given the male-on-female number of crimes held my interest in the *Times* series. I knew that women were often the victims in cases involving veterans, PTSD, and violence. The story of the Vietnam veteran who strangled his wife during the night and later claimed he had had a nightmare or flashback and thought she was a Viet Cong was a cliché in the anthology of legal alibis. As is the power of cliché, however, the late-night parry of the bed-mate enemy endured as a kind of lore, crossing generations and leeching into broader spectrums of popular culture. The cartoonist G.B. Trudeau gave it new life when he brought his character Army Specialist "Toggle" home from Iraq with PTSD. Released from the hospital, Toggle begins a relationship with Alex, and just after the affair turns serious, Toggle experiences his first flashback. Curiously, or so it should seem to discerning readers, the combat scene revisited in the nightmare is unrelated to the bombing incident responsible for his injury. Has Trudeau gotten careless or is he signaling something else about the mismatch between Toggle's experience and his symptoms?

Toggle awakes with his hands on Alex's head—"Can you let go of my head?" she asks. The next day, Toggle wonders aloud if he should check into a vet's center for counseling but tells Alex that he doesn't like to talk about personal stuff. "Personal stuff," she wryly asks, "like a serious new girlfriend?"[5]

With the inimitable nuance of Trudeau's work, it's no surprise that the skepticism of PTSD as medical nomenclature and the latent danger in it to mask misogynist impulses, conveyed through Toggle, would be missed by those with a stake in the more conventional and sympathetic representations of war veterans. When the "Toggle" series was collected for the volume *Signature Wound: Rocking TBI*, the foreword to it, written by former Chairman of the Joint Chiefs of Staff, Marine General Peter Pace, was filled with platitudes about the service and sacrifice of those who "volunteered to protect the freedoms we hold dear."[6]

In fact, Toggle's story—at both its literal and subtextual levels—had some basis in fact. For a 1988 documentary on PTSD, CBS News featured the case of "Steve," a supposed veteran of the Navy Seals who had attacked his mother during the night as Viet

Cong. B.G. Burkett investigated the case of "Steve" for his book *Stolen Valor* and discovered he had never been a Navy Seal. Other legal cases involving claims of PTSD as alibis for violence had also been later discredited. Joseph Yandle, for example, was returned to jail after it was discovered he had never been in Vietnam. Most provocative for its bearing on domestic violence was a 1994 article on the effect of combat experience on future marital relations in which authors Cynthia Gimbel and Alan Booth reported a tendency for Vietnam veterans to exaggerate their military experiences in order to explain their troubled marriages. It was a finding that reversed the expected sequence of war trauma leading to post-war marital problems to suggest that veterans' personal troubles led them to "discover" that they had been traumatized by combat— perhaps just as Toggle had.

WALTER SMITH'S STORY

The second edition in the *Times* series appeared a week later. Front page again, this long article by Deborah Sontag featured the case of Walter R. Smith, a combat veteran who drowned the mother of his twins, according to the caption beneath his photograph. Smith was a 25-year-old Marine Corps veteran of the war in Iraq who had deployed to Kuwait with the First Marine Division early in 2003. His Fox Company was involved in the invasion of Iraq and saw heavy fighting near Nasiriya on April 8. Returning stateside later in the year, Smith volunteered for marksmanship instruction at the Quantico marine base in Virginia. On the rifle range he was overtaken by what Sontag called "vivid, hallucinatory images of Iraq." Shortly thereafter the Marines began the process leading to his discharge for PTSD.[7]

On July 1, 2004, Smith argued with his father and then took a shotgun and ammunition, walked toward the nearby Wasatch Mountains, and left what Sontag called "goodbye messages for everyone" in his cell phone directory. One of his former Fox Company buddies called the police who intercepted him near a trailhead. He later told a friend that he had been "hoping for 'suicide by cop.'"

Later in the year, Smith reported to police that he had thoughts of killing a girlfriend; he acted in a threatening manner toward another. He also began dating Nicole Speirs who shortly became pregnant with twins. Smith doubted he was the father and left the relationship for yet another woman whom he threatened with abuse. Seven months after Speirs delivered twins, Smith returned but resisted her desire for love and marriage. On March 25, 2006, Smith drowned Speirs in the bathtub. Smith took the twins out of town for a day and then returned to report her death to authorities who subsequently ruled it a suicide.

On December 3, 2006, after a few months of co-parenting the twins with Nicole Speirs's parents, Smith checked himself into the local Veterans Administration hospital and confessed his responsibility for her death. The prosecutor, Gary K. Searle, however, began collaborating almost immediately with Smith's attorney, Matthew Jube, to construct a "duress" alibi for the killing that cited trauma suffered by Smith in Iraq and allowed him to avoid a charge of murder by pleading guilty for manslaughter.

The Speirs were upset with the sentencing, telling Sontag that war was not an excuse for the killing. Their feelings were understandable but my thoughts were as much on the way the *Times* had covered this and the Sepi story—indeed, I wondered, what was the story the newspaper thought it was covering? The loss of a daughter to the Speirs family and the tragedy of veterans' descent into crime were newsworthy at the time of their occurrence but what was the story the *Times* was deriving from the Smith and Sepi cases, now two and three years old?

Within days after the *Times* series began, letters poured into the paper complaining that Sontag and Alvarez were exaggerating the problems and generalizing from the cases they reported in a way that damaged the reputation of all veterans of Iraq and Afghanistan. In his January 27, 2008, column, the *Times* Public Editor Clark Hoyt addressed the critics and shared his own qualms about the series. Hoyt's intervention was telling because the public editor's position was only about five years old, having been created as a firewall to journalistic malpractice. The missteps assigned to Sontag and Alvarez didn't rise to the level of malpractice, and the inquiry into their reporting by Hoyt was confined to narrow issues like how they had handled the comparison of veterans' crime rates with rates for the general population. Although Hoyt himself puzzled over what it was that the reporters had really been after with the series, he never pressed the issue. In any case, my interest in the stories was different.[8]

GLANCING BACK ON PTSD

Sontag and Alvarez weren't working the court-reporter beat for this series so much as a human-interest angle on post-war culture and the way that trauma experienced in Iraq was now playing out at home. But they seemed to be taking the merits of PTSD as an alibi for murder at face value, concerning themselves only with the traumatic effects of war and the inadequacy of care available to veterans. Again, echoes of *Times*-stories-past crossed my mind. I recalled the *Times* having been seminal in the formulation of PTSD as a diagnostic category 35 years earlier. For my book *The Spitting Image: Myth, Memory, and the Legacy of Vietnam* I had written critically of the part played by the *Times* in bringing PTSD to the fore as a way of talking about veterans' homecoming experiences that downplayed political issues.

In the early years, the return of soldiers from Vietnam was unremarkable. Writing in *Shook Over Hell*, his study of PTSD, Eric Dean says veterans were finding jobs so readily that the GI Bill was under-utilized. The *New York Times*, he wrote, actually complained editorially that the favoritism being lavished on returnees risked creating a "permanent privileged class of veterans." Newspapers, he said, reported "strangers on the street approaching the Vietnam vet to thank him for his service" or pick up his check in a restaurant. All that changed in 1968 when the Vietnamese Tet Offensive fought the United States to a standstill, raising questions about the certainty that the war could be won. Simultaneously, reports of atrocities like My Lai in 1969 cast a shadow over the public image of veterans, and the disillusionment of troops returning by then put them in closer alignment with the anti-war movement.

In solidarity of the fall 1969 Moratorium Days against the war, some units in Vietnam refused orders to go on patrol; having returned from the war, some veterans formed Vietnam Veterans Against the War (VVAW) and joined the protests. These anti-war warriors were a troubling sight for many Americans, one that coupled with observations by conservative critics that the nation had grown soft in the years since World War II, permissive even, and that the kind of robust masculinity that had "fought the good fight" against fascism was being eroded by liberal parenting, feminism, and government entitlement programs. Men of "The Greatest Generation" had won their war but the long-haired veterans in the streets with the protesters were losing theirs; they weren't "real" men, averred some conservatives, better that the memory of them be expunged.[9]

Liberal observers, inclined toward opposition to the war themselves, were more likely to align with the military dissenters while at the same time precariously toeing a line that distinguished between legitimate political dissent on one side and expressions of emotional suffering wrought by the war on the other side; one side of that line called forth mutuality and solidarity, while the other side evoked empathy and help in healing. As the war wound down and the anti-war movement dissipated, some veterans made common cause with the help-in-healing workers for what would emerge from the American Psychiatric Association in 1980 as the new diagnostic category, Post traumatic Stress Disorder.[10]

The process leading to the inclusion of PTSD in APA's Diagnostic and Statistical Manual, the so-called "bible" used by clinicians to make judgments on mental health cases, was a hard-fought political one, waged on the field of public opinion and in the committee rooms of the APA. The famous psychiatrist Robert J. Lifton weighed in with *Home from the War*, a book about war trauma; churches sponsored conferences on the needs of veterans, and mental health professionals lobbied for and against the need for nomenclature specifically designed for veterans. Looking back on that struggle, however, psychiatrist Chaim Shatan, one of the principle architects of PTSD, pointed to the importance of the *New York Times* coverage of the Dwight Johnson story and its 1973 decision to publish an opinion piece on what was then called "post-Vietnam Syndrome," an op-ed that it had previously rejected. The Johnson story, recalled Shatan, became "the first public acknowledgement of a post-Vietnam Syndrome" while the op-ed produced what he called a "mushroom" of attention that energized the professional community's interest in war trauma.[11]

What the *Times* had in fact discovered was a mode of discourse that enabled political authorities and opinion shapers to pathologize the radical behavior of veterans opposed to the war, and thereby discredit it, while simultaneously appearing sympathetic to the plight of veterans. Going into the future, it was a discourse that shifted the focus away from controversies surrounding the war itself to easier-to-agree-upon concerns about men who fought the war, and began the rewriting of the war's history as a "mistake" that Americans and Vietnamese both paid dearly for. As a case of psychologizing the political, the construction of PTSD is a textbook illustration of how "badness" can be reframed as "sickness."[12]

PTSD: REENLISTED FOR NEW WARS

By the time President George H. W. Bush sent troops to the Persian Gulf in the fall of 1990, the image of the Vietnam-era soldiers and veterans at war against the war they were sent to fight was fading from public memory. In its place, most Americans saw the trauma-stricken victim-veteran, an image that was by then tangled with myths about home-front betrayal of the mission in Vietnam, and veterans traumatized by the hostility they felt when returning. [13]

Political and popular cultures are not so easily separated from the way mental health problems are thought about. The symptoms of PTSD, including flashbacks, appeared on theater screens at least fifteen years before they entered the DSM, a finding that made me question the firmness of the boundary between science and art. Looking downstream from the mid-1990s and the time when I speculated that the origins of PTSD lay beyond the realm of medical reasoning, I worried also that PTSD was evolving into a cultural category whose meaning as a signifier of mental health status could be overshadowed by other considerations. Its use by the defense in a homicide case, for example, could prompt prosecutors and relatives of the victim to cross the line questioning its *use*, to questioning its validity. From there, especially when rendered through the media and coffee-shop chatter about the news, the very "realness" of war trauma could become a discussable topic rather than a terrible reality needing public attention. It seemed possible, in other words, that the overextended application of PTSD could produce a backlash that diminished its potential to help the victims of war trauma it was intended for. [14]

In a different direction, was there a danger that the diagnostic purpose of PTSD could be supplanted by its power to actually *infuse* diagnostic situations with its own assumptions and logic? Would mental health professionals "find" PTSD because that was what they were looking for? Would returning soldiers adopt the symptoms of PTSD and a war-story biography that conformed to what they thought family and friends would expect to see and hear? And would newspaper reporters "find" sick veterans because they knew their readers would be trying to fit the aftermath of war and the coming-home experience of veterans into that mold?[15]

The imperious qualities of PTSD had been driven home rather dramatically to me at Clark University in the mid-1990s where I was giving a public talk about the myths and legends of war. Having laid out my thesis that spat-upon veterans were mythical, a fellow in the back row rose to object. Introducing himself, he began, "I'm 100 percent PTSD." The "I am" conjunction caught my ear because it said something different than what could have been said, such as, "I have been awarded a 100 percent disability claim from the V.A. for PTSD" (or some variant of that). In any case, PTSD had no place in my presentation that evening so I could only imagine he had reached for such cryptic medical phrasing as a way of credentialing what was to follow. Even more, the "I am" was delivered with a prideful intonation, a personal identification with an illness I would have expected to be shunned for the stigma it carried—was PTSD taking on an ontological character, morphing, in a sense, into something larger than its authors ever intended?[16]

I finished writing *The Spitting Image* as the symptoms reported by returnees from the Persian Gulf War were being bundled as "Gulf War Syndrome," a collection of ailments that included PTSD and cancer as well as new and mysterious maladies attributed to exotic weaponry like depleted uranium. I speculated in the last chapter of the book that the image of the victim-veteran had become such a compelling element in the American imagination of what the return from war should be that it was evoking the very health problems that it proposed to describe. It was a speculation that seemed all too justified when the soldiers dispatched to Iraq in the Spring of 2003 began returning.

Actually, the coming-home story of the Iraq War generation began to be written for them before they left the war zone. Science reporter Joseph B. Verengia framed the storyline that would shape news coverage of veterans for years to come when he asked in his April 18, 2003, story for the Associated Press, "How many soldiers will require mental health treatment?" Suggesting that past conflicts offered clues to the answer, he went on to report that one-third of Vietnam veterans returned emotionally wounded. Traumatized soldiers, he stated, "relive their horrors through flashbacks and nightmares, often followed by depression and fury." And like Vietnam, he pointed out, this war is colored by controversy and protests.

Unbeknownst to himself, Verengia was making prophetic words written by Dr. Robert H. Fleming for a 1985 article in the journal *Psychiatry*. Noting the emphasis given the psychological impact of combat by the media, Fleming wrote that, "In some instances there appears to be an almost neurotic need to regard the Vietnam veteran as being traumatized by war." But Verengia's extension of the Vietnam-era homecoming story to foretell the shape of post-Iraq coverage was missing one important detail: the outcome of the war. The war in Vietnam had been lost whereas the mission to Iraq was declared "accomplished" by President George W. Bush when he spoke on the aircraft carrier USS Abraham Lincoln on May 1, 2003.[17]

The first veterans of the war arrived stateside just in time for the Fourth of July. The 4th that year fell on a Friday, virtually ensuring that the holiday would be a flag-flying three-day weekend. The war was over, and won, so front page headlines blended patriotic themes with those of community pride and family reunions. A *St. Petersburg Times* story on June 29 reported the happy return to Florida of the Marine 365th Squadron—with no trauma cases in sight. *USA Today* followed with a celebratory July 2 story by Rick Hampson that contrasted the feel-good present with the bad vibes met by Vietnam veterans. On July 3 the *Kansas City Star* told of returnees anxious about their buddies still in the war zone but made no mention of PTSD or its symptoms. The most telling news account was a July 3 Associated Press story whose headline seemed to fulfill Verengia's forecast: "In 'unprecedented' effort, military prepares to screen soldiers for war illness." But the "illnesses" being screened for were coughs, rashes, and diarrhea with the problems of depression and insomnia given a past-tense association with "Gulf War syndrome" from ten years earlier—no trauma or PTSD in this report either.[18]

Was it really possible that the appearance of trauma, in newsprint or the clinic, was correlated with social, political, or cultural matters such as the perceived outcome of a war? It seemed so when ten days later the tone of the "homecoming" story changed: the 3rd Infantry Division's 1st and 2nd Brigades were unexpectedly given extended commitments in Iraq, their returns "postponed indefinitely." Sprinkled with references to soldiers "abandoned" and "marooned" with their "morale shattered" and their families "lied to," news about the delayed homecomings signaled a war not yet over, not yet won. And, as if on cue, PTSD returned to the vocabulary of news reporters and editors. "The Other Battle: Coming Home" announced *The Christian Science Monitor* on July 9 before reminding readers that 50 percent of Vietnam veterans suffer PTSD and that the longer time soldiers are in a battle zone, as was foreseen for the troops still in Iraq, the more likely they were to carry "mental burdens" from the experience.[19]

As the country settled into a war-without-end, the media settled into storylines displacing controversies over what the war was about with numbers from opinion polls, comparisons with the war in Vietnam, and casualty counts. Many of the stories about war veterans with PTSD appearing in the press during the first year of the war in Iraq were really about Vietnam veterans although one could imagine that reporters and editors intended them for readers anxious about soldiers in the Middle East. Stories of that type could have derived from a December 10, 2003, American Legion press release that found "a high rate of PTSD" among "Vietnam combat veterans" in the American Legion, and identified as a risk factor, "a perceived negative community attitude about their service in the war"—a nod to Americans believing that Vietnam veterans had been ill-treated upon their return.

The number of returnees in the summer of 2003 proved to be token, a byproduct of the President's May 1 photo-op staged on the carrier deck. The more authentic homecomings would follow, after the twelve to fifteen months of actual service in Iraq that the invasion forces would serve. Their return in the summer of 2004 and the likelihood that the going and coming of GIs and Marines would continue for months and years called for press coverage with sufficient emotional draw and narrative arc to catch and sustain their readers' interest. With the war in Iraq already being filtered through public memory of Vietnam, and PTSD topping the lists of many lunchroom conversations about the cost of war, it was no surprise that the second coming of the homecoming story would get a medical framing.

The medical hook wasn't the only choice, even for journalists with imaginations limited to storylines inherited from the Vietnam era. Prior to 1972, after all, the image of veterans marching arm-and-arm with other antiwar activists dominated the American view of their return. Even after the threat they posed to the orderly conduct of the Republican Party National Convention in Miami Beach that summer catalyzed the recasting of their "badness" as "sickness," the historical significance of GIs and veterans having turned against the war of their generation was indelible, its presence in the playbook of reportorial choices unavoidable. So, why hadn't Joseph Verengia asked if soldiers home from the war would be tearing up Eighth Avenue to prevent the renominaton of George W. Bush as president at the 2004 Republican convention? Why did he choose the medical framing, over a political one, for his speculations on veterans? And what were the consequences of his choice for the way returnees, their families and friends, imagined the homecomings to come?

CHANGING THE SUBJECT: FROM THE WAR TO THE WARRIORS

Other and even more powerful developments were converging on news organizations to push the political and economic issues surrounding the war off screen using the veteran homecoming story. By the summer of 2004 the *New York Times* was facing an unfolding scandal featuring its reporter Judith Miller and the role her reporting played in the rush to war during 2002. Miller's reports that Saddam Hussein was pursuing a nuclear weapons capability were wrong but government officials at the highest levels in the Bush administration pointed approvingly to her stories in their propaganda campaign to swing public opinion behind the invasion. Later, she would falsely claim that the U.S. military *had* found weapons of mass destruction (WMD), and be roundly renounced for relying on a sketchy and secret source known as "curveball" for the erroneous stories she had filed. [20]

To its embarrassment, the *Times* was revealed to have abided Miller's indiscretions for months, perhaps out of its own uncertainties about supporting or opposing the war. Now, with the war going badly and public support for it souring, the paper had no choice but to separate itself from Miller and the war she had used its pages to promote. She was fired in November, 2005, after an ugly standoff with federal prosecutors over the Valarie Plame CIA leak scandal and her 85 days of self-exile in prison that followed.

With that, the *Times*'s priorities shifted from the war and its ill-conceived ends, to the means of war, the men and women sent to fight it, and the damage done to them by service in Iraq. Counting the months back from January 2008 when the Sontag-Alvarez series was reader-ready, it makes sense that resources were committed to that project at about the time the *Times* looked in the mirror and reached for the makeover kit.

The *Times* series on veteran homicide cases ended a phase of my own thinking begun in the mid-1990s when it appeared to me that the narrative of veterans-as-victims, incubated during the closing years of the war in Vietnam and grown to maturity with the myth of veterans disparaged by the public and abused by protesters, the images of trauma-stricken veterans popularized by Hollywood film, and recognition of the diagnostic category PTSD, was being extended to frame the coming-home story of Persian Gulf War soldiers. Virtually every news organization in the country would do a "special" on "wounded warriors," many of them with a focus on the mental and emotional damage coming home in the uniforms.

One concern that I carried away from that period was the symbiosis of PTSD with other images, such as the spat-on veteran, that lent its use, even if unwittingly by the clinicians who championed it, to the construction of larger betrayal narratives for lost wars, and table-turning accounts from which "we," the perpetrators of military aggression and occupation, emerge as the victims of "them." In a similar fashion, PTSD's power to evoke the very symptoms it was trying to identify fit nicely with the apparent public need for heroes and willingness of pundits and some veterans to cash in disability as a credential for military accomplishment.

More troubling was that the hegemonic presence of PTSD in press coverage of the homecomings after the summer of 2003 not only displaced what might have been more political and authentic expressions of what returnees were feeling but virtually inoculated them against a political interpretation of their own experience. The possibility of a successful veterans' movement against the war under those conditions was slim.[21]

There was, finally, the eerie popularity of PTSD as a cultural category, a kind of seductiveness even, that drew some men to embrace it as an identity and their countrymen to assign it to whole cohorts of veterans as a badge of honor. In that light, PTSD becomes a kind of phenomenon that taps a cultural vein running through the American dark side to something very primal, a vein that will be mined for the coming chapters.

NOTES

1. The psychiatrist Chaim Shatan who is recognized for his work with Vietnam veterans, would later say that the trail of events leading to the professional acceptance of PTSD as a diagnosis began with Nordheimer's 1971 *Times* news report (Scott 1993, p. 643).

2. Frankel (1994, p. 321) wrote, "The content of a flashback appears to be at least as likely to be the product of imagination as it is of memory."

3. The details of Matthew Sepi's case are all drawn from Sontag and Alvarez (2008). Sepi killed Sharon Jackson, 47, and wounded Kevin Ratcliff, 36. Sepi claimed he had shot in self-defense but the reporters say it was never clear who shot first.

4. Alvarez and Sontag reported Sepi working as a welder in Phoenix in January 2008.

5. Other themes in the Toggle series, such as his dysfunctional family background, hinted at factors other than his experience in Iraq as playing into his post-war condition.

6. Trudeau (2010).

7. These details about Smith are drawn from Sontag (2008).

8. Eleven days before Hoyt's column, the January 16, 2008, edition of the *Times* printed seven letters that on balance conveyed a more positive and apparently misleading sense of how the readership was receiving the series. Responding to the first two weeks of the series, four of the letters were of a "support the troops" variety complaining that not enough was being done to help veterans and thanking the *Times* for pointing out the problem. Two writers said the articles had discredited soldiers, one saying: "it is contemptible to pander to the worldview that American troops are drunken, debt-ridden psycho killers." One of the letters, from a Vietnam veteran, reiterated the symptoms of PTSD from which he said he suffers 40 years after the war.

9. The conservative position on the war, as with the liberal position that follows, was not monolithic. An ultra-rightist wing that included the John Birch Society, for example, actually opposed the war. Nuances like this will be fleshed out in subsequent chapters.

10. Conrad and Schneider (1992) argue that the distinction between what is considered "criminal" and what is considered "sick" or "mad" is the outcome of social and political process.

11. Before PTSD, news media and popular culture had helped legitimate Shell Shock during World War I, and after PTSD, Traumatic Brain Injury in the early 2000s. The history of those cases will be reprised in subsequent chapters. In his 2012 (p. 154) book *Agent Orange: History, Science, and the Politics of Uncertainty*, historian Edwin Martini cites a 1978 documentary produced by Chicago television station WBBM-2 as "completely changing the political landscape of veterans' allegations about the exposure to Agent Orange."

12. Scott (1993) has the best account of the political wrangling leading to PTSD as a diagnostic category. The *Times* op-ed was Shatan's own (1973). The Johnson killing was reported by Nordheimer (1971). Martini (2007) has the best account of U.S. attempts to falsely balance the war's effects.

13. By the 1990s, a show of hands in my college classes would reveal that most students "knew" about Vietnam veterans with PTSD (or that they had been spat on by protesters), while few had ever heard of Vietnam Veterans Against the War, the largest single membership organization of that generation's veterans.

The co-mingling of war trauma with traumatic homecoming experiences in the discourse of PTSD *ala* veterans of Vietnam is seen in Raja Mishra's 2004 *Boston Globe* report: "The most recent studies found that about 30 percent of Vietnam veterans had developed psychological problems after the war, as condemnation of soldiers by stateside critics exacerbated combat stress in some." Mishra didn't cite the "recent studies" he was referring to.

14. See Gieryn (1999) of the interpenetration of science and non-science cultures. Mnookin (2011, pp. 79, 81-82) applies that critique to the way the vaccine-autism controversy gained media attraction.

15. The details in the origins of PTSD as a diagnostic category will be reprised in later chapters.

16. This fellow's apparent desire to conflate his PTSD identity with that of the alleged spat-on veteran is important because it suggests the "victim-veteran" identity that is the common denominator to both the medicalized lexicon provided by PTSD and the social-stigmata form provided by the spitting image. Going forward, PTSD would be claimed by some as a "wound" deserving of a Purple Heart; still others would claim PTSD as a credential for heroism. With admiration for Vietnam veteran and poet Lamont B. Steptoe in 2012, Horace Coleman wrote, "He got a CIB [Combat Infantry Badge], a Bronze Star, and eventually, a 100% PTSD rating."

17. Verrengia (2003); Fleming (1985, p. 123).

18. See Bynum (2003a), Bynum (2003b), Pendygraft (2003), and Robertson (2003). A LexisNexis search of Major US and World Publications, and News Wire Services, on August 4, 2009, for (Iraq War Homecoming PTSD) between July 1 and July 10, 2003, resulted in "No Documents Found." Repeating the search with "homecoming" dropped from the terms sought, produced no documents. Repeating the search again with "homecoming" retained but PTSD dropped from terms sought, resulted in 114 items returned.

19. Tyson (2003). The discrepancy in Tyson's reference to 50 percent of Vietnam veterans suffering from PTSD and the 33 percent cited by Verengia is

typical of the data on PTSD and war veterans, a matter addressed in later chapters.

20. Friel and Falk (2007) have the best account of Miller and the *Times*. Rich (2006) is also helpful.

21. With remarkable candor, Jon Myatt, spokesman for the Florida Department of Military Affairs, explained to *New York Times* reporter Jan Hoffman (2009) that today's dramatic and public homecoming receptions featuring spouses and children (sometimes staged at elementary schools) help separate emotions about the troops from feelings about the war. These "mini-dramas," as Hoffman called them, are an institutional response to the politicized climate created by the war in Vietnam.

Chapter Two

Post Traumatic Stress Disorder: The Coming-home Story for a New Generation of Veterans

By January 2008 the country was already awash in news reports on veterans framed by mental health issues. Among the news organizations and city newspapers that had done a series or special report on the subject were the *Pittsburgh Tribune-Review* (February 2005), the *Washington Post* (November 2004), and *USA Today* (October 2007). The *New York Times* itself wasn't a wallflower in the months and years leading to the Sontag-Alvarez series, having run major stories in January of 2006 and an op-ed, "For some, the War Won't End" by Sally Satel.[1]

One of the largest and most powerful examples was the *Boston Globe's* four-part series in 2006. Written by Thomas Farragher and entitled "The War after the War," the series began on October 29 and featured troubled men prone to violence, men with substance abuse problems and difficulties maintaining home and work lives after service in Iraq. Coupled with an online photo gallery, the 20,000 words given the articles ending on November 1 left little space in readers' minds for thinking about the return from war outside the PTSD frame of reference. But was there an outside?

NO DIFFERENT DRUMMER

The anti-war coffeehouse named "The Different Drummer" opened in Watertown, New York, near Fort Drum in November 2006. Started by veterans of the war in Iraq with help from the anti-war organization Citizen Soldier, Different Drummer revived what had begun as "the coffeehouse movement" during the war in Vietnam.

Founded by Vietnam veteran Fred Gardner, the first Vietnam-era coffee house opened near Fort Jackson, South Carolina, in 1967. Soon, others opened at sites near Fort Hood, Texas, Fort Lewis, Washington, Fort Bragg North Carolina, and other military posts. The coffeehouses provided GIs a space free from the watchful eyes of military authorities where they could commiserate, get legal services, and organize resistance to the war. They also provided a meeting ground where veterans of the war, back from duty in Southeast Asia, could talk to and educate those who were about to be shipped to the war zone. Community anti-war activists, too, frequented the coffeehouses to build alliances with uniformed dissenters.

The Drummer started up in Watertown in 2006 almost simultaneously with the *Globe*'s series, providing a cue to a different coming-home narrative that reporter Farragher could have developed, a storyline more resonant with the one that dominated news coverage of Vietnam returnees from the late-1960s through veteran protests at the Miami Beach Republican convention in August, 1972. Indeed, with so much of the Iraq War reportage filtered through references to Vietnam, an account of disaffected veterans emboldened by their experience in war, like their predecessors, would have reconnected readers with historical subjects relevant to political campaigns gearing up for the 2008 elections. But Farragher didn't go that way and it's worth a moment's reflection to consider why.

It's possible, of course, that he didn't know about Different Drummer. Or he did, but did not know the history and legacy that it was part of. It's unlikely, though, that he could have missed the related, and larger, formation of Iraq Veterans Against the War that had formed at Boston's Fanuel Hall in the days before the Democratic Party convention in July 2004. Virtually all news reports of that founding tagged it to Vietnam Veterans Against the War, the organization that candidate-in-waiting at the time, John Kerry, had been instrumental in forming thirty-three years earlier. Members of VVAW were prominent at the IVAW founding, and in the weeks and months that followed, news reports on IVAW's activities commonly mixed in references to its predecessor.

Still, having written a book on the way CNN producer April Oliver ruined her career and almost destroyed the news organization she worked for by bungling the investigation of a Special Forces raid in Laos in 1971—because she didn't know the background of the story she reported—I knew that the professional standards for journalists' familiarity with history were pretty low. As was the case with Oliver, however, I suspected that what Farragher *didn't* know was only half the problem: the other half was what he *did* know, or thought he knew, which was that war veterans come home traumatized, victimized by their experience. The image of veterans moved to political action against the war they had just fought didn't fit with the then-dominating public image of veterans returning as damaged goods.

That image was so prominent that it would have been difficult for Farragher to develop a counter-narrative to it even if he had wanted to. By the fall of 2006 the antiwar movement was being driven by a "cost of war" discourse that diverted attention from the political, economic, and military imperatives that were driving the war policies of the Bush administration. Early IVAW efforts to "bring the war home" through guerilla theater enactments in public spaces were overshadowed by humanitarian appeals for mental health care for veterans and public displays of boots and crosses depicting American losses in lives and limbs. The emotional appeal of the "cost of war" approach interfered with the integration of veterans as allies in the anti-war movement to a degree that some-times frustrated activists. At a New London, Connecticut, stop of the IVAW "base tour" in 2006, Thomas Barton, editor of *G.I. Special Newsletter* complained to me that public preoccupation with PTSD made it harder to organize. "Everywhere we go," he said, "all people want to talk about is PTSD." Motioning to his comrades drinking beer and chatting with the local hosts, he asked me, "Do these guys look fucked-up to you?"[2]

If there was a different drummer to be heard when *Globe* report-er Farragher wrote in the fall of 2006, its beat was but a discordant tap in the din of med-speak about veterans by 2009. The Thoreau-inspired coffeehouse outside Fort Drum had closed leaving an elec-tronic vestige with a homepage that headlined "Army suicides" and "violence by returning GIs," with sidebars on "the new Gulf War syndrome" and the "record use of anti-depressants" by troops in Iraq and Afghanistan. There was a link to an Associated Press story about Sgt. Andre Shephard's protest of the war in Iraq through his desertion in Germany but there was nothing on the page about organizing.[3]

Under the Hood coffeehouse opened near Fort Hood, Texas, just as Different Drummer closed its doors. Managed by Army spouse Cindy Thomas, the cafe signaled its commitment to the health-services agenda that had by that time overrun the culture of the veterans' movement. Its marquee nailed to a tree at streetside read-ing "There are no Unwounded Soldiers in War," captured the pow-er of PTSD to medicalize the image of veterans even in the absence identifiable injuries. A video presentation of the café's mission began with Ms. Thomas talking about the "cost of war" through oblique references to her husband's PTSD and Traumatic Brain Injury. A few veterans who frequented Under the Hood spoke about their marital problems and other adjustment issues and ex-pressed their dislike of the military and war but the 28-minute clip was bereft of political analysis or strategy.[4]

Coffee Strong outside Fort Lewis in Lakewood, Washington, likewise reflected the approaching hegemony of the mental health paradigm. Its September 2009 five-sentence web page announced Coffee Strong as a service provider with PTSD mentioned twice as something visitors might get help with. Further on the page, the Vietnam-era coffeehouse movement was acknowledged as an inspiration for the new venture but the words "anti-war" or "organizing" were not used. A two-month-old link to a screening of *Sir! No Sir!*, the documentary film about the GI antiwar movement of the 1960s and 1970s, did bring to mind the more radical history of that period but nothing on the Coffee Strong homepage recalled that the Fort Lewis coffeehouse of those years, The Shelter Half in nearby Olympia, had been effectively shut down by military authorities who declared it off limits to troops. The Coffee Strong manager, Iraq War veteran Seth Manzel told reporter Jon Anderson for a 2010 *Army Times* story that, "We tried to keep the place very neutral in terms of our views on the war."[5]

There's no gainsaying that veterans have personal and health-related problems and that service providers, be they professionals working in institutions or volunteers in informal settings like off-base coffeehouses, play an important role in their lives. The news stories about the health needs of veterans, moreover, can catalyze social movements for better funded services and, in the course of doing that, broaden the agenda of public discussion about war-related issues.

Nevertheless, the treatment of war trauma is different than the prevention of war trauma and humanitarian appeals in behalf of wars' victims are different than appeals for solidarity *with* them to solve international problems through negotiated settlements rather than war. Soldiers and veterans approached as men and women with political agency can be leaders in a campaign for peace; approaching them as casualties deserving of sympathy, however, diminishes their status and sidelines the capacity they bring to the cause.

A "SHRINK" OR A SOCIAL MOVEMENT?

The foregrounding of mental health issues on the same Coffee Strong homepage that slid *Sir! No Sir!* into a sidebar creates some poignant irony. The film compiles the historical record of the rank-and-file rebellion that grew during the War in Vietnam and reached the level of mutiny by the war's end. Question and answer sessions following the film's screenings often lead to comparisons between then and now—the resistance of soldiers and veterans of the Vietnam years as portrayed in the film, compared with the more compliant posture of troops today toward political and military authority.[6]

Not surprisingly, the audience drawn to the anti-war flavor of *Sir! No Sir!* uses the past as a basis for criticism of the present, leading participants to ask why so few uniformed Americans are moved to resistance today when so many were in a state of insurgency just a generation ago? Typical responses to the question take the form of there is "no movement" today, by which discussants seemed to mean there is no larger, more general movement for social reform that might succor the efforts of would-be in-service resisters. That answer, though, would bend back on itself into more questions: *why* is there no movement? Why isn't there a movement now like there was then?

The "no movement" response packs a bit of nostalgia for times that may be better in memory than they were in reality, and romance for "the day" can diminish awareness that the mobilizations against the invasion of Iraq that loomed in February and March of 2003 were enormous. Similar questions can be raised about the claim that the news media was more forthcoming with information about the war in Vietnam than current conflicts. A quick comparison of newspaper coverage of the two wars suggests that the public got *far more* information about the war in Iraq than it did about the war in Vietnam. The real problem may be more Huxlian than Orwellian, more a problem with what *is* in American living rooms— *American Idol* and ESPN—than what is not.

By seeing the GI movement as an appendage of other oppositional efforts of the time, moreover, one of *Sir! No Sir!*'s most important points is obscured, namely, that in-service opposition to the war in Vietnam had a degree of autonomy from developments in the civilian world. Donald Duncan quit the army in 1966, at a time when, as he recalls in the film, he was unaware of the anti-war movement; and it was in-service resister Howard Levy's vision of an alternative to the Bob Hope variety show that inspired Jane Fonda, Donald Sutherland, and others to form *FTA* (variously: Fun Travel Adventure or Free/Fuck the Army) that toured military bases in the U.S. and the Asian Pacific during 1971. It would be a mistake, though, to flip the analytical coin over and credit the early dissidents like Duncan with spawning the Vietnam-era movement that followed their path-breaking actions. Rather, the focus should be on the chemistry between military and civilian dissent and what is different decades later that helps account for the disinterest of many Americans, both in and out of uniform, in what their wars are all about.

One difference is the absence now of an embraceable enemy-other, an avuncular leader like Ho Chi Minh and a hardscrabble underdog like the National Liberation Front. In 1965, within weeks of the first Marines landing at Da Nang—when the U.S. government was still demonizing the Vietnamese as terrorists—"Women's Strike for Peace" saw something else in the "enemy" and sent a delegation to Hanoi to talk to them; a year later but still early in the war, the Quakers were taking medical aid to the communists; and by the end of 1967 American civilians acting independently of their government had negotiated the first prisoner releases. Within the military there was a similar recalibration of reality taking place. In *Sir! No Sir!* David Cline recalls looking at the Viet Cong soldier he had killed and thinking that that guy was fighting for his country too, and that he (Cline) had an obligation to honor what he died for and help end the killing.

Another difference lies in the cachet carried by veterans from previous wars. Some of the most credible voices in the early movement against the war in Vietnam were World War II veterans who could see that the U.S. war of aggression in Southeast Asia was perverting, turning inside-out, the principles of the "Good Fight" they had waged in Europe and the Pacific. Following the bloody battle for the Ia Drang Valley in 1965, for example, 500 veterans of previous wars signed a full-page November 24 advertisement in the *New York Times* protesting the expanding U.S. involvement in South Vietnam. Formed into a group called Veterans for Peace, these older-generation veterans helped distribute Donald Duncan's "I Quit" resignation from the Army and provided support for the Fort Hood Three who refused deployment to Vietnam in 1966.

Vietnam veterans, by contrast, cut a more complex figure in the eyes of today's military-eligible population. The image of activist Vietnam veterans was disparaged during the 1980s through the canonization of Post Traumatic Stress Disorder by mental health professionals and its use by the media to associate political dissent with psychiatric disorder. Thanks to Hollywood for having imaged Vietnam veterans almost universally as dysfunctional, troops in today's military would understandably find it hard to assess the credibility of the anti-war perspective coming from that generation of veterans; with their image of having gained in self confidence and political maturity through their experience in Vietnam all but obscured in popular culture by the figures of homeless and strung-out head cases, it is easy for the younger minds to smoosh "the political" and "the pathological" into one broad category of stigmata to stay clear of.

It's an image that *Sir! No Sir!* corrects for. The turning point of the film comes early when veteran Bill Short tells that he was sent to the unit shrink in Vietnam for refusing his assignment to conduct body counts of enemy killed. Taped for the film thirty-five years later while sitting in his own office, Short demonstrates how the psychiatrist turned to take something from a desk drawer, something that will determine Bill's future—and, we sense, frame the rest of the film's story. It's a pregnant moment that also locates the metaphorical fulcrum around which the construction of the veterans' image in post-war culture would turn.

Were the film to be paused at that moment, and the audience quizzed, many in the theater would say, "and the doctor pulled a diagnostic manual from the drawer and sent Sergeant Short stateside for psychiatric rehabilitation." A few might add some riffs from Charlie Clements's autobiography *Witness to War* about his confinement to a mental health ward for refusal to fly in Vietnam. Other viewers would remember that the Diagnostic and Statistical Manual used by mental health professionals at the time did not have a category for war-related trauma, so they might guess that the rest of the film tells the story of how Bill Short and the doctor joined forces to lobby for the new diagnostic category that became known as Post Traumatic Stress Disorder. But it's not the DSM that comes off the shelf and that's not the story that filmmaker David Zeiger thinks we need to know.

After his own pause, Short says the doctor pulled out a copy of the November 9, 1969, *New York Times*; Bill doesn't need treatment, he needs a social movement and here it is: a full-page advertisement against the war signed by 1,365 active-duty soldiers—[up-tempo music] the GI Movement is born.

FROM BADNESS TO MADNESS

The crossroad that was only a premonition in the moment when Bill Short's psychiatrist reached for the *New York Times*—one path leading to therapy, the other to organized resistance to war and the military—would become explicit with the formulation of PTSD, a process just then getting under way. We know now that the steps taken by Bill Short and his psychiatrist were not followed by the press and medical community. Rather, as the war and anti-war movement wound down, the dominant views of how soldiers and war veterans should behave were reasserted, and veterans' dissent in the post-war years would be redirected onto the path to therapy.

On October 15, 1969, the anti-war movement had reached new heights with its first Moratorium Day. Intended to be a day when business as usual would stop for teaching, organizing, and reflection about the war, Moratorium Day was a success by most measures: students stayed out of classes, workers stayed home, church bells rang, and hundreds of thousands of people turned out for protest activities.[7]

The Nixon administration's response in the following weeks was to try to drive a wedge between radicals and liberals in the movement, hoping to isolate the left. The "wedge" was rhetoric alleging the anti-war movement was betraying the military mission, a charge the government hoped would give liberals pause about their support for the movement.[8] The problem with the strategy was that by that time, thousands of GIs and veterans had come out against the war. Some GIs in Vietnam wore black arm bands in support of the Moratorium and refused orders to fight. Stateside, scores of servicemen and women joined civilians for rallies and marches against the war. By the end of the fall, Vietnam Veterans Against the War would be a major force within the antiwar movement.[9]

The anomaly of veteran and GI opposition to the war when the Nixon Administration was telling Americans that they should support the war because of the soldiers, required that the government neutralize, if not silence, the voice of these antiwar warriors. The initial efforts to do that involved statements raising suspicions about the authenticity of the anti-war vets and casting aspersions on their manliness. The administration also launched a campaign of disruption against VVAW that involved infiltrating informants and provocateurs into the organization. [10]

The attempts to gay bait and criminalize in-service and veteran resistors was short lived, displaced within a few months by a strategy to stigmatize anti-war soldiers as emotionally impaired casualties of the war who deserved sympathy and treatment but not political support. It was a strategy that moved the thin line separating badness from madness, widening the span of "treatable" behavior. It was a strategy that evolved into a campaign for a new diagnostic category that ended in 1980 when PTSD gained acceptance as professional terminology. The capacity to manage dissent inherent in the new concept lent its use to later generations of policy makers, mental health workers, and political pundits looking for ways to handle the tensions rising inside the military from new wars in the Middle East.

One of those new-war programs is the Army's "three-week soldier 'reset' program" that uses cranial massage, yoga, and acupuncture to alleviate the hyper-vigilance said to accompany combat stress. Eric Jasinski was sent for "resetting" after fifteen months in Diyala Province north of Baghdad, with an intelligence unit collecting data used in air strikes. Jasinski returned home in late 2007 and experienced bouts of anger, depression, and excessive drinking. A doctor told Jasinski he had PTSD and prescribed antidepressants. When the Army scheduled him for return to Iraq, he took the advice of his parents to stay home. He deserted, then turned himself in to authorities and was checked into Fort Hood's "mental ward." [11]

There is little in the press coverage about Jasinski to convince readers the he was "combat stressed." He was collecting data, not

counting bodies, but like other service members his choices were to
a) march back into a war he didn't like, b) do jail time, or c) accept
commitment to the mental ward. By 2007, moreover, the antiwar
movement was ensnared in the same discourse: to leverage its opposition to conflict, its leaders reached for the rhetoric of risk and
loss, toting the human damage of war in order to build a case for
peace, a calculus in which soldiers were worth more as victims than
allies. The military authorities were making the same calculations:
better to embrace Jasinski as a mental health problem than push
him into the organized resistance movement where the power of his
political views might be amplified.

THE "RIGHT STUFF" GOES WRONG

On Thursday November 5, 2009, U.S. Army Maj. Nidal Malik
Hasan killed twelve soldiers and gunned down thirty-one more at
the Soldier Readiness Processing Center at Fort Hood, Texas,
where troops were preparing for overseas service. With headlines
like the *Chicago Tribune*'s "Motive is a Mystery," speculation in
the next-day news reports began laying groundwork out of which
four contending explanations for Hasan's shooting spree would
grow: arrested personal development that left him maladjusted, a
resentful loner vulnerable to the rejection of peers and susceptible
to religious appeals; religious extremism rooted in the shooter's
belief in Islam, an explanation that associated his actions with terrorism in some versions; dissidence centered in his opposition to
the U.S. wars in the Middle East; and trauma he suffered as an
Army psychiatrist assigned to council service personnel returned
from overseas deployments.

Some of the early speculation mixed elements from more than
one of the explanations. The *Tribune*, for example, composed a
headline for its page 29 profile of Hasan putting "suspect" and
"stress disorders" together over a subhead reading "war stories

turned him against the military." The stories the major heard from soldiers returned from the wars had made the prospect of his own deployment a nightmare but the report didn't indicate if those stories stirred in him *political* opposition to the wars, *fear* for his own safety, or *moral* objections rooted in religious values. The story did say Hasan was "raised a Muslim" and cited a *Washington Post* report that he was "very devout" and often attended prayers in uniform. The paper's portrait of Hasan ended with the report that he had "looked for a wife through the center's matrimonial seminar" but that he "never found a match."

On that same day, the weekend edition of *USA Today* led with a front-page headline "Army doctor, opposed war" that pointed more directly to the shooter's political motivation. That tone continued with reports of Hasan having taken extra weapons-training classes, and his opposition to the U.S. mission in Afghanistan. According to the story, U.S. officials were interested in the suspect's possible ties to "foreign agents" but made no mention of his religion or concern by authorities that religious belief may have been a factor in the shootings. Islam was not mentioned in the story. The story described the major as "disgruntled" because of poor performance evaluations but did not relate that, as did the *Chicago Tribune*, to more deeply-seated personality issues.

The *New York Times* began its probe of Hasan's motives on the front page using the phrase "Feared Deployment" for a headline counterpoised to *USA Today*'s more politically suggestive headline. The story continued in that personal vein reporting, as did the *Chicago Tribune*, his cousin saying veterans told the major on a daily basis of "the horrors they saw over there." Like the *Tribune*, though, the *Times* made no attempt to identify for readers whether "the horrors [seen] over there" referred to atrocities committed against Iraqis and Afghanis that might have spurred Hasan's anger at the war, or experiences of their own that left them traumatized— a distinction that, read as the former, would be consistent with the

USA Today anti-war interpretation of the shootings versus the latter, a psychologized reading that problematizes the mental state of the veterans.

These four interpretive frameworks vied for space in the newspapers for about a week before the *New York Times* dropped the hammer with reporter Erica Goode's lead article in the November 8 "Week in Review" section. Dramatically presented on the front page with a full half-page black-and-white photograph of a soldier sitting forlornly with his bandaged head in hand over the title "When Minds Snap," one didn't really need to read the text to get the point: the Fort Hood shooting was a psychological event. [12]

But the photograph held my eye. There was something incongruous about its alignment with this story, a ghost-from-the-past air about it, as if transmigrated from some different but similar context. Was this the same photograph that accompanied a *Times* story on August 21, 1972, with the headline, "Postwar Shock Besets Ex-GIs"? The story that followed on that day claimed that 50 percent of the soldiers returning from Vietnam needed professional help to adjust, and peppered its full-page continuation on the inside with phrases such as "emotional stability," "psychiatric casualty," and "mental breakdowns." Even in its attempt to appear discriminating in its characterizations, the story managed to cast a pall over veterans: "The men who suffer post-Vietnam syndrome are not dramatically ill. They do not go berserk or totally withdraw. Instead they are bewildered, disillusioned, unable to cope."

That 1972 photo-headline-story combination appeared on the very day when Ron Kovic (whose memoir would later be made into the movie *Born on the Fourth of July*) and hundreds of other Vietnam veterans disrupted the Republican Party National Convention in Miami Beach to protest the war and the anticipated renomination of Richard Nixon as the party's presidential candidate. The juxtaposition of its imagery that pathologized Vietnam veterans with the news of the day about veterans whose wartime experiences had been anything but disabling was a jarring discordance, a clue as to how the homecoming narrative of that war's veterans would be rewritten.

Coming just days after the paper had printed psychiatrist Chaim Shatan's opinion column advocating the professional acceptance of PVS as a diagnostic category, this news story would be viewed in hindsight as having launched the forerunner to PTSD into public discourse and, as such, the story that began the displacement of the GI anti-war movement from public memory.

A quick check confirmed that the *Times* was not *so* clumsy as to use the same photograph again, thirty-seven years later. Nevertheless, the repetition of the photo-text technique it had used earlier— dejected veteran paired with a psychologizing headline to frame the story that followed—seemed indicative of something besides bad editing. And the 2009 photo itself still seemed out of place for me. Had the soldier in the photograph really been to Iraq or Afghanistan? I was skeptical enough to pursue its provenance: who took it, when, and where? Who was this soldier? As I tapped the keys for advice from my friend the photojournalist, my eyes caught the caption that told me enough: "An American considers the misery of war in South Vietnam in 1968."

The use of an old photograph to tell a new but familiar story would be lazy journalism but that was not what this was about. The words betraying its four-decades-old identity were removed from the photograph and merged with the caption for another, smaller, photograph of three men said to be attending a recent suicide prevention class at Fort Riley, Kansas. The oddly composed caption that resulted wasn't a matter of false or even misleading attribution so much as a window into the minds of the writer and editors responsible for it, a window through which we can see how totally the abilities to think about the current conflicts are conflated with the socially constructed memories of the war in Vietnam. Put more simply, the photo-headline setup for Erica Goode's November 8,

2009, story in the *Times* had inadvertently created an exhibit for the case that thinking about the present wars was utterly inseparable from thinking about the war in Vietnam. [13]

Goode's story that followed seemed an exercise in avoidance. After reviewing the basic details of the shootings at Fort Hood, she acknowledged that Hasan had not yet been to a war zone and that "officials had not yet ruled out the possibility that his actions were premeditated or political." The first of those facts—the absence of Hasan's exposure to combat—conflicted with the inference of the headline—that "his mind had snapped" due to the stress of combat trauma—while the fact, as reported by many news organizations by that time, that he had purchased the guns days before he used them pointed toward premeditation, if not political intent. Rather than go down that fact-based path, however, Goode's story slid into a sketchy history of wartime psychiatry. [14]

PSYCHOLOGIZING THE POLITICAL

Just as psychiatric disorders, themselves, are sometimes understood to be signs of avoidance, disquieting thoughts about the goodness or security of a society can be unwittingly suppressed by cultural workers who shape the public consciousness; journalists fall into that broad occupational category. News stories about wartime atrocities that are couched as the failure of individual soldiers to meet the national standards, or reported as forms of personal "breakdown," are a kind of spin put on violations of human decency so as to shift the blame away from public policy and social norms for which members of the public would otherwise have to take responsibility. Psychological spin of that type can be read, then, as a diversion from the collective anxiety that all is not well with the peoples' war. [15]

That the *Times* would seize an individual's case to construct a psychological storyline that obscured its racial, religious, and social dimensions would not surprise anyone familiar with its coverage of the Dwight Johnson story in May, 1971. What was remarkable about that story was that the paper had ignored the Winter Soldier hearings into allegations of U.S. war crimes held in Detroit a few months earlier. But the April protest in Washington by Vietnam Veterans Against the War that featured decorated veteran John Kerry's eloquent denunciation of the war before Congress, and hundreds of veterans returning the medals they had been awarded for service in Vietnam, made the need for attention to Vietnam veterans more urgent. Then too, white fears of militarily skilled black veterans who had been politicized by the war were growing, making the story of a war-crazed black veteran like Johnson good copy.

In retrospect, however, it appears that the greater attention to Johnson's story was due to it being an individual case. Whereas the story of organized radical veterans was a sociological phenomenon with vastly broader political implications, Johnson's story lent itself to a psychological interpretation. Spun as a microcosm of all Vietnam veterans, it could provide a new starting point for interpreting the coming-home experiences of Vietnam veterans. Mental health professionals did not miss their cue. [16]

Johnson's story became a prominent anecdote in psychiatrist Robert J. Lifton's writing on survivor guilt and PTSD. Another psychiatrist, Chaim Shatan, also read the *Times* story on Johnson and later identified it as the "first public acknowledgement of a Post-Vietnam Syndrome." Personally moved by the story, Shatan approached the *Times* and the paper agreed that it was an "opportune time" to publish his op-ed on post-Vietnam syndrome. May of 1972 was opportune because the credibility of anti-war veterans was high and the Republican convention was approaching. Originally scheduled for San Diego, the convention was rescheduled for Miami Beach where it was thought security would be easier to maintain. The announcement of the rescheduling came on the same day that Shatan's (1972) piece appeared. The timelines of Shatan's article, in other words, had to do with the timeline of political developments of the largest magnitude. [17]

Johnson's story has obvious parallels to that of Iraq War veteran Matthew Sepi, making it possible that the paper's reporters and editors came upon Sepi's case while trolling for a Dwight Johnson update. But Sepi didn't have the armed-and-dangerous-racial-minority value common to Johnson and Hasan that resonated with white anxieties about the stability of domestic racial relations or, what Hasan brought to the equation: the fear that, like the war in Vietnam, Iraq and Afghanistan could be producing a generation of soldiers disaffected by their military experience in ways that raised their political consciousness and emboldened them to resist and even rebel.

The possibility that Maj. Hasan's shootings were intentional and motivated by his anger that U.S. policy was killing innocent people, many of them Muslims and Arabs with whom he felt some ethnic identity, was disturbing. In the first place, it blurred the lines dividing "us" and "them," an essential boundary for the legitimacy of any war. Even more so, his identity spotlighted the presence of three million other Arabs in the country, a forth of whom were Muslim. Those facts, known to Americans already jumpy from the periodic reports of post-9/11 Islamist-Arab-terrorist sleeper cells operating in the country, set off alarm bells in some quarters. Additionally, the Army's training of Hasan and acceptance of him in its own ranks raised the possibility in some minds that an organized unit of angry and armed Arab Americans might actually be incubating within the U.S. military. [18]

The armed ethnic/racial Other inside the gates with righteous anger is the ultimate haint in the imagination of an America built with the backs of the enslaved ancestors of twenty million African Americans, and stoked today by the cheap labor of thirty-seven million immigrants. And the potential rationality in acts even as reprehensible as the slaughter of a dozen defenseless people fueled by that righteousness comes with unthinkable implications: there but for the grace of God . . . so let's *not* go there. And yet the threat represented by the physical "them" is a reality that calls forth *some* form of denial, a form that admits to their corporeal presence while denying the rationality of those acts, the rationality at the very core of our humanness. Viewed as "bad," they invite rebuke as one of us gone wrong (but retain that humanness); seen as irrational, they lose that humanness and fall into the ranks of them, the "mad."

Hasan's position as an Army psychiatrist added poignancy to his case. Even more than Vietnam—a war remembered as America's first for "hearts and minds," for which psychological operations played a larger role than they had in previous wars—the early twenty-first century wars against terrorism waged by the United States were propaganda campaigns conducted with the tactics of "shock and awe" against whole populations of Iraqis and Afghanis. But as the Fort Hood shootings appeared to evidence, the battle line for the emotional and mental fidelity of American fighters cut right through military ranks and the hearts and minds of soldiers themselves. Just as Dwight Johnson, the blue-collar tank gunner, was a front-linesman in the Vietnam War, Hasan, qua psychiatrist, had been deployed to the lines of battle in the new century where military authorities feared political casualties as much as physical. That one of its own "right stuff" would be felled in that battle was profoundly upsetting.[19]

• • • •

It was Kafkaesque: the diagnostic category PTSD evolved as a response to Vietnam's psychological casualties that, latently, functioned to help manage the resistance of anti-war Vietnam veterans by dismissively associating them with mental health stereotypes; an Arab American Army major is schooled, years later, to apply PTSD clinically to keep U.S. troops mentally stable enough to wage another war of questionable legitimacy; through the troops he counsels, he's led to question the morality of the mission he's been assigned; he rebels, commits murder, and has the political nature of his act rewritten by a press corps using the medical lexicon of PTSD.

The same evolution of military strategies and tactics that made psychiatrists more decisive to the outcome of wars than ground-pounding grunts and track-mounted gunners also redefined the meaning of "combat" and blurred the distinction of being a soldier. And it wasn't just mental health workers who were displacing the "GI Joes" of yore that many American minds still associated with going to war. The front line of the war against the Taliban and al Qaeda in Southwest Asia ran across keyboards in the American Southwest where computer operators sitting at Fort Huachuca guided pilotless drones on assassination missions. Fighting wars that had dramatically reduced the chances of physical casualties in a societal context in which "the purple heart" for a combat wound was still the gold standard for manliness virtually required that meaning and measure of that standard be rethought.

NOTES

1. The *New York Times* op-ed (Satel 2006) presents a case study for media scholars in how "form" can override "content" in the *Times*'s practice of "agenda setting." The content of Satel's piece expressed her skepticism of PTSD's widespread application by the medical community. Its form, on the other hand, given by its title ("For some the war won't end.") and the follow-up set of letters printed five days later under the heading "For Veterans, a Longer Battle," ran counter to the point she was making. Moreover, six (out of seven) letters published attacked her position, some of them taking the kind of spurious approaches she was criticizing. In "form," in other words, the *Times* used Satel's op-ed to say that PTSD, pro *or* con, is what the nation should be talking about.

2. The accuracy of Barton's observation is reinforced by Clyde Haberman's November 24, 2009, column in which he notes that veterans of Iraq and Afghanistan in an NYU writers program "didn't like being treated in the mass media as if

they were damaged goods." One of the veterans told Haberman, "We don't come back with our souls excised . . . filled with nothing but violence."

3. Todd Ensign's "G.I. Joe: Lessons for the Coffee House Movement" posted on the War Resister League's homepage in 2009 has a thumbnail accounts of Different Drummer's demise and the coffeehouse efforts at Fort Hood and Fort Lewis.

4. Anderson 2010.

5. Even Vietnam Veterans Against the War (VVAW) was overtaken by the power of PTSD to frame the homecoming story of the new generation of veterans. Twenty-two of thirty-seven pages in the spring 2012 edition of its newspaper *The Veteran* carried at least one reference to PTSD or related terms.

6. I participated in some post-screening discussions, sometimes with veterans of the war in Iraq.

7. Wells 1994.

8. Wells 1994

9. Wingo 1969; Halstead 1991.

10. The clumsy concoction of a conspiracy case against VVAW backfired, however, when the trial of the Gainesville Eight, accused of planning an armed attack on the 1972 Republican Convention, revealed that it was the government, not VVAW, that was guilty of conspiracy to break the law. A month after the Gainesville defendants were acquitted, Spiro Agnew resigned in disgrace to be followed a year later by the president himself.

11. Dao 2010.

12. Goode 2009.

13. Mnookin (2011, p.165) has an excellent discussion of the way photographs and t heir captions are used to manipulate news readers.

14. Dao and Frosch (2009) wrote that Hasan had "wanted to report soldiers who had admitted in counseling sessions that they witnessed or committed war crimes in Iraq or Afghanistan" but that "Major Hassan was discouraged from filing reports on his patients."

15. Freudian theory sheds light on the connection between emotional repression and physical illness. C. Wright Mills (1967) made the distinction between "personal troubles" and "public issues."

16. Katzman (1993, p. 7).

17. Scott (1993, p. 43).

18. On December 11, 2009, *Times* reporters Waqar Gillani and Jane Perlez reported the arrest of five Americans in Pakistan while trying to join Pakistani militants to fight against the U.S. military in the region. The parents of one of the Americans were immigrants from Pakistan. In their report, Gillani and Perlez recalled other then-recent cases involving immigrants or first generation Americans in anti-American activities. Scott Shane's front page report on the arrests in the *Times* the next day continued on page 9 with the subtitle "The Call of Extremism, Echoing at Home, Worries Experts on Terrorism."

19. The phrase "hearts and minds" was made popular by the 1974 film of that title. The phrase "shock and awe" was used by U.S. authorities to describe the

invasion of Iraq in 2003 and analyzed by Naomi Klein (2008) as an essential strategy of neoliberal policy.

Chapter Three

Combat in the American Imagination: What Did *You* Do in the War?

On August 17, 2009, President Barack Obama spoke to the Veterans of Foreign Wars convention in Phoenix, Arizona. For two consecutive hours in mid-day, newscasters for National Public Radio reported that the president was speaking before an organization of "combat" veterans.

A casual identification of the VFW with combat veterans would be understandable. After all, service abroad in the U.S. military for the last hundred years has most often involved a relationship to the wars it fought on foreign soil. But not all foreign service, even in war zones, involves combat. Among other things, military organizations are huge bureaucracies that require legions of clerical personnel to keep the records. The mechanization of warfare during the twentieth century created the need for maintenance crews to keep the trucks rolling and the planes and choppers in the air. And the age-old aphorism that "an army runs on its stomach" is no less true in Afghanistan than it was at Flanders Field, making the troops who move the food and cook the meals as essential to the mission as those walking point. Eighty-five out of every one hundred soldiers in Vietnam did not see combat, a proportion that was about the same in World War II and remains the same today. If experience in combat was a necessary credential for membership in the VFW, it would be a pretty small organization—too small for a presidential visit. In fact, the VFW is open to all veterans who have served abroad.[1]

VALORIZING COMBAT

What's interesting, then, is what it is that presses the term "combat" into inappropriate usage, even by the carefully edited NPR newscasters. Beyond its use as a noun for occasions of military engagements, "combat" is sometimes used as an adjective to connote something positive, superior even, about the veteran or group of veterans referred to. So, calling the VFW an organization of "combat" veterans is a way of saying its members are *special*, a cut above ordinary veterans. In turn, the president's stature is raised by his appearance before this august gathering.

In Western culture, the designation of combat refers to more than the role or performance of someone in a military setting. Military duties have been assigned to men for so long that the societal sense of what it means to be a man is virtually synonymous with martial accomplishments. Nietzsche is said to have written that service in war is for men what childbirth is for women—the rite of passage from boyhood to manhood. With the same boundary defining gender identity and adulthood for men, it's no surprise that military experience becomes a recognized measure of manliness. Indeed the phrase "What did you do in the war, Daddy?" has achieved the status of a trope, a saying embodying the cultural importance of military service.[2]

The status of wartime service makes it a credential as well, a form of documentation called forth in conversation and displayed on the uniform with medals worn for ceremonies, parades, and anniversary events. The need for affirmation of self is basic to humankind but the dependence on military experience for affirmation grows as access to other sources is diminished. The mechanisms used to recruit large numbers of people for military service include the draft and proffered economic benefits, both of which virtually insure that people from the lower middle class, working class, and the chronically poor will comprise a large portion of veterans. For many of them, separation from service marks a return to humdrum lives, leaving the years in uniform remembered with pride and fondness as the best of their lives. With the passage of time and the dearth of other markers in the life course, the inclination to foreground for others what a veteran did in the war, maybe with some inflation, is hard to resist. Indeed, the term "war stories" has become a metaphor for men's exaggerations of their accomplishments, be they on the battlefield or football field.

Combat experience can also become a credential for authority on military matters or even broader social and political issues. Despite having no previous political experience, Dwight D. Eisenhower oversaw the invasion of Normandy, France, as Commander of the Allied Forces in 1944 and, on the basis of that, won the presidency in 1952 and reelection in 1956. As a Navy Lieutenant in the Solomon Islands in 1943, John F. Kennedy won decoration for heroism after saving a crew member from his Patrol Torpedo boat (PT-109) that was hit by a Japanese destroyer. Like "Ike" before him, Kennedy parlayed that record of heroism into a political asset that took him to the White House. Several veterans of Vietnam including Senators John McCann of Arizona, John Kerry of Massachusetts, and Jim Webb of Virginia bounced off their records in combat for successful political careers.

The use of military service as a stepping stone for careers in politics or business has implications that aren't always recognized. Until recently, combat was a singularly male experience which means that the voices of women, youth, and those who may for religious or other reasons have "not seen combat" are sometimes devalued. Questions were raised during the 2008 presidential campaign about Barack Obama's suitability to be Commander in Chief, one of the president's responsibilities, because he had never been in the military. Hillary Clinton, who challenged Obama for the Democratic Party nomination, had no military experience either and when during the campaign she claimed to have been exposed to sniper fire and bombs in Bosnia during the 1990s she was accused of overreaching for a combat credential. Richard Blumenthal, the Connecticut Attorney General, ran for U.S. Senate from that state in 2010 reiterating a claim made over the years that he was a Vietnam veteran. Press revelations that he had never been to Vietnam cost him some public embarrassment but not the election.[3]

False claims to battlefront valor led to the passage in 2006 of the Stolen Valor Act that made it a federal crime to lie about being a military hero. Thousands of cases are reported each year according to Doug Sterner who tracks down the phonies, and 60 have been prosecuted under the Act that he helped draft. In 2010, however, a court ruled in the case of Xavier Alvarez that the law was "overly broad" and unconstitutional. Alvarez had bragged about being wounded in combat and receiving the Medal of Honor although he had never been in the military.[4]

SEEN COMBAT? WHO'S TO SAY

If "combat" credentials manhood and authority, who or what credentials combat? A Google search for "Jerry Lembcke" "combat veteran" turns up a thread from "Vietnam Studies Group" wherein a 2003 posting refers to me as a "combat veteran of Vietnam." The attribution is made in reference to my book *The Spitting Image* with the connotation that it should be taken seriously because I'm a *combat* veteran. In fact, I was a Chaplain's Assistant in Vietnam and never saw combat. Or had I?

I returned from Vietnam in February 1970 at the time the country was between the Moratorium Days against the war four months earlier, and the spring mobilizations against the invasion of Cambodia that was just ahead. My thirteen months in Vietnam had been a time of personal and political growth and I was ready to help end the war. Even if I *had* seen combat, my emerging pacifist values would have discounted any glory to be had in the experience, my identity as a war veteran limited to that of the anti-war variety. In any case, I don't recall hearing the "combat?" question until years later and when I did I always answered it with "no," followed by a brief description of my duties in Vietnam. It wasn't until working on a book in the mid-1990s that I came across a "Combat Index" that I begin to wonder if I had been telling the truth.

The index was in *Legacies of Vietnam: Comparative Adjustment of Veterans and Their Peers*, a 1981 study prepared by the Center for Policy Research for the Veterans Administration. It was a list of twelve items, some weighted more heavily than others and each weighted by frequency of occurrence: rarely, sometimes, often, or very often. The second item read, "Flew in aircraft over South or North Vietnam" for which the combat score was 1 with a multiple of 1–4 depending on the frequency of occurrence. Hmm, I thought, playing along; I flew about once a week by helicopter to landing zones (LZs) and fire support bases in the 41st Artillery Group to which I was assigned in the Central Highlands. In comparison with most troops who only flew in and out of the country for R&R, this item, I thought, deserved a multiple of 3(often) or 4(very often), either of which put me over the 2.99 total points needed to qualify me as a "low combat" veteran.

Item four read "received incoming fire." I did. Well, maybe I did, depending on what counts as incoming fire. If a mortar round had landed on the bunker I was in for guard duty, it would count. But that never happened. If a mortar round had landed ten feet from the bunker, it would still count—right? But what about twenty feet? An enemy rocket landed 300 feet from my friend Denny one night. That's a football field away and too far to count for the combat index—except that shrapnel from it tore away half his face. That's combat; that counts. A few weeks later I was at a battalion head-quarters camp near Phan Rang when several mortar rounds landed inside our perimeter. Whap, whap, whap, they sounded, each of them kicking up a puff of dust 300 feet or so from where I stood. Combat points for me?

If the line for manhood was drawn between *no* combat and combat, albeit "low" combat, I was safely across it—a combat veteran. Gaming the index like that was a useful exercise in decon-structing the meaning of combat so I kept playing. "Saw Vietna-mese killed" was worth two points but what does it mean? I once saw a dozen or so dead Vietnamese, killed and piled in a village center, but I hadn't seen them *getting* killed. But then what Americans would have knowingly seen a Vietnamese getting killed? Hit and wounded maybe, but when does seeing someone getting wounded get redefined as seeing them "killed"? Do I get the points or not? Who's to say?[5]

In the hands of VFW members at the clubhouse bar, this index might produce hours of animated disagreement but its relationship to controversies surrounding PTSD is serious. By the 1980s it was common to read that 30 percent to 50 percent of Vietnam veterans suffered from PTSD, figures that lacked credibility alongside esti-mates that only 15 percent of Vietnam veterans saw combat. How could men who never saw combat be suffering its traumatic ef-fects? The credibility gap could be narrowed, of course, by down-sizing the 30–50 percent figure but that would entail a challenge to medical science and the credibility of veterans claiming the effects of war-born trauma. The politics of that approach seemed unten-able, with the thought of attacking combat veterans' sense of the trauma in their own experience being especially distasteful. The other approach to the combat-trauma gap was to expand the defini-tion of combat so that the 15 percent figure could rise.

Definitions of combat bedeviled the discourse on war trauma well into the conflicts in Iraq and Afghanistan. In an August 2011 article, *New York Times* reporter Benedict Carey, citing a new article in *Journal of the American Medical Association* about the use of an antipsychotic drug, Risperdal, to treat PTSD wrote that, "Up to 20 percent of those who see heavy combat have lasting signs of post-traumatic stress disorder." Skeptical of categories like "heavy combat," and knowing the powerful subtexts they carry, I searched the news story for how it was defined—but found nothing. Looking at the *JAMA* article cited by the reporter, I saw that the researchers had used no such category. I asked a doctor at a Veterans Administration hospital how and why the reporter might have come up with the term, and she said, "I don't know—he made it up."[6]

On one level, the reporter's invention of "heavy combat" for his story might seem to be of little consequence since he seemed to have reported the rest of the *JAMA* article accurately. On another level, though, it clouds the interpretation of the data: if at most 20 percent of *heavy-combat* veterans have PTSD, that could reduce the number of plausibly traumatized veterans of all levels considerably—depending, again, on how the term is defined. The more likely (and serious) fallout from what the reporter wrote, however, was another instance of "combat" and PTSD being used circularly to credential each other. In the context of two decades of PTSD and combat being tangled through popular, medical, and political culture, it's as likely as not that the association between PTSD and "heavy combat" in the story registers with the casual reader as, "all veterans with PTSD saw heavy combat," as the way the journal article was meant to be read which was that some veterans who saw heavy combat will have PTSD.

THE PROBLEM OF EXPECTATIONS

The temptation for men to exaggerate their records in combat is understandably greatest for veterans whose actual performance in war does not live up to what they think the society expects of them. Sometimes those expectations, having been formed by Hollywood film or other fictional sources, are unrealistic inventions intended to entertain rather than inform. In Vietnam, for example, a GI with his helmet unbuckled, cigarette dangling from his lip, and a bandolier of ammunition draped around his neck might pose for a photograph knowing that the pose would interest the folks back home. Behind the camera, however, his buddies, who knew he had no machine gun for the band of ammo he showed off, were ridiculing him for trying to look like "a John Wayne."[7]

Showing off has a long presence in studies of masculinity, perhaps deriving from the term "Napoleon complex," said to be a feeling of inadequacy due to size or other physical attributes. The colloquial form of the term, "little-man complex," is sometimes employed to account for the behavior of braggarts whose boastfulness is attributed to insecurities about their bodies. In the vernacular of boy's locker rooms, the guys who have really done "it" supposedly don't talk about it—the "it" being the batting average on the field or the social "it" scored (or not) at the post-game keg party. Those who talk about "it" the most may be regarded as phonies by their peers, setting off a dynamic that can compound the needs of "the phony," leading to more exaggerations.

The problem of unrealistic expectations put on male veterans has grown over recent decades because war has become automated to a point where the soldier has been reduced, in some cases, to a joy-stick appendage delivering remote-controlled weaponry to targets miles away. In March 2009 reports surfaced of drones operated from Arizona being deployed against suspected al Qaeda targets in Pakistan: the operators went home to their families for evening dinner. That's an extreme example of war so automated as to deprive the men involved of any meaningful sense of soldierly accomplishment; but it's really just an extension of trends underway for most of a century. Bombing runs over North Vietnam in the 1960s and 1970s often originated in Thailand or the Philippines where pilots and crews lived in air-conditioned quarters with amenities like swimming pools and libraries located well beyond the range of enemy retaliation. Sometimes, the flyers knew nothing more about their targets than the coordinates for the bomb drop—and even less about the people they were killing.[8]

KILL RATIOS AND BRAGGING RIGHTS

Ground war, too, has changed. The last war involving the United States against standing armies, more or less equally outfitted with long-range artillery and mechanized transportation, was in Korea from 1950 to 1953. Since then, it has waged wars of counterinsurgency and occupation against irregular forces that blend uniformed personnel with civilians and guerilla units, an asymmetry resulting in kill ratios of 30–1 in Vietnam. The imbalances on the ground are multiplied by U.S. domination of the air war, of course. The 1990–1991 war in the Persian Gulf, for example, was fought almost entirely from the air against an Iraqi regime with no air defense, a one-sidedness resulting in a kill ratio that was all but incalculable; the attacks of U.S. fighter planes on retreating Iraqi ground troops was referred to as a "turkey shoot."[9]

A kill ratio for the war that followed the 2003 invasion of Iraq is hard to arrive at because in the early days of fighting the United States claimed to not be counting the enemy dead. In the absence of "official" figures, observers developed creative methods to fill the information gap. In July 2007, the web site *Free Republic* cited a line from the 2001 film *Blackhawk Down* claiming 1,000 terrorists had been killed in Somalia compared to 18 U.S. service members. From that ratio of 55.5 to 1, the writer extrapolated to Iraq for a claim that 200,000 "terrorists" had been killed based on the figure of 3,600 U.S. fighters known to have been killed at the time.[10] In a May 12, 2005, posting at "The Greater Jeneration," the blogger "Jen" wrote approvingly of the 100:3 kill ratio claimed for Marines in Operation Matador then underway in western Iraq.[11]

The British medical journal *Lancet* reported in 2006 that 655,000 Iraqi deaths had resulted from the invasion and occupation that followed. That number, put in a ratio with the approximately 3,000 U.S. deaths at the time, yields a figure of 218:1. But critics pointed out that the *Lancet* made no distinction between civilian and military deaths of Iraqis and that the attribution of civilian deaths to the invasion distorted the kill ratio and maligned the U.S. military.[12]

The counterpoint to that criticism advanced by Naomi Klein in her book *The Shock Doctrine* was that the "shock and awe" campaign against Iraq, as it was called by U.S. Secretary of Defense Donald Rumsfeld, had targeted the civilian population with the intent of inducing human emotional trauma. The bombing of basic infrastructure like power plants, communication buildings, and sanitation facilities was a form of armed propaganda that terrorized the people, and resulted in thousands of deaths: civilians and combat casualties, not "collateral damage."[13]

Many of the U.S. dead, on the other hand, *were* non-combat casualties. Reporting data available from the Pentagon, Thomas Frank wrote in *USA Today* that "about half" of U.S. military deaths in Iraq during the first year of the war were non-combat related—a percentage that was down from the Persian Gulf War of 1991 when non-combat deaths actually outnumbered those in combat. Traffic accidents were the most common cause of non-combat deaths, followed by other accidents, friendly fire, and suicides. By 2007, when Frank wrote, non-combat deaths were down due to troop movement on the roads being limited, but they rose again, outnumbering combat deaths in the period September 2008 to April 2009, according to the *Boston Globe*.[14]

Combat casualties are loaded with emotional and political meaning which makes them subject to interpretation and use by individuals and organizations with different agendas on matters of war and peace. People supportive of the U.S. wars in Iraq and Afghanistan, for example, sometimes allege that exaggerated enemy losses appeal to humanitarian sentiments *against* war. Anti-war activists, meanwhile, suspect that the government and military authorities generally skew body counts of U.S. losses downward lest higher counts spawn popular opposition to the war. But the politics of war and body counts don't always align in those ways. Some war supporters like blogger "Jen" (above) believe that biases against the war will result in artificially low counts of enemy dead that are then used to demonstrate the futility of the war, while some the anti-war voices on the left contend that exaggerated U.S. losses can feed some "don't let them die in vain" feelings that will be used as a reason to keep the war going.[15]

The calculus connecting kill ratios and the political economy of war is different, in any case, than the way they play out in the political culture of the country. While a high kill ratio might bestow bragging rights of a kind to the veterans with the biggest numbers, military service and the pride of having given it are freighted with the values of discipline and sacrifice that make the risk of defeat, not the margin of victory, the measure of accomplishment in battle. It's hard to say you looked death in the face and didn't flinch while hurling bombs from miles away at an enemy whose face you can't see. Just as a major college basketball team doesn't take much pride in the score it ran up against the small school it played for a pre-conference tune-up game, it's hard to find accomplishment in wars with double-digit kill ratios—unless that imbalance can be spun as an entree for the warrior resume. [16]

THE ATROCITY AS CREDENTIAL

In his book *War Stories*, historian Gary Kulik has a chapter entitled "False Atrocities" filled with stories about GIs and Marines killing unarmed Vietnamese who were so inadequately provisioned that their killing would have constituted war crimes—if the stories were true. But the stories are loaded with exaggeration, some of them preposterous and unbelievable. He begins the chapter with a vignette about "Turk." Turk tells of being a tunnel rat for the 1st Infantry Division in the Iron Triangle north of Saigon. On one mission to ferret Viet Cong from their underground lair, he goes deeply into the tunnel complex and then risks his own life, pulling the pins on several hand grenades by his teeth and tossing them into a hole where he is sure there are enemy soldiers. Reluctant to finish the story about his heroic action (which listeners are certain must have earned him a medal), Turk eventually responds to a request: no medal, he explained, "I blew up a teacher with a classroom full of kids."[17]

Kulik, the author, then reveals to us that Turk was "a wannabe vet" who had never been in Vietnam. What's more, Turk wanted to have killed children, a perversity that Kulik finds pervasive in post–Vietnam War culture. "Dead children are everywhere in Vietnam narratives," he quotes another author saying.

Kulik's chapter is full of phony atrocity stories like Turk's, and he puzzles over why historians and reporters so often buy into them when details like pulling grenade pins with teeth happen only in screenwriters' imaginations; their gullibility, he speculates, stems from their belief that the war in Vietnam was immoral, a liberal bias they find validation for in the atrocity stories. The small number of soldiers responsible for those reprehensible acts, he says, sought out by the media are all too willing to exploit their desire for attention. Although Kulik speculates that veterans tell interviewers what they want to hear, he concludes that we don't know much about why men make up war stories.[18]

"I liberated Dachau." "Well, I was at My Lai."

Kulik is undoubtedly right that veterans or even men like Turk who are not veterans sometimes attempt to curry favor with their listeners by trying to meet the expectations of their audience. That's why "war stories" might be as old as time. Prior to Vietnam, though, a war story was likely to associate the teller with something positive and heroic. World War II veteran Paul Parks, for example, was exposed in 2000 for falsely claiming to have been present at the liberation of Dachau, a Nazi death camp in 1945. The desire for connection to something as momentous and universally celebrated as that is easy to understand.

But the counterparts of Parks's overreach for glory in the years after Vietnam and the wars in Iraq and Afghanistan pervert the logic of that motivation. Take the case of Joe Ellis as an example. As a history professor and distinguished scholar at Mt. Holyoke College, Ellis regaled his students for years with stories of having been "almost" present at the 1969 My Lai massacre in Vietnam. Ellis was in the Army during the war but not Vietnam. So why would he lie to associate himself with something as *in*glorious as My Lai?[19]

Joe Ellis has been recognized for years as one of America's most esteemed writers, so Kulick's "did it for the attention" explanation won't explain him. The better explanation for Ellis is found in an analogy with Turk. Ellis, like Turk, was reaching for a combat identity that in America's twisted lost-war culture became attached to atrocities. The atrocity story reverses the polarity of the veteran-as-hero equation, casting the veteran as anti-hero for having done something so awful—and thereby insulating him from the accusatory, "Oh, you're just trying to sound like a hero." Simultaneously, the veteran's placement in the story can be read backwards to reinforce the war-is-hell narrative: it was the terror of the war that numbed Turk to the dangers that lurked below the ground and his sensitivity to the conditions that forced innocent Vietnamese into the tunnel for shelter. We "know" Turk is the real deal because only the trauma of war could have dehumanized him in this way. [20]

Turk's dehumanization makes him a victim of the war, a biography in which the enemy Vietnamese is held responsible for his depredation. And within that Devil-made-me-do-it calculus, the more awful he can make his atrocity sound, the more demonic the Vietnamese can be made to appear, and the more valid his claim to combat-veteran status becomes. Both of those elements in the victim-veteran narrative shore up ideological pillars important for the national sense of self left damaged by the loss of the war: we really were the "good people" confronting an evil other in Vietnam, and our men did our collective masculinity proud over there.

For years before the first U.S. soldiers shipped out for Iraq in 2003, American memory of the war in Vietnam and post-war culture was steeped in the representations of traumatized veterans as combat heroes. The troops embarking for Baghdad and later Kabul went with the images of themselves coming home symptomatic, as Vietnam veterans did—and therewith credentialed as combat veterans. The place of "the atrocity" in that narrative was just as established in their minds through films like *Platoon* that pictured GIs putting their Zippo lighters to grass huts *ala* My Lai, and *Casualties of War* that portrayed the rape of a Vietnamese girl. The public sense of the war in Vietnam was also dominated by memories of atrocities, so much so that My Lai had displaced almost everything else from memory.

"I was at Abu Ghraib—with the pictures to prove it."

With veteran identity and the national expectations about war so entangled with images of atrocities, it should have surprised no one that stories about GIs and Marines committing atrocities in Iraq would reach home before the story-tellers did. Soon after the troops landed, news reports of execution-style killings, rapes, and mutilated bodies began trickling out. Those reports elicited lots of "like

Vietnam" commentary, but the atrocity of Vietnam having been normalized, the shock that might otherwise have been elicited by photographs on the Internet and YouTube footage of soldiers posing and gloating about criminal offenses was itself missing.

Just as the early efforts to explain war crimes in Vietnam attributed them to young soldiers unhinged by an enemy using terror as a tactic in a primitive environment, so did some commentary use the "fog of war" framing to make sense of atrocities in Iraq. That extension of Vietnam-era thinking was okay but it missed one important difference between the cases: the photographs, video tapes, and digitally-recorded images of crimes committed in Iraq was a record created by the soldiers themselves, showing themselves perpetrating the offenses. While there were photographs of what happened at My Lai, Vietnam, in March of 1968, most them were taken by Ronald Haeberle a photographer for the Army's Public Information Detachment and few show GIs in the act of killing or maiming. The atrocities committed in Abu Ghraib prison in 2004, on the other hand, were recorded as they happened by the criminals themselves. Moreover, the photographs have a contrived motif about them, documenting the crimes being committed while suggesting, as well, that the tortures were *staged* to create the photo opportunity for the soldiers. The now infamous "electrical wires" photograph showing a hooded detainee wired up for shock treatment was, for example, set up "as a joke" according to Army investigative files. In one of the photographs, we see SSG Ivan Frederick, one of the torturers, holding a Cyber Shot camera.[21]

The crimes captured in those photographs were rightfully decried for the ethno-religious hatred they exhibited, but little attention was given to the narcissism evinced by the act of photographing the brutality—indeed, sometimes photographing the picture-taking torturers who had arranged the scene for photographing. Many of the photographs show the U.S. soldiers in the act of torturing prisoners while turning to face the camera with "two thumbs up." The important pathology revealed by the photographs is not the racism and sexism of the soldiers torturing Iraqis, but the self-conscious intent of the posers and the picture takers, their need to document, apparently for purposes of credentialing their combat bona fides, that they had experienced war so heinous that they were driven to inhumanity.

The pictorial record of Abu Ghraib provides valuable historical and legal documentation for the crimes committed there, but it is also a cultural coda for a post-empire society turned in on itself. The traditional trophies of war coming home with soldiers like surrender agreements and expressions of gratitude from their war-time allies affirmed the nation's sense of goodness, but they are missing from Iraq, as they were from Vietnam. In the absence of those externalities that might provide meaning for the war, the interiorizing of the search finds only a dark hollowness registering the *meaninglessness* of it all, a vacuum to which the fantasized Otherness of our enemies returns and finds the space to germinate a new and terrifying Self.

The woman too can fight

The acquisition of combat experience on the resume for manhood has been further complicated by the integration of women into the armed forces. The dichotomy of man as protector, woman as pro-tected, is so embedded in Western culture as to be definitional of sexual and gender categories. It's a dichotomy that makes the idea that women can protect themselves, and maybe even men, a chal-lenge to the very definition of what it means to be a man. Women serving alongside men in the uniformed services leads to a "what's the point, then?" kind of questioning for men having grown up thinking, now , their time in the army, is when they differentiate themselves from women. [22]

Some of the reasons for the recruitment of women into the mili-tary only compound the unease their presence creates in what had become over the years a male preserve. For one thing, they are often assigned to missions involving contact with local women who need to be searched and interrogated, an unspoken and even, for some men, an unthinkable confirmation that girls and women are among the enemy they are fighting, some of whom are combatants, some not. For another, wars for hearts and minds such as those now being fought make language translators and psychologists as critical to their outcomes as ruck-humping ground-pounders used to be; the joy-stick weaponry of war today doesn't know a man's hand from a woman's.

The sadism inflicted on Iraqi prisoners at Abu Ghraib may have been intensified by the gaze of women in the ranks of U.S. prison guards. With confidence in their own masculinity shaken by the sight of women filling what the men grew up thinking were male-defining roles, the male guards did what men do when they feel insecure around women—they acted out. By "showing off" their brutality, they reaffirmed the traditional boundary between men (aggressive and insensitive) and women (passive and empathetic). Meanwhile, being seen by their own women as capable of dominating the racial and ethnic Other embodied in the Iraqi men bolstered their self-image as defenders and protectors of the "weaker sex." By incorporating the women guards in the degradation of the Iraqis, the male guards not only assured the presence of the audience they wanted, but demonstrated their control over the women.[23]

Not your father's war

Service in a war zone has lost the rite of passage designation it once had. Going "overseas" for World Wars I and II meant parting from parents and other adult relatives for long periods of time. Those separations forced young men into self-reliance and dependence on age-group peers, changes that accelerated their "growing up." In psycho-sexual terms the break with home also terminated the reliance on mothers and other female figures for emotional nurturance;

it was the ultimate male bonding experience, the transition that begat generations of humor about the sergeant being your mother now—or not.[24]

But the rite of passage function that military service once provided has itself been passed by, it's relevance a reminder of times when soldiers were younger than they are today. Precise data on the ages of U.S. soldiers deployed abroad is hard to come by but the names and ages of the dead are reported daily in the *New York Times* and scrolled nightly on the PBS *NewsHour*—and few of them are on the youth side of the generational line. The mean age of the U.S. dead in Iraq was about 26, the median a bit lower; the average age of the first 700 killed in Afghanistan was almost 28. Although news stories regularly sprinkle words like "kids" and "young" into their stories on deaths in the war zones, readers' eyes are as struck by the numbers of soldiers over thirty who have been killed as those under twenty. Presently, military forces are comprised of volunteers, and the observation that some of the older men enter the military to escape dishes and diapers at home raises questions about their place along the line dividing boys from men.[25]

The "mail call" scenes that were stock footage for war films up through the Vietnam era were representative of the miles separating soldiers from family and friends, but they are now icons of war the way it used to be. War today comes with Internet connections and regular phone calls home. In his article "Back from Iraq" for *Worcester Magazine*, December 23, 2009, reporter Jim Keogh quotes Julie Ugalde, mother of Neal Bakerlis, 20, a "combat engineer" in Iraq, as saying, "About every two weeks he's able to place a call." In Vietnam, by contrast, there was no telephone contact except for emergency purposes through something called the MARS system for which permission was needed and travel to a special facility was required—GIs and Marines in Vietnam had to wait six months or more for their one out-of-country R&Rs to hear

Mom's voice. For the "doughboys" of WWI and many of their sons in WWII, no phones—period.

"FAT CONTRACTS"

The mall life that troops deployed to Iraq might have thought they left behind—maybe even looked forward to leaving as they embarked on their search for manhood—followed them to Al Asad Airbase in Iraq and Camp Phoenix in Kabul. A *CBS News* report on February 7, 2005, began with the line "a soldier's life isn't what it used to be" and quoted Terry McCoy recalling he had "opened the first Burger King at Baghdad airport in May 2003 before the U.S. military had set up its first mess tent." McCoy worked for the Army & Air Force Exchange Service that at the time operated 23 fast food franchises at 16 bases in Iraq. Thirty-six months later the *Los Angeles Times* reported 73 outlets operating in Iraq including Pizza Hut and KFC.[26]

The junk food provided by McCoy's AAFES came with thousands of calories unbefitting the fitness of any army, but comfort was its point, not nutrition. The bloated troops and swelled profits of the venders contracted by Kellogg, Brown, and Root, until recently a subsidiary of Haliburton Corporation, to furnish the burgers and pizzas is widely recognized by critics, but the social relationships involved in providing those comforts might be more important. The manual labor needed to pamper the palates has been offloaded from the arms and legs of uniformed personnel onto the backs of low-paid civilians employed by the high-paid contractors. The degradation of peeling potatoes before meals and scrubbing pots and pans after, known as "kitchen police" or KP, once a test to be passed by the boy on his climb to manhood, is now passed down to people who are going nowhere.[27]

The fat contracts going to KFC are not resulting in union-scale jobs for laid off U.S. workers or even subsistence-level jobs for

Iraqis living dirt poor in an economy the Americans promised to rebuild after the invasion. Rather, the contractors subcontract to labor brokers who ply the most desperate pockets of humanity in Africa and South Asia for workers who are sometimes recruited on the false promises of good jobs someplace else but end up working on U.S. military bases in Iraq or Afghanistan. Thirty-five thousand of these third country nationals, or TCNs as they are known, hailing from Uganda, Nepal, Bangladesh, and Pakistan were living in "substandard" conditions and working for Kellogg, Brown, and Root in Iraq in 2005.[28]

The use of TCNs constructs for U.S. military personnel, no matter what their rank, an appearance of privilege they can enjoy over the manual laborers who do their dirty work. It's an illusory sense of privilege but it draws attention away from the indignities of life in a military hierarchy. It also works, as historian Chalmers Johnson points out in *Sorrows of Empire*, as an in-your-face exercise of cultural and political hegemony that fosters in U.S. troops a sense of status superiority while at the same time reproducing in the TCNs the feelings of dependency characteristic of colonized people.

Calorie counts and status points aren't the only measures of payoff for compliant service. Writing at truthout.org in February 2010, retired Marine Corp officer Carlton Meyer used Department of Defense data to show that 20-year-old sailors at an E-2 pay grade earned an average $37,637 while civilian Americans, age 16–24, earned an average $22,308. With a wife and two kids after four years and promotion to an E-4 pay level, the sailor earns $48,180 a year which is about $14,000 more than the earnings shown for workers of all ages in any of the Bureau of Labor Statistics categories for civilian occupations. Additionally, Meyer points out the childcare benefits, guaranteed vacation and holiday time, and educational opportunities that are more available to military personnel than most other workers.[29]

The possibility that the greatest damage done to men deprived of real-war deprivation is cultural is a comment on their socialization and the society that sends them off to war. Part of the coming home experience fantasized by young men entails the telling of the journey, the trials faced, and the victories won; it's a narrative as old as Homer, with an appeal to the ear of the listener that matches the pride in the voice of the warrior returned. With war's degree of difficulty downgraded and the mystic surrounding much of the rest dissipated by the presence, now, of women in the ranks—the gendered Other from whom webs of obscurity woven by men over centuries have occluded the realities of military life—the emotions connected to those unfulfilled fantasies are blocked, turned back into their bodily element to resurface symptomatically at a later date.

The fanfare with which troops were dispatched for the 2003 invasion of Iraq ratcheted to still higher levels the already inflated expectations that members of the military had for the duty ahead. Countless segments of local television news broadcasts showed reserve and guard units assembled in high school gymnasiums and surrounded by spouses and children as they were lauded as "heroes" by mayors and congressional representatives before they had even left town. With promises they would be welcomed home "this time," troops were sent off against the backdrop of supposed hostility greeting returnees from Vietnam

The matter of expectations and military service is complex because they are mediated by so much myth, legend, and popular culture. The authenticity of military experience is beyond the reach of most Americans; what they "know" about it has been filtered through the pens of historians, screenwriters, novelists, and graphic artists who downplay the mundane and exaggerate the drama and storylines of heroism. It is those unrealistic portrayals of war that have set the expectations of friends and families, as well as themselves, that veterans feel they have to meet when they come home.

As unpleasant as their weeks in the desert were, and as competently as they carried out their assignments, it's easy to picture men and women returning from service in Iraq without the pride and satisfaction they thought they would have, the feelings they *imagine* that World War II veterans, or even Vietnam veterans, returned with. Sensing, probably correctly, that listeners don't want to hear stories from a veteran who shuffled paperwork for fellow Marines moving in and out of Al Asad airbase, the large percentage of veterans who did not do "it"—see combat—feel the pressure to make something up. For some, the gap between expectations and accomplishments is unbearable. Marine Cpl. Wade Toothman committed suicide in October 2012 after service in Iraq. In a note left to his mother he wrote, "I was really hoping for some crazy, noble, heroic death" and apologized to her for his weakness and failure. [30]

The disappointment of having missed their once-in-a-lifetime shot at battlefield glory can be especially intense for troops serving during the withdrawal stage of a military commitment. Two years after President Obama's 2011 announcement that the U.S. would begin drawing down its commitment to Afghanistan, there were still 60,000 troops there assisting the transition to an independent Afghan fighting force. "The younger soldiers," according to a *New York Times* report on a 101st Airborne Battalion still in Afghanistan, "are struggling with their relegation to a support role. Some feel that they had missed the war and were consigned to cleanup duty." Maj. Tyler Anderson, battalion executive officer said, "I tell these guys they were just born a decade too late." [31]

The discrepancy between the 15 percent of soldiers seeing combat, and the 30 percent or more of soldiers claiming mental disorders due to combat, closes if the definitions of what counts as combat is expanded and the combat credentials of individual claimants are enhanced through the "war stories" they tell. As it turns out, reasoning about combat and combat-related illness becomes circular when the illness itself becomes a credential for combat, a circularity deconstructed in the next two chapters.

NOTES

1. At vfw.org and the link to "Am I eligible?" one finds the criteria for membership in Veterans of Foreign Wars, some of which entail having a "campaign medal" for service in a military unit assigned to a place for a certain operation. A clerk-typist assigned to a headquarters unit in Vietnam, and not normally exposed to combat, would qualify for membership, as well as an infantry rifleman.

A campaign medal for "Operation Uphold Democracy" in Haiti, September 16, 1994, to March 31, 1995, entitles the holder to membership. (One U.S. soldier was killed during the operation.) A two-day Vietnam "campaign" called "Frequent Wind" on April 29–30, 1975, earns eligibility for the holder.

2. Shephard (2000, p. 18) recalls the words of military historian Sir Michael Howard about Edwardian England: "For the best part of a hundred years, war did indeed 'define masculinity' in British society. War was a test of Manhood."

3. Susan Faludi wrote approvingly of Barak Obama in 2008 that he was refusing to give "the traditional answer" to the "are you man enough?" question that is asked of men who want to lead America. At the time of her keynote address to the "Tea Party Convention" in 2010, republican Sarah Palin speculated in a February 6 interview with Fox News journalist Chris Wallace that President Obama might be a formidable candidate in the 2012 election campaign if he "toughened up" in his war against terror.

4. Frosch (2011). The sense of the court decision on Alvarez was that lying is not a crime, and that misrepresentation of military service is no different than, say, misrepresenting one's age on a job application. Other court cases upheld the validity of the Stolen Valor Act. In June 2012 the Supreme Court ruled in favor of Alvarez. The problem of false combat records combined with disability claims is addressed below.

5. Soldiers returning from current deployments fill out a "Post-deployment Health Assessment" questionnaire, DD Form 2796, APR 2003, which asks the follow questions: #7) Did you see anyone wounded, killed or dead during this deployment; #8) Were you engaged in direct combat where you discharged your weapon; #9) During this deployment, did you ever feel that you were in great danger of being killed; #10) Are you interested in receiving help for stress, emotional, alcohol, or family problems? Each of the questions had boxes to check for yes and no. Questions #7 and #8 had additional boxes for more qualified answers.

6. I messaged the reporter, Benedict Carey, on August 28, 2011, to ask if he had some other source for the "heavy combat" designation but I have not heard back.

7. Urbina (2009) reports on the problem of false military identities and disability claims: "In April 2009 the Department of Veterans Affairs was paying disability benefits to 286 supposed prisoners of war from the Persian Gulf War . . . and to 966 supposed prisoners of the Vietnam War. But Defense Department records show that only 21 prisoners of war returned from the Gulf War, and that fewer than 600 are alive from the Vietnam War." Urbina goes on to write that "tales of physical or psychological suffering can influence whether a veteran receives some money or nothing at all in disability payments."

8. With all apparent earnestness, *Times* reporter Christopher Drew (2009) wrote that "some pilots [as the air force calls the remote control drone operators] said it can be a hard transition from being a computer-screen warrior to dinner at home or their children's soccer games." The memoirs written by the pilots shot down over North Vietnam and held as POWs in Hanoi contain numerous references to the upscale living conditions they enjoyed before making their last and fateful bombing runs. Lair (2011, pp. 76–86) writes that conditions for GIs even within Vietnam were often as good as stateside. To provide fresh dairy products, including ice cream, the military contracted the operation of several dairy plants located throughout the South.

9. Troops of the National Liberation Front in South Vietnam had only small caliber artillery like mortars and virtually no means of transportation besides human and animal. The North Vietnamese mustered heavier artillery for a few set-piece battles like Khe Sanh in 1967, and mixed truck transport with human labor to move material and troops along the Ho Chi Minh trail in Laos and Cambodia. The U.S. faced very little air power from the Vietnamese other than the MiG fighter jets (acronym from their Russian manufacturer) deployed by Hanoi for defense of the North; the surface-to-air (SAM) missile defense of the cities was formidable.

10. See "How Many Terrorists Have We Killed in Iraq" www.freerepublic. com. The writer offered his own "belief" that even more than 200,000 terrorists had been killed.

11. "Jen" attributed the claim to "the command" of the operation.

12. In a September 5, 2007, interview with *Democracy Now*'s Amy Goodman, Anthony Romero, head of the American Civil Liberties Union, said that Vice President Dick Cheney had stated that Iraqi dead were not being counted. Secretary of Defense Donald Rumsfeld is also credited with saying the same thing. The *San Francisco Chronicle* reported on March 23, 2002, General Tommy Franks saying at a Bagram, Afghanistan, Air Base press conference, "You know we don't do body counts." The counts of U.S. dead and wounded are also distorted by the use of private security companies like Blackwater whose personnel carryout some dangerous duties and suffer some losses. It is not clear if their dead are factored into the kill ratios.

13. The idea of "armed propaganda," also known as "propaganda by deed," is captured by the expression that "actions speak louder than words."

14. Frank 2007; Bender 2009. By comparison, about 20 percent of U.S. military deaths in Vietnam were non-combat related.

15. Support for the continuation of the war in Vietnam during its closing years was mustered around the "don't let them die in vain" sentiment that used casualities as a reason for more war.

16. One perspective on the atrocity at My Lai, Vietnam, in 1968 was that it was *lack* of combat—not revenge for previous loses—that left troops of the U.S. Americal Division feeling deprived of the experience they wanted that led to their orgy of killing. Threads of that analysis can be found in Frederick's *Black Hearts*, 2010.

17. Kulik (2009, p. 181) reconstructs Turk's story-telling from Samuel Haynes's book *The Soldiers' Tale.*

18. As Nick Turse documents in *Kill Anything that Moves*, atrocities were a terrible reality of U.S. operations in Vietnam. Careful as he is, however, Turse, too, falls prey to "war stories" when he writes (p. 156) that "running down [Vietnamese] civilians with jeeps, trucks, tanks, and other armored vehicles was a commonplace occurrence," or when he repeats (p. 173) what has now become a kind of folklore about some prisoners being thrown out of helicopters in order to make others talk.

19. Farragher and Robinson (2009).

20. Kulik avers (pp. 190–91) that veterans tried to please interviewers by telling stories they thought would be recorded and reported. He concluded, "We'll never be sure why men embellished, exaggerated, and lied about such matters. But we know they did, and that's enough."

21. One of the best collection of Abu Ghraib photographs is Michael Scherer and Mark Benjamin "The Abu Ghraib Files" at Salon.com March 4, 2006.

22. See Faludi (2007) for the way the protector-protected dichotomy works to mutually construct gender identities.

23. Most of the interest in the women guards at Abu Ghraib prison has focused on how and why they could have forsaken the stereotypical female image as care-giving nurturers, and become accomplices in sexual violence. The centerpiece of those studies is that the military is an authoritarian and male dominated institution and for women to be successful in it, they have to become "one of the guys" (McKelvey, 2007). Rajiva (2007) rejects the "showing off" thesis, fearing that it supports conservative views that women in the military are a problem and should be banished from the ranks.

24. Merrill A. McPeak, Air Force chief of staff from 1990 to 1994, wrote in 2010 that the "military lifestyle . . . prepares warriors for a life of hardship . . . a kind of adventure apart from the civilian world and full of strange customs. To be a fighter pilot or a paratrooper or a submariner is to join a self-contained, resolutely idealistic society, largely unnoticed and surprisingly uncorrupted by the world at large."

25. Musheno and Ross (2008) capture the mixed motives of men deployed to Iraq. The closing scenes of the 2009 film *Hurt Locker* substitutes clogged drain spouts for "dishes and diapers" as the home-front unpleasantries to which some men prefer war. On the day this was written, March 9, 2010, the PBS *News Hour with Jim Lehrer* reported ten new deaths of U.S. soldiers in Iraq and Afghanistan: the mean age of those ten was 26.1, the median 26, and the mode 24. The youngest was 19, the oldest 40. The 19-year-old was the only death under 22. I wrote at greater length about the American fantasy of "kids" in war in "The Facts about Soldiers' Ages."

26. Hennessy-Fiske (2007). In April, 2010 after this paragraph was written, MSNBC reported that Burger King and Popeye were being withdrawn from Afghanistan. The report poked fun at the French fries that soldiers had been noshing and said priorities had shifted to more gyms and Internet availability. While the logic of the change was not apparent (i.e. gyms and Internet availability aren't exactly the same set of anything) the coincidence of the change with the coup d'état that destabilized neighboring Kyrgystan that week may have anticipated harder fighting ahead and the need for some hardened bodies to do it.

27. Chrandraskaran (2013) reports on the benefits provided to stateside military members by the commissary/PX system. See Lair (2011) for a historical perspective on the same.

28. Brown (2008) writes about the provisioning of TCNs for the U.S. military as "forced labor" but shows that it is a system interwoven with debt peonage and elements of slavery. Naomi Klein in Part 6 of *Shock Doctrine* (2007) illuminates the deeper ideological and policy dimensions of privatized warfare in Iraq, with specific attention to the use of foreign labor in pages 355–357.

29. Meyer's February 27, 2010, article at truthout.org has easy-to-use links to the Department of Defense "calculator" for military pay and the U.S. Bureau of Labor Statistics data he cites. Meyer acknowledges the difficulties of family separations for deployments and the dangers faced by soldiers in war zones.

30. Dao and Lehren (2013).

31. Ahmed (2013). The "just missed" feeling that can be devastating to the psyche of the individual returning to civilian life can also fuel the politics of resentment and loss in the post-war years. For his 1994 book *Warrior Dreams: Violence and Manhood in Post-Vietnam America*, James William Gibson found a large number of American men in the rightwing armed militia groups during the 1980s who felt deprived of a combat experience for having been too young for Vietnam.

Chapter Four

The Legacy of Salpêtrière: Art in the Science of War Trauma

Narrator (Charles Osgood):

World War I. Doctors see soldiers with unexplained tremors, some gone blind or deaf overnight, others mute, paralyzed, crying. Charles Meyers, a British doctor, speculates that their behaviors are somehow related to exploding shells on the front. So he calls it "shell shock." But then soldiers who have yet to see combat appear with similar symptoms.

Michael Roth:

Shell shock in many ways resembled hysteria. That was very embarrassing. Hysteria was something that happened to women. Doctors tried to find another name for it so as to spare their patients the shame of being called hysterics.

Narrator:

War neurosis; buried-alive neurosis; soldier's heart. All names to describe male hysteria. Doctors look long and hard for a physical

explanation for the symptoms . . . . Among a pioneering few familiar with Freud's theories, were those who believed that shell shock
is psychological.

Anne Harrington:

Shell shock is the body language of powerlessness . . . the body
will convert feelings of powerlessness into symptoms. Soldiers
who were brave, fit, and patriotic found themselves dealing with
fear, grief, loneliness, feelings that were not part of society's definition of what it meant to be a man. [1]

Anything but psychological. That was endpoint to which medical
studies of World War I veterans were driven by the culture of the
time. Decades later the historian of psychiatry Elaine Showalter
reflected on those times, saying that doctors were "so persuaded
that there must be an organic cause, so prejudiced against a psychological cause that they just kept looking and looking." The missing
"organic cause" they wanted, she said, was something physical,
some kind of visible wound on the body, or at least evidence of an
observed event, like a bomb blast, that could be responsible for the
symptoms they were faced with.

The doctors were men who had long associated hysteria with
women. Hysteria as a female disorder dated at least from its naming
by the Greeks who thought the uterus was anatomically unanchored
and capable of migrating throughout the body. Wherever the "wan-
dering womb" settled, it caused disturbances: paralysis of a leg
when it was there, limpness if it sat in the wrist, a facial tic if it was
in the neck. Men had no womb. How could they be hysterical? [2]

MEN, MODERNITY, AND RAILWAY SPINE

Prior to the nineteenth century, the social isolation of rural life that came with peasant and family-farm production and scattered-site small-scale manufacturing likely resulted in injuries to single workers that went unreported or even unrecognized. The cultures of self-sufficiency that those conditions bred, moreover, meant that treatments for the emotional effects of accidents—"nerves" was the expression common to the times—were the responsibility of the injured parties, a practice that sometimes made victims easy targets for hucksters selling "nerve tonics."[3] In fact, some of those symptoms were consistent with hysteria, the female disorder that men couldn't have.

It was the developments in transportation and communication associated with the industrial revolution that began breaking down the taboo on male hysteria. Railway accidents were among the first appearances of modernism's downside: large numbers of people were gathered together by the new technology in ways they had never been before and put at risk in relatively fast moving wood-frame train cars, people whose injuries following accidents were then widely publicized by the new medium of mass-produced newspapers.

The new and growing phenomenon of financial claims for accident injuries added to the public awareness that people were being injured in train wrecks, an awareness filtered through the newspapers and other impersonal sources. Soon, a new disorder known as "railway spine" appeared, its claimants not always evincing physical injury, or even with evidence of having actually been in a train accident. The defending railway companies in such cases understandably reacted to the claims for compensation for "back pain" by alleging that claimants' ailments were psychological, a form of "mass hysteria" brought on by the unsettling newness and dangers of railroad technology and the contagion effect of mass communications. Litigation over the cases went on for decades before the triumph of psychological interpretation both relieved the transportation companies of financial responsibility and legitimated further inquiry into the power of the mind to cause physical aliment.

The common symptoms of "railway spine" included spinal rigidity that prevented bending forward; an exaggerated concavity of the lower back, with the pelvis thrust forward and the shoulders thrown back as if the body was bracing for impact from behind; unsteadiness when standing or walking; a "peculiar gait" with one foot appearing to flop uncontrollably to the ground, and a leg that seemed to drag the ground in less than full strikes. John Eric Erichsen, the doctor who became famous for his study and treatment of the condition, also noted the "disproportion that exists between the apparently trifling accident the patient has sustained and the real and serious mischief that has occurred." In some cases, he remarked, there is no sign of external injury whatsoever. In fact, he said, the symptoms "seldom occur when a serious injury is inflicted on one of the limbs" unless, of course, the spine itself had been directly impacted.[4]

The origins of "railway spine" being associated with the public sphere of mass transportation, rather than the more private space of the home, and many actual victims of railway accidents being men who worked on the trains, increased the number of men brought under the scrutiny of Erichsen and other doctors. The appearances of symptoms in men when no physical injuries were evident pointed to a psychological dimension in "railway spine," the study of which eventually breached the reluctance of doctors to put "male" and "hysteria" in the same sentences.

Working at the Hospital Salpêtrière in the early 1880s, the French psychiatrist Jean-Martin Charcot considered the cases of men impaired from industrial accidents, and theorized that fright alone could be the cause of their symptoms. In effect, Charcot was suggesting that men could be hysterical and that, in keeping with their nature of being more physically active than women, their symptoms were more likely to take the form of bodily contortions—like railway spine. He even called one type of male hysteria "clownisme," a name that Showalter says reflected his lifelong fascination with circus clowns.[5]

The ability of social and economic environments—the "times," in effect—to influence medical diagnoses, aptly suggested by the early-nineteenth-century context in which "railway spine" appeared, was made still clearer by Charcot's studies of female hysteria.

WOMEN, MODERNITY, AND HYSTERIA

With the distance of many more years, it's easy enough now to see that it was the culture of the times, the years approaching the apex of modernism, that were responsible for the epidemic of "railway spine." The closer we get to our own time, on the other hand, the harder it is to treat war trauma in those coming home from Iraq and Afghanistan as a cultural and historical phenomenon—or, to invert the matter, easier to dismiss the reality of war trauma even if it appears in forms we do not recognize. Fortunately, the intervening decades provide other well-studied examples in which we can see the interplay of culture, technology, and medical science, examples that help bridge the gap between what is seemingly common sense and the sense of a more analytical approach.

Charcot was a neurologist by training and came to his study of hysteria with a theory that physical impairment of the brain, such as might be caused by an injury or a wound, was responsible for the bodily disorder exhibited by his patients. Known as the "brain lesion" theory, this idea came under attack after doctors practicing hypnosis were able to show that physical symptoms could be induced in otherwise healthy subjects by the utterance of suggestive words or commands, and that ailing patients could be relieved of their symptoms by other suggestions. The odd and inexplicable behaviors associated with hysteria, in other words, had a more attenuated relationship to the physical condition of the brain than the lesion theory would predict.

Charcot also collected classical paintings and was an artist in his own right who continued a centuries-old tradition of doctors sketching their patients. Sander Gilman notes the cross-influences of insanity, medicine, and art in his cultural history of madness and art. According to him, "The visual representations of the insane in medical texts [at the end of the seventeenth century] are identical with those in fine and popular arts of [the thirteenth century]."[6] To demonstrate his point, Gilman displays a diagram from the Middle Ages showing the postures of the maniac, the epileptic, the melancholic, and the frenetic, postures similar to those treated for hysteria in the late nineteenth century.[7]

The invention of photography led to its use by Hugh Diamond in the women's department of the Surrey County Lunatic Asylum in the 1850s. The photograph, Diamond argued, could record with greater accuracy than hand-drawn portraits the external manifestations, observed on the body, of internal derangements, although Gilman observes that the photographs chosen by doctors for inclusion in textbooks of the time sometimes resembled the same postures and positions established by the tradition of portraiture over the years.[8] Charcot hired photographer Albert Londe to record the postures of hysterics and some of those were sold with sketches for public consumption. A showman, Charcot turned his lectures at Salpêtrière into public performances using his artwork to decorate the "stage" and hysterical patients as the stars of the show. Patients would be hypnotized by Charcot's interns and made to crawl and bark like dogs for the entertainment of his noontime audiences, even though the doctor himself believed hypnosis only "appeared" to work as advertised—the susceptibility to hypnosis was itself a symptom of hysteria.[9]

Critics would eventually allege that Charcot had "invented" hysteria through the power of his theatrics but, just as railway spine was a product of its times of origin, so too hysteria was propelled to prominence by the technological and cultural forces changing Europe in the late nineteenth century. To begin with, Charcot worked within the milieu of medical science already altered by modernism and the influence of railway-spine studies. Moreover, Charcot was also in harmony with secular movements against Catholicism and the church's practice of exorcism to treat diabolic possession and other precursors to hysteria. Additionally, the centralization of manufacture and transportation in the early decades of the century had changed the relationships between workers, employers, media, and the state. Factory production was pulling women off farms, putting them into cities where their presence in the workplace challenged the traditional boundaries of sex and gender—men at work, women at home—putting stresses on working-class women who were alone and sexually vulnerable in urban environments new to them.[10]

Above all else, it was the primacy of "the visual" that the camera brought to its symptomology that reinforced the idea that psychological states could register visually on the body—and specifically as facial expressions—bolstering the foundation on which the subgenre of psychosomatic illnesses would be identified, studied, and treated. The aestheticism that attached to the photographs, moreover, lent hysteria the necessary cachet for appeal to popular cultural interests outside the narrow community of professional diagnosticians.[11]

It's not so certain, of course, that photography had to precede hysteria in the same sense that there could have been no railway spine before there were railroads, but there is no doubt that the photographs of Charcot's patients enhanced the allure that his practice had for the public and other professionals. At that level, though, Charcot was merely demonstrating, seventy years ahead of

Marshall McLuhan, that the "medium is the message," whereas the real significance of Salpêtrière was that the *medium was the method*: it was the presence of the camera that evoked from the patients the bodily expressions that were then said to be symptoms of hysteria.[12]

Historians who study the influence of Charcot's work on the practice of psychiatry going forward emphasize the interactions of the doctor, his artwork, his female patients, and the presence of the camera. The course of that influence ran through the worlds of art, theater, and novels from where they looped back into the cultures of medical practice and public policy. One of Charcot's patients was Blanche Wittman who historian Elaine Showalter describes as the daughter of a carpenter who worked as a laundress, furrier's apprentice, and a nurse, and whose convulsions and "nervous cries" began after the furrier attempted to rape her. At Salpêtrière, her fits were "painted, displayed, and photographed" and reported in detail for the Western medical community. Another was Augustine who began having seizures after being raped by her mother's lover; in the hospital at Salpêtrière she became the most photographed of all of Londe's subjects and the inspiration for playwrights and screenwriters.

In turn, the images of Wittman and Augustine "taught other women how hysterics looked," according to Showalter. She quotes historian Jan Goldstein saying, "'The 'iconography' of hysteria as defined by Charcot—with all its vividly theatrical contortions and grimaces—seems to have been so widely publicized . . . in both pictorial and verbal form, as to constitute for that historical moment a reigning 'cultural perception' of how to act when insane.'"[13]

The classical paintings of demonic figures that surrounded Charcot and the women may have suggested to them the poses that he wanted to see, according to Michael Roth. But the more serious criticism of Charcot was that he actually "coached" his patients, and that by proffering them a "warped celebrity" when they executed his script—while yet keeping them confined in the hospital—he was coercing from them the presentation of symptoms that he then used to define hysteria. In time, novelists who may once have found their subject matter in Augustine found it in the practice of the doctor himself, the impresario who made it all happen. [14]

Charcot's brain lesion theory of hysteria had its moments in the treatment of World War I veterans but, by then, his use of photography had had the unintended consequence of exposing the interplay of mind and body in the production and presentation of patients' symptoms. With the mind in play, so to speak, it was a short step to consider the power of patients' imaginations in creating the symptoms seen by doctors, and the influence of cultural forces on those imaginations. If art prompted Charcot's patients, is it possible that the body language treated as "shell shock" in soldiers was cued by some other cultural form? Is it possible, even, that doctors acculturated to Charcot's syntheses of *pre*sentation and *repre*sentation were unable to distinguish one from the other in their observations of "shell shock"? [15]

Charcot's protégés would take more literally the possibility that hysteria was a form of body language, expressions of feelings that social norms had banished from the mind and tongue to a level of the psyche called the "unconscious." From there, emotions stemming from the "unspeakable" and "unthinkable" reemerge as unwanted physical symptoms. The linkages made between mind, body, and society in that emerging paradigm provided a model for understanding how the news media, popular culture, and medical science fit together in the studies of war trauma, a paradigm that holds the key to understanding those same war-born maladies a century later. [16]

THE SOCIAL IMPERATIVE IN SHELL SHOCK

Between Charcot's theory of physical causation and the idea that hysteria was a kind of "body speak" lay twenty years of thinking about what brought it on and whether hysteria was the proper way to think about veterans' ailments. The recognition that minds and bodies interacted with societal influences in the production of symptoms was an enormous step forward but, left at that, the field was open to a simple power-of-suggestion theory that dismissed patients as clever agents of their own symptom making or even outright "fakes." After watching Charcot's patients as a student, Joseph Babinski thought that they had persuaded themselves that they had a disease and then presented the symptoms they thought the doctor wanted to see. Thus, the symptoms viewed as shell shock, he reasoned, were "brought about not by the war itself but either by unintentional suggestion from doctors or by the patient's auto-suggestion and imitation."[17]

Babinski's theory of suggestion gained support with the more frequent appearance of shell shock symptoms in German soldiers who had never been under fire, compared with those who had. The Freiburg physician Alfred Hauptmann, moreover, reasoned that soldiers with actual physical wounds should exhibit shell-shock symptoms—but they seldom did, a fact leading him to search for psychogenic explanations. Moreover, he thought, if shell explosions did directly cause neuroses, then soldiers would surely suffer these symptoms from firing their own weapons, a phenomenon that he had never observed." And there were those cases that could be cured by hypnosis, an indication that their disorders must be psychological, not physical in nature, something akin to hysteria. Referring to the suggestion theory as "copper" and the psychological theory as "gold," Sigmund Freud tentatively "alloyed" the two for a psychoanalytic approach that was just emerging out of the wartime experience with shell shock.[18]

Freud had attended Charcot's lectures in Paris, but he wasn't sure that patients participated so consciously in the making of their own illnesses. For one thing, they didn't always remember when their symptoms first appeared, much less why, and yet under hypnosis they would remember. It was as if the memory was there, thought Freud, but the patient couldn't willfully call it forth. Oftentimes, the memory that seemed inaccessible to the conscious *un*-hypnotized mind was an unpleasant memory, one that the patient must have "put away" to a part of the mind where it would not be a bother.

Working with a colleague, Joseph Breuer, Freud's treatment of women with hysteria was oriented around the idea that the mind was divided between levels of the conscious and the unconscious. He thought it was memories of early childhood sexual experiences involving incest that patients had repressed to the unconscious from whence they then reemerged in unwanted physical expressions. When the patients were able to talk about those experiences, their physical symptoms would often disappear. But Freud was seeing more female hysterics than he thought there could be sexually abusive fathers and uncles, and thought it more likely that his patients had repressed childhood *fantasies* of socially forbidden sexual acts and that, under hypnosis, it was these fantasies that reemerged as "memories."

It was the rethinking of Freud's ideas by other therapists that etched them into the repertory of mental health professionals. British psychologist W. H. Rivers, for example, concluded that repression of something to the subconscious was related to shell shock but that it was conflict between fear and duty, not something sexual, that soldiers and veterans repressed; it was that conflict, Rivers said, that caused the Freudian "flight into illness." Likewise, it wasn't *sexual* fantasies that reemerged as memories, but men's fantasies of the martial experiences and accomplishments they thought were expected of them that came out as false memories of those things having actually happened. In a sense Rivers put *social* in the place where Freud had *sexual*, opening the way to understanding how the minds of soldiers could generate physical symptoms of shell shock prior to exposure to combat, and the role played by culture as the consummately social ingredient in that process. [19]

In no sense did Rivers's neo-Freudian perspective on shell shock imply that the illness of veterans needing to be understood was not "real." Rather, it shifted the diagnostic gaze from causes external to the victim, like exploding shells, to causes that were internal to the mind and emotions of the veteran. What the patient was *really* afraid of was his own shortcomings that might result in him being seen as a failure by friends, even his comrades in arms, and family. [20]

Just as retrospective studies of Charcot's work at Salpêtrière pointed to the influence of art and culture on what the patients were exhibiting and the doctor was seeing, reviews of shell shock's origins see it cradled in the popular culture of the times. Writing in *A War of Nerves*, historian Ben Shephard calls shell shock an example of "a common modern phenomenon: a medical debate, hedged with scientific qualifications, taken up by public opinion and the media in an oversimplified way." With shell shock thus imbedded in the public imagination, wrote historian J.C. Dunn, the "lurid journalese of home [news]papers . . . prepared the minds of the draft[ees]" for receptivity to suggestions that they would soon be suffering from it. Or, in the words of Doctor William Johnson who had studied as a neurologist, won commendation for bravery at the battle of the Somme, and later treated war casualties, "Young soldiers prepare to become a case of shell-shock almost before the first shell drops near them." [21]

The doctors themselves were not impervious to the influence of popular culture. Charcot's photographs had made their way into the public realm but Janet Browne notes their particular popularity among doctors working in Salpêtrière. And there may have been a feedback loop running from the doctors in the asylum where the photographs were taken, through the public's fascination with them after they were published and distributed, back to doctors working in subsequent years in hospitals. In his 1985 essay "Shellshock and the Psychologists," Martin Stone wrote of the early war period that "shellshock had, it seemed, caught both the sympathy and imagination of the public who [in turn] 'raised the psychoneuroses to the dignity of a new disease before which doctors seemed well nigh helpless.'" In short form, Browne and Stone are suggesting that art, if not having led science in the making of the diagnostic category known as shell shock, was a powerful additive. [22]

The gendered threads of shell shock are also traceable through the connection of art to psychiatric diagnosis but in this case the threads get a twist. The utility of the shell shock diagnosis was cultural as much as medical because it diverted the search for the cause of symptoms away from issues with sex or gender implications. The idea that the symptoms observed could be due to fear of either bodily injury or failure was objectionable because it linked, in the minds of psychiatrists, to hysteria which led in turn to the photographic images left by Londe's camera—which were women—and the paintings in Charcot's clinic that prompted Londe's subjects—which were paintings of women. Those graphic images formed a paradigmatic barrier to the ability of the doctors to follow a train of thought leading to either psychological or socio-cultural explanations for the symptoms they observed—anything but psychological. [23]

Two other technological determinants converged to bend the search away from psychological explanations for the symptoms to physical causes external to the patients. One was the industrial nature of the war that brought petro-powered vehicles like tanks, airplanes, and long-range artillery into battle. The manufacture and transportation of mass quantities of ammunition like those expended in the war were beyond the imaginations of war planners prior to the era of factory production and the roads and rails criss-crossing Europe by 1914. Called the "war of machines" in some accounts, World War I proletarianized the armies, reducing skilled fighters to little more than bodies in the trenches, the life or death of which provided a means of measuring the productivity of the machines.[24]

The combination of men and machines for medical considera-tion summoned to mind, for doctors and patients, the relevance of "railway spine" as a starting point for understanding what was hap-pening to soldiers. Dr. Henry Head believed that men under fire in the trenches had to suppress their instinct to survive by running away, and that the body then converted that conflict into a paralysis of the legs, a condition recognized as a "symptom" that could jus-tify his removal from danger. Others speculated that paralysis was a positioning in place of arms and legs that fixed them as they were at the time of exposure to explosions—sort of like bracing for the impact of a train collision. Like the paralysis of a limb, other forms of immobility such as dumbness or insensitivity to stimuli were thought by William Rivers to be reassertions of instincts dormant since earlier stages of human evolution, vestigial responses to dan-ger calling for silence and stillness.[25] The attraction of the railway-spine paradigm was enhanced by the way it, first, placed cause on the train accident itself, outside the mind and body of the patient, and, second, privileged physical symptoms such as paralysis as more in keeping with a "man's malady," a bias that easily trans-ferred to its diagnostic appropriateness for war casualties.

The other technology coming into play was the movie camera. Historians are in wide agreement that Londe's still photographs were able to capture the facial contortions of Charcot's female patients, and thereby magnetize the attention of doctors on "the visual." In a sense, that part of what went on at Salpêtrière lends support for the idea that doctors believed, not just what they could see, but the visuals they could document. But it was the impairment of motion associated with railway spine that would frame doctors' observations of shell-shock patients, and motion (or the lack of) could not so easily be documented by still photography. While there was a lot of overlap between the symptoms associated with hysteria—muteness and deafness, for example—it was the presentation of *paralysis* that signaled something more specifically like railway spine, something more man-like that called forth a new diagnostic category tailored for veterans of modern war. The moving picture camera only being developed when Charcot died in 1893 was just what the doctors ordered for the men felled by the Guns of August.[26]

SHELL-SHOCK CINEMA

In his 2010 book *Shell Shock Cinema: Weimar Culture and the Wounds of War*, Anton Kaes recalls that the German psychiatrist Hans Henns pleaded in 1909 for "the wider use of film in the recording and diagnosis of mental patients' behavior." Kaes continues with the suggestion of a kind of synergy between the technologies of early film itself—jumpy, abrupt juxtapositions, and silent—and the symptoms it purported to capture—spastic movements, contortions, and muteness. Nearly a century later, one can imagine that the oddness of body images appearing in these rough-hewn films, even healthy bodies, as seen for the first time by young men, perhaps even before the war years, suggested to them that certain positions and postures carried mental health implications when viewed by the public.

Tellingly, the soundless property of early film correlated with the absence of the startle response presented by veterans of later wars who claimed that a sharp and unexpected noise like a firecracker caused them to relive wartime experience and respond as they would have in battle. It was a symptom that would be closely associated with PTSD after the war in Vietnam—and well after sound was married to motion pictures in the 1930s.

The certainty that film influenced patients and doctors in the shell-shock wards of hospitals and asylums to the same degree that Londe's photographs shaped the construction of hysteria cannot be established, of course. But the 1920s were verdant years for comingling art, science and new technology. In her book *God or Gorilla: Images of Evolution in the Jazz Age*, Constance Clark documented the way scientific thinking was popularized through cartoons and illustrations, noting as well that "visual images colored the way scientists themselves thought about evolution." In particular the metaphor of "seeing evolution" by running a succession of photographs through a "moving picture machine" was likely inspired by the movie *Evolution* circulating in theaters at the time. According to Clark, "Visualizations like [*Evolution*]—or the existence of movies in general, and the acute awareness of moving pictures as a way of seeing—affected the way people, including scientists, conceived of evolution."[27]

Kaes, accordingly, is certain that the post-war cinematic representation of World War I veterans as victims of shell shock was an essential element of political culture, especially in inter-war Germany. The 1920 film *The Cabinet of Dr. Caligari*, for example, was one of the first and most influential films of that genre. In it, the character Cesare is a veteran representing the horrors of the war he carries into Germany's future. Metaphorically, shell shock was the unseen wound carried as well by the body-politic as the silent disease of national trauma demanding vengeance through more war. Cesare appears early in the film, standing but inanimate, in an open and upright coffin. Haltingly, under the influence of the mysterious Dr. Caligari, Cesare begins to move, stepping from the coffin in a stiff and jump-cut motion that resembles the movement of the recovering shell-shock victims that we see in the public television program *Odyssey* cited in the epigraph for this chapter. Kaes's blunt identification of the real-life Charcot as the model for the filmic Caligari fills in a matrix of mutually influencing relationships in medicine (between doctors and patients), developments in communication technology (photography and film), the interaction of means and modes of modern warfare with cultural influences (media representations of medical and military events), and artistry (painters, photographers, screenwriters) across several decades, shaping, as they move, public memory of wars past and imaginations of wars to come.[28]

THE UNITED STATES: WHEN JOHNNY CAME MARCHING HOME

In the United States, shell shock, or "war neurosis," became an even more common ailment after the armistice of November 11, 1918. Writing in *Hystories*, Elaine Showalter speculates that the rise in post-war symptoms was due to veterans' resentments of the war and the political sentiments that had placed them in harm's way. That anger might have found fuel in the lingering public disaffection manifested during the war through strikes and the spread of pacifist activity and organizations. But the crack-down on political dissent triggered by fear that the Russian Revolution would instigate insurrection in the American Heartland, and the reneging of the government on its payment of veterans' benefits undoubtedly left many Doughboys, having already suffered combat, feeling vulnerable in a hostile environment. [29]

World War I and the years that followed produced evidence that veterans' development of medical or psychological symptoms depended on more than the events of the war themselves. The level of societal divisiveness wrought by the war, for example, effected veterans' perceptions of how much their service was respected. With thousands of Americans having been arrested and deported for opposing the war, and hundreds more jailed for labor strikes, it

was easy for veterans to imagine their sacrifices going unappreciat-
ed by the very people for whom they had fought. The stock market
crash that sent the country into deep depression a mere eleven years
after the war pushed tens of thousands of veterans out of their jobs,
homes, and farms, leaving them feeling rejected and forgotten.
They responded by marching on Washington in July 1932 as the
"Bonus Expeditionary Force" to demand payment of the benefits
promised to them. Instead, they got the points of bayonets wielded
by U.S. troops mustered to drive them from the capitol mall.

The outcome of World War I, moreover, left its mission less
than accomplished. Sold to Americans as "the war to make the
world safe for democracy" and "the war to end all wars," it resulted
in massive violations of civil liberties at home, and post-war settlements in Europe that remilitarized the continent and propelled the
triumph of fascist dictatorships in Germany, Italy, and Spain. In
short, ten years after the war, veterans would have seen few results
to take pride in; in twenty-five years they would be looking at a
Second World War whose butchery was growing from the carnage
they had left behind.[30]

Before they looked ahead to the next war, however, they had to
look at the way public memory of the last was being constructed
through film, theater, and novels. The signature product of those
efforts was *All Quiet on the Western Front*, Eric Remarque's anti-
war novel about the illusions of patriotism that drew young Ger-
mans into the war, and its cruelty that left them maimed and embit-
tered. In 1930 it was made into a film by the same title, considered
by some critics to be one of the great films of the twentieth century.
In Irwin Shaw's 1936 play *Bury the Dead*, six dead soldiers refused
to stay buried, their persistence to live a metaphor for the unsettled
conscience that burdens societies that have made war. For his 1938
novel *Johnny Got His Gun* Dalton Trumbo created the World War I
veteran Joe who lost all his limbs, senses, and face in an artillery
explosion. Joe's mind is fine, however, and by tapping Morse code

with his head, he manages to tell the world the class realities of modern war.

NEW WARS, DIFFERENT POST-WAR STORIES

World War II provided a contrasting case in the matter of its soldiers' and veterans' psychiatric welfare. Its brutality registered on the bodies of 416,000 U.S. dead and 566,000 wounded; the evacuation rate for U.S. psychiatric casualties was much higher than it would be in Vietnam. And yet curiously, observed one doctor, "In the Second World War hysterical symptoms disappeared almost entirely." The absence of shell-shock-type damage could have been due to the improved practices of doctors who, "forewarned and forearmed," as Showalter put it, "could prevent epidemic hysteria in the trenches"—nip it in the bud, so to speak.[31]

More likely, World War I itself had acquainted the Western world with modern military technology, thereby diminishing the social and psychological impact that long-range artillery and airpower would have on the next generation of fighters, and the way the public would imagine World War II. The greater accessibility of photojournalism to Americans through mass-circulation magazines like *Look* and *Life*, and the filmic images brought to theaters through newsreels helped, too, to demystify the war. The popularity of the war also made service in it less troubling.

World War II would eventually be remembered as "The Good Fight," the war that a large majority of Americans supported as a righteous cause: the liberation of the death camps in Europe, and payback in Asia for the sneak attack on Pearl Harbor. But those feel-good memories emerged slowly in the post-war years, competing for a time with discomforting images of veterans with lives torn up by the war. An August 7, 1944, *Time* magazine article exposed the difficulties facing soldiers returning from the war. The article became the basis for *The Best Years of Our Lives*, the 1946 film about three veterans who return with no fanfare and problems that included unemployment, alcoholism, and divorce. Sociologist Alfred Schutz wrote the same year about veterans as "strangers" at odds with their communities. The journalist Hunter Thompson later rode with the Hells Angels and described them as World War II veterans who had been unable to settle back into civilian life.

But the overwhelming reality was that World War II had ended with unambiguous victories on the European and Pacific fronts that cast the admiration of the world on the United States and bequeathed it twenty-five years of economic prosperity, for which veterans could take prideful credit.

Post–World War II American culture was triumphalist with the material means to do well by the men who had pushed the Nazis back into Berlin's Fuhrerbunkers and taken Japan's surrender on the battleship *Missouri*. The GI Bill passed in 1944 paid tuition to veterans' colleges of choice and provided them with home loans and a year of unemployment compensation. Jobs in manufacturing that had been filled by women were reopened to men upon their return; the engines of propaganda that had romanticized "Rosie the Riveter" as an industrial warrior keeping the supply lines full were reversed to justify her reassignment to the kitchen. Construction projects and consumer demands postponed for wartime production and service now manifested as economic demand that spurred investment and job growth into the 1970s.

The privations of war visited upon soldiers and their families during the war years of the early 1940s receded in the rearview mirror as the nation raced into its glory days.[32]

The 54,000 U.S. soldiers killed in Korea from 1950 to 1953 were more than a speed bump in the road to the American Dream but the headiness of triumphs over Hitler and Tojo, relived in the weekly televised episodes of *Victory at Sea,* documented the military might of the United States—and the moral rectitude that it licensed. The newness of television in itself conveyed the message that World War II was a threshold through which the country had passed from "old" to "new," more a cultural boundary than a political economic event. The generation growing up on the new media of the 1950s and early 1960s would know World War II through televised images of valor but, as well, through sitcoms like *Hogan's Heroes* and *Gilligan's Island* that lampooned military life while erasing any sign that the horrors of war lived on in the psyches of the men who fought it. Early post-war films like *The Best Years of Our Lives* (1946) hinted at veterans' adjustment problems but Hollywood, sensing perhaps the rising tide of optimism that many years of economic growth would bring, refocused its lens on figures of heroic masculinity like John Wayne's Sgt. Stryker in *Sands of Iwo Jima* (1949), and then kept filmgoers comfortable with more stories about the last war like *From Here to Eternity* (1953) that *Variety* called "socko entertainment."[33]

DRIVE-WAR-DISCHARGE

In his book *No Man's Land*, Eric Leed describes the "drive-discharge" psychoanalytic approach to war trauma that sheds additional light on why the symptoms of hysteria were less common for GIs in World War II than World War I, an approach that, in turn, helps us understand the reappearance of shell shock/hysteria in the guise of PTSD after the war in Vietnam—and its third act as Traumatic Brain Injury in the next century.

Leed wrote about the confining and channeling nature of modern society that required the denial and suppression of libidinal drives. It was a theory of modernity not unlike that of the sociologist Max Weber who thought the deferment of gratification, regarded as virtuous by Protestantism, was the psychological basis for capitalism. The instinctual primitivisms of earlier stages of evolution were retained by humankind, requiring the periodic releases of "the insubordinate libido" in a "field of instinctual liberation," sometimes taking the form of war. In the words of German play-wright Carl Zuckmayer, war provided "liberation from bourgeois narrowness and pettiness, from compulsory education and cramming, from the doubts of choosing a profession and above all . . . from the petrifaction of our world."[34]

The peace-war binary played out classically in World War II as spasms of violence in the Nazi death camps, the suicidal assaults on Normandy, the fire bombings of Dresden and Tokyo, and the atomic bombings of Nagasaki and Hiroshima. But World War I had been a slow and grinding affair, deathly but inconclusive and unsatisfying. The oppositions distinguishing peace and war across which the accumulated frustrations of life in modern society could be discharged were blurred by the invisibility of the enemy positioned behind its artillery miles away—or dug into trenches only yards away; the ambiguous identity of "no man's land" given the ground separating the dug-in troops that could as well have been called "the commons," a metaphor for the lack of hostility normally felt by warring parties. The rapidity with which "recruits" were ushered into the ranks lacked sufficient ritual to bounder the civilian life of the inductee that *had been* from the military life that *was now*, a boundary that blurred again at the end of the war with a lack of consensus about what it had all been about and how the men returned from war should be received. [35]

• • • •

Shortly after it was produced for public television in 1998 I began using "Science Odyssey: In Search of Ourselves" for a unit on Freud in a sociology course at Holy Cross College. The program's segment on Charcot's work on female hysteria at Salpêtrière and the application of Freud's insights to shell shock in World War I veterans illustrated points about mind-body-culture connections that are at the core of sociological interest.

But it was the program's reprise of shell shock that had me enthralled. I had just finished an early phase of writing on PTSD and the words of Michael Roth and Anne Harrington, as quoted for the epigraph for this chapter, were not only resonant with what I had written, but articulations of what I thought needed to be said about PTSD, thoughts for which I needed their words. Writing in his 2001 edited volume *Traumatic Pasts*, Mark Micale, another contributor to "Science Odyssey", emphasized the similarity in the provenances of "shell shock" and PTSD. "The congruities in both narrative backgrounds and clinical descriptions between these nineteenth- and twentieth-century cases," he wrote, "are conspicuous."

The following chapter reveals the congruity linking shell shock and PTSD to be, in turn, the core narrative in PTSD's extension to twenty-first-century wars and the emergence of Traumatic Brain Injury.

NOTES

1. The foregoing epigraph is transcribed from the 1998 PBS broadcast "Science Odyssey: In Search of Ourselves." At the time, Michael Roth was a historian at the Getty Research Institute. He is currently the President of Wesleyan University. Anne Harrington is Historian of Science at Harvard University,

2. Showalter (1997, p. 64) quotes a French physician saying in 1819: "A man cannot be hysterical; he has no uterus."

3. Shephard (2008, pp. 15–16).

4. Erichsen (1867, p. 73).

5. Working at the Hopital de la Salpêtrière in Paris, Charcot published sixty-one case histories of male hysteria, cases which Showalter says were "crucial to understanding the construction of masculinity." Those writings remained obscure, however, because they were not translated into English until the 1990s, a delay in time that allowed hysteria in war veterans to be hidden under euphemisms such as shell shock and Post Traumatic Stress Disorder.

6. Gilman (1982, p. 21).

7. Charcot's own drawings, writes Gilman, were indebted to sketches published by Jean Etienne Dominique Esquirol in the early 1800s.

8. Gilman (1982, p. 164).

9. Showalter (1997, p. 34). A detailed description of the artwork decorating Charcot's stage is found in Sander L. Gilman's *The Image of the Hysteric*. (Note on the citation: A UC press "E-books Collection" found as a PDF file on line.)

10. Showalter (1997, p. 32) notes Charcot's interest in debunking the church's "miracle cures." Showalter (p. 34) elaborates the socioeconomic conditions that accounted for many of Charcot's patients being working-class women.

11. Janet Browne (1985, p. 158) opines that psychiatric photography was popular in part because of "the attractions of the art of photography itself." Sander Gilman (2004, Pp. 716–717) wrote of "facial expression as an infallible indicator of psychological states."

12. The results of Charcot's use of photography may also have presaged recognition of "the Hawthorne Effect," the alteration of a research environment by the research process itself. Coincidentally (perhaps), the studies at the Hawthorne factory giving rise to that concept in the 1920s were conducted by Elton Mayo who according to Martin Stone (1985, p. 248) began his career as a "shellshock doctor with the Australian army."

13. Showalter (1997, p. 36).

14. "Warped celebrity" is Showalter's phrase (1997, p. 36–37). Showalter cites Leon Daudet's *Les Morticoles* as a "savage novel [that] portrayed Charcot as the sinister Doctor Foutange who manipulates his patients like a puppeteer." Roth in "Science Odyssey" says the resemblance between the poses struck by Charcot's patients and classical paintings was "not an accident."

15. Shepard (2008, p. 98) recalls that Herman Oppenheim in Germany believed that shelling created microscopic lesions in the brain and nervous system, causing the paralysis seen in veterans. Although Oppenheim's idea was soon discredited, according to Shepard (2008, p. 99), it would be resurrected in the early 2000s for a successor to shell shock, Traumatic Brain Injury (TBI). For a 2012 *New York Times* column, Nicholas Kristoff wrote about Iraq War veteran Ben Richards who is being treated for PTSD/TBI, reporting prematurely that lesions have been found in his brain.

16. Shephard (2008, 98). As late as 2013, the search for "biomarkers," something physical that could be connected to PTSD, was ongoing (see Dao, 2013).

17. Shepard (2008, pp. 11–12, 98).

18. Shepard (2008, p. 106, 112). Given the uncritical acceptance in popular culture decades later that shell shock was a valid diagnostic category for World War I soldiers—and thus a base-line from which inquiries into PTSD can meaningfully begin decades later—it is surprising to look back and see that, at the time, some doctors rejected it. The official inquiry into "shell-shock" by the British War Office Committee in 1922 (their quotation marks on the term) summarized its findings with the following words:

> On all the main issues there is unanimity of opinion. "It is demonstrated that 'shell-shock' has been a gross and costly misnomer and that the term should be eliminated from our nomenclature. . . . The war produced no new nervous disorders, and those which occurred had previously been recognized in civil medical practice."

19. Harrington (2008, pp. 75–76) has an accessible account of Freud's break-through. See also Stone (1985, p. 255) for Rivers's reworking of Freud's insights. *New York Times* columnist Maureen Down (2010) made clever use of Freud's insight in writing about Connecticut Attorney General Richard Blumenthal's false claim to being a Vietnam veteran.

20. Rivers' insight would be reprised by Hyer et al. for a 1990 study that found low self-esteem rooted in parental practices was a better predictor of suicide among Vietnam veterans than was military experience. Controversies over veteran suicides are touched on in other chapters.

21. Dunn (1987, p. 250); Johnson is quoted by Shephard (2008, pp. 58-59).

22. Browne (1985, p. 158); Stone (1985, p. 254).

23. The details of World War I battlefront realities provided by Reid (2010, pp. 58–70) make it understandable that doctors and military authorities had a hard time sorting out cases of malingering, self-mutilation, hysteria, and imitation from actual shell shock—which itself was still an emergent concept.

24. The 2011 film *War Horse* set in World War I provides a dramatic contrast between the old horse-drawn technology that began the war and the twentieth-century machines that brought it to an end. The skills of horsemanship and hand-wielded weaponry like sabers were no match for artillery and tanks.

25. Hunters are familiar with the ability of animals, like rabbits, to sit motionless in order to disguise their whereabouts. If evolutionary development has programmed a startle response into humankind, it's as likely to be the instinct to "sit" when threatened, writes psychologist Susan Cain (2010), as to more actively engage the danger.

26. Young (1995, p. 41) captures the power of railway spine to frame doctors' thinking on war casualties: "A half-century after the publication of Erichsen's first book on railway accidents, physicians . . . were witnesses to an epidemic of traumatic paralyses, contractures, anesthesias, and aboulias . . . as if a hundred colossal railway smashups were taking place every day." Anesthesias, contractures, and aboulias are all associated with difficulty in moving. In Caruth (1996, p. 16) we can see the presence of the railway spine studies in Freud's thinking.

27. Clark (2008, p. 159–60).

28. Kaes (2010, p. 66) says Cesare "might have been case number 365, as recorded in a 1919 medical collection called *Shell-Shock and Other Neuropsychiatric Problems Presented in 589 Case Histories from the War Literature, 1914–1918*. Whether Cesare's herky-jerky motions are performed by the actor Conrad Veidt, or are an artifact of the film's jumpy quality, they can be compared with documentary images of shell-shock patients seen in the 1998 PBS "Science Odyssey" cited above. In *Caligari to Hitler* (1947) Siegfried Kracauer developed the political role played by films like *Caligari*.

29. Showalter (1997, p. 74) says that 36 percent of British veterans receiving disability payments in 1932 were psychiatric casualties and 58 percent of patients in U.S. veterans hospitals in 1942 were psychiatric cases. She does not footnote her source.

30. Although it did not address the American cases of shell shock, the most universally cited primary document on shell-shock is the Great Britain 1922 *Report of the War Office Committee of Enquiry into "Shell-Shock."* In its section "Summary of Findings of the Committee," the authors cited "the inculcation of morale and discipline" as effective measures for the prevention of shell-shock and included in their definition of morale "belief in the cause" and "the feeling that a man is part of a corporate whole."

31. The average psychiatric casualty rate per 1,000 troops for the years 1965–1969 was 11.96 as compared with 37 for the Korean War. Rates for World War II ranged from 101 to 28 depending upon the unit reported (U.S. Senate, 1972b). Bourne (1972) reported that 6 percent of the evacuations from Viet Nam were for psychiatric reasons as compared with 23 percent in World War II. Showalter's (1997, p. 74) claim that hysteria disappeared in WWII is supported by Anderson et al. (1944) who found that psychiatric casualties from the invasion of Normandy recovered quickly and without the "conversion disorder" (to somatic symptoms) associated with hysteria. The Normandy study cited higher unit morale, commitment to the mission, and confidence in leadership as reasons for the lower rate of hysteria.

32. More formally the GI Bill was The Servicemen's Readjustment Act.

33. Brogdon (1953).

34. Leed (1979, p. 17).

35. Smith and Pear (1917, Pp. 9–10) draw a graphic distinction between what they call "natural and primitive means of fighting" involving face-to-face combat and "impersonal, undiscriminating, and unpredictable . . . methods of modern warfare" characterized by trenches of World War I. In the former, they say, "the effect of every blow would be visible, and the intense excitement aroused in the relatively short contest would tend to obliterate the action of other instincts such as that of flight, with its emotion of fear," whereas the latter would not.

Chapter Five

Flashbacks: War Trauma Refashioned for PTSD

World War II was an orgiastic deliverance that left the United States satisfied and free to focus on its birthright as the City-on-the-Hill. But its idea of modernity—and its own sense of that as a better way for others as well—was soon met with objection from the traditionalism of the less developed world and the opposition of visionaries looking for a route to industrialization that bypassed the "satanic mills" of early capitalism. Those impulses toward pre- and post-capitalism, respectively, converged in Vietnam, spawning a multifarious strategy that blended military and political tactics against U.S. designs for that country's development. After burying imperial Japan's Greater Asian Co-prosperity Sphere, and turning back French efforts to recolonize Indochina in the 1950s, the Vietnamese movement for independence would hasten the end of the American century.

The war in Vietnam and World War I have been portrayed as opposites for so long that the contrast is widely accepted as a truism: the latter's fixed-piece artillery and troops dug into trenches symbolic of modernism; the former's highly mobile and irregularly uniformed guerrilla units, often indistinguishable from civilians, countered by helicopter-borne units and stealthy special forces trained for clandestine operations as uncommon to traditional forms of battle as it is modern.

But in the study of war trauma and post-war culture, the war in Vietnam fits better as a type with World War I than with World War II: plagued with controversy, lacking a definition of objective, blurred perceptions of friend and enemy, and a post-war narrative that displaced the war itself with the figures of emotionally and psychologically damaged men who had been sent to fight it. In turn, the image of the trauma-stricken veteran that "shell shock" helped fix in public memory eclipsed cultural interpretations with more political implications.

SIEGFRIED SASSOON, DONALD DUNCAN, CHARLIE CLEMENTS

In 1917, Siegfried Sassoon, a decorated Lieutenant in the British Army, wrote a letter to his commanding officer titled *Finished with the War* in which he declared his refusal to fight any longer. After his letter was read in Parliament by a sympathetic M.P., he was considered for punishment by Court Martial but was remanded instead to Craiglockhart Hospital for treatment for shell shock. There, Sassoon came under the care of W.H.R. Rivers, the British neurologist whose medical views were tempered by Freud and the anthropological field work he did in South Asia. Rivers saw the normality in Sassoon's opposition to the war: avoiding the dichoto-mizing of the soldier's pacifism as either criminal or medical, the doctor suggested (surely with a chuckle) the label "anti-war com-plex."

It's hard to read about Siegfried Sassoon's letter of resignation from World War I and not think about its similarity to the procla-mation made by Donald Duncan in 1965. Duncan was a career Green Beret Sergeant who left the Army after service in Vietnam. "It's all a lie," he wrote of the government's stated reasons for the war. A striking photograph of him under the large block letters I QUIT comprised what is now the iconic February 1966 front cover of the antiwar magazine *Ramparts*.[1]

And Sassoon's commitment to a mental ward brings to mind Charlie Clements's story. Clements graduated second in his 1967 class at the Air Force Academy. In Vietnam two years later, he concluded that the Nixon administration was lying to the American public about the war. After a stateside leave, he refused to return to Vietnam. Facing prison time for disobeying orders, Clements accepted hospitalization for mental problems and was then given a psychiatric discharge. His military career over, Clements became a doctor and the subject of the Academy Award–winning film *Witness to War* for his medical work in war-torn El Salvador in the 1980s.

Despite their one-time celebrity status as war resistors, Donald Duncan and Charlie Clements are, like Siegfried Sassoon, lost figures in the history of twentieth-century wars, their stories, like Sassoon's, casualties of the war on public memory waged with the images of soldiers and veterans with minds and emotions broken by war.

VIETNAM AND THE RETURN TO WARTIME LIMINALITY

If World War II was less a shock to America's individual and collective psyches—waged, as it was, within a modernist motif already made familiar by World War I and remembered through the feel-good representation of "The Good Fight," and its veterans the beneficiaries of advances in medical practice and social policies— the war in Vietnam redirected that cultural trajectory, pointing it back toward the liminalist experience that war had been before.

The United States slid into Vietnam under political and cultural radar spinning with post–World War II narratives and projections of boundless global expansion; it also went in with confidence in the approaches to war that had delivered the victories in Asia and Europe. If there was ever a stage-setting for fighting a war with the lessons learned from the last, it was the one set by American expectations for how things would go in Vietnam. The Vietnamese struggle for independence against the French and Japanese had honed guerilla tactics informed by the Maoist principles later known as "asymmetrical warfare"—the reluctance to "fight fire with fire" in favor of doing the opposite of what the enemy did. Outgunned by American artillery and bombers, the Vietnamese took up lightweight small arms like the AK-47 and perfected hit-and-hide ambush tactics that deprived the big guns of targets; under-outfitted in comparison with the uniformed and well-shod GIs, the Vietnamese made do with pajama-like peasant garb and sandals cut from U.S. Army truck tires—happy to have someone else's wet feet rotting in factory-made boots.

By the end of the war, the generals schooled at West Point had made some adjustments—M-16s that sprayed small-caliber bullets had replaced the aim-and-squeeze 7.62mm standard issue carbines from World War II, and nylon "jungle boots" with holes to let the water run *out* had replaced the old-style leather wear. Rhizomic guerrilla maneuvers were countered with some success by the versatility of helicopters, but the American adaptations to the unconventionality of Vietnamese inventiveness resulted less in an abandonment of modernism's limitations for war against an agrarian society than a kind of post-modern pastiche with fixed-place artillery supporting air-mobile infantry, and slow and lumbering technological marvels like B-52 bombers stirred into the tactical mix with small-team counterinsurgency operations. But tactics changed little. As late as 1969 the U.S. Army was still spending nighttime hours tucked behind barbed wire fences and perimeter floodlights while the Vietnamese stole through the dark by foot and hoof.

Most importantly for the way it shaped the American post-war experience, however, was the inability of the Americans to adjust psychologically to the unpatterned and decentralized military tactics of the Vietnamese, and American inability to do more than vilify as "terrorism" the Vietnamese use of deception and duplicity as a counterweight to their deficiencies in modern matériel. Americans thought the war in Vietnam to be about "communism," and the generation coming of age during the 1950s and early 1960s had little sense of the enemy as a socioeconomic system with a base of popular support among workers and peasants. Rather, they thought of it as a pernicious belief system, a set of vile and corrupting ideas that were spread by trickery. Like the biblical Antichrist that presented himself as "good" in order to fool God's people into following him, communism was an incarnation of evil that deceived good people into doing bad things. Communism was duplicitous and commun*ists* were dupes.

The war against North Vietnam was premised on the belief that its leaders maintained their control and command of the people through a system of lies. If the people could see and hear the truth, American planners thought, they would abandon the war effort and turn on their leaders. The strategy growing out of that theory entailed the imposition of enough hardship on the people through bombing that the leadership in Hanoi would be discredited by its failure to protect the people; simultaneously, a propaganda campaign would be waged to bring the truth to the populous. Suspecting that the North was infiltrating secret agents into the South to stir up the peasants, the CIA adopted the view, "If they can do it, so can we" and began infiltrating teams of friendly Vietnamese agents into the North. Contact with many of those teams was soon lost, however, leading to speculation that they had defected to the North and maybe reinfiltrated to the South as counterspies.[2]

In short, the U.S. war for hearts and minds, based as it was on the notion that communism was first and foremost a social system of lies and deceptions grew into a classic case of what is known in the espionage business as "blowback"—the very paranoia that the United States hoped to induce in the North came home to haunt the Americans, infecting everything about their conduct of the war.[3]

Postmortems on the United States' lost cause in Vietnam revealed that high levels of the South Vietnamese military and government had been infiltrated by the enemy agents but that was only the tip of the iceberg. The hardships wrought by the war caused people to move from one side to another and back again in search of security and daily sustenance, a fluidity to the situation that made it difficult to stabilize the loyalty of large numbers of people. American combat units sometimes complained about the reliability of their South Vietnamese allies, reporting that they would flee rather than fight. In cities and base camps, GIs were routinely warned by officers to watch what they said around the Vietnamese civilians lest some of the friendly camp workers turn out to be imposters spying for the Viet Cong.

Lines between friend and foe blurred in other ways, as well. In World War II, military units moved into an area, defeated the enemy, and then moved on; but Vietnam was a body-count war. A hill on which a hundred enemy Vietnamese were killed today could be abandoned by the Americans only to be retaken a month later. The same U.S. units stayed in the same areas of operation, sometimes taking and retaking the same hills and valleys for years. The 25th Infantry Division moved into Cu Chi west of Saigon in January 1966 and stayed until April 1971, establishing a large sprawling complex that, over the years, employed thousands of Vietnamese and mediated the off-base contact between thousands more GIs and civilians.[4]

Unlike the World War II units that kept lines of combat clearly defined as they moved—spawning terms like "the front" and "rear echelon"—U.S. units in Vietnam were perpetually immersed in a stew of military and civilian activity that blurred the distinction between combat and noncombat, friends and enemies. At guard posts and checkpoints throughout the country, local kids on a first-name basis with the Americans appeared daily as if by appointment, looking for handouts or selling whatever they could. The danger in those situations was that security could be compromised by the "loose lips" of GIs overly eager to make friends, and the familiarity with the architecture of military sites that kids in service to the Viet Cong could come away with. Met with questions such as "did you see combat?" or "were you at the front?" questions that would have made sense for World War II veterans, Vietnam veterans were often at a loss for answers: there was no front. Combat in Vietnam was everywhere and yet nowhere in particular.

The murkiness of the war experienced by Americans in Vietnam diminished the "drive-discharge" function that it might otherwise have performed, leaving the United States profoundly frustrated. It was a long war with an indistinguishable beginning and an ending that dragged out over years. Twelve months was the standard term of service in Vietnam which meant a neighborhood waving anxious goodbyes to a favorite son leaving for war in the morning might be joyously welcoming someone else's son home in the evening—or helping a third family grieve the death of their son. What does the collective Self emote in those circumstances?

For troops returning from Vietnam uncertain about what they had experienced, the representations of the war made by popular culture were unlikely to have clarified things. To begin with, most soldiers returned while the war was still going on, its outcome unknown. Hollywood stayed away from the war except for the cartoonish 1968 film *Green Berets,* and films with Vietnam veterans as characters in their après-war situations. The early examples of the latter, however, usually featured feel-good post-World War II storylines developed around a character who just happened to be a Vietnam veteran. The 1964 film *The Lively Set* was a slice of southern California kitsch giving us the clean-cut Casey who goes from the college parking lot to road-racing fame with the girl next door in his passenger's seat and Bobby Darin music on the radio.[5]

There was a spate of films from 1968 to 1970 that portrayed Vietnam veterans in political fashion, the most interesting of which was the 1969 *Alice's Restaurant* in which Arlo Guthrie plays himself as a draft resister who befriends a veteran. Political films with veterans reach a temporary apex in 1970 with Elliot Gould in *Getting Straight* and Jon Voight in *The Revolutionary*. By 1971, the political Vietnam veteran was all but gone, displaced from the big screen by the criminal, crippled, or crazy, the images of social and psychological wreckage through which Americans would come to remember what the war was all about.

The images of deranged veterans fixed over time in remembrances of the war may not have been, however, just passive reflections of film makers' work. Writing in 1985, Robert Fleming noted elements in our society that "really do not want to see the Vietnam veteran 'come home.'" Veterans themselves, he wrote, have too often accommodated that societal need by "taking on the role of 'the sick child in the family.'"[6]

The synergy Fleming described between society and the returnees from Vietnam framed the issue of post-war trauma more sociologically then psychologically, a framing recently employed by historian Michael Roth to describe the prominence of trauma in late-twentieth century American culture. Writing in *Memory, Trauma, and History*, Roth describes the ways in which trauma has become a central feature of communal identity, attention to it "regarded as a virtue, as character building, even as morally uplifting." Roth is speaking here of political identities based on commonly shared experiences of a traumatic nature, a form of identity building that extended in the United States after the loss in Vietnam to a new national identity for which the war veteran stricken with PTSD provided the grounding image.[7]

Incisive though it was, that sociological view would be overtaken by powerful developments in the fields of mental health that galvanized the attention of journalists and the American public. In September 1969 a Vietnam veteran told a social worker named Sarah Halay that his company had killed women and children at a village called My Lai. He described how he was now unable to sleep, had nightmares, and was easily frightened. Halay reported her interview to her staff meeting and was surprised to learn that the *Diagnostic and Statistical Manual* (DSM), published by the American Psychiatric Association to classify mental conditions, contained no language to cover the case of a war veteran like she had just seen. The condition known as war neurosis and treated as "gross stress reaction" in the years following World War I, had been dropped from the manual after World War II. Her colleagues dismissed the veteran's story as delusional and classified him as paranoid schizophrenic.[8]

Soon thereafter, Halay joined forces with psychiatrists Chaim Shatan and Robert Lifton in a campaign to regain formal recognition of war neurosis as a condition for treatment. That campaign ended in 1980 when "Post Traumatic Stress Disorder" was added to the DSM.

THE FREUDIAN TRADITION V. THE MEDICAL MODEL

From its inception, PTSD was a composition of already recognized disorders, each of which had an independent standing in the existing mental health literature: depression, anxiety, and paranoia among them. Each of those, in turn, came with an associated set of symptoms such as lethargy, insomnia, and obsessive-compulsive behavior, all known to be treatable separately or in combination with each other. While no one would doubt that experience in a war zone—or even the impact of the draft and military authoritarianism without deployment to Vietnam—could bring on feelings that could unsettle the mind and emotions, there were disagreements about what was to be gained by bundling those disturbances into a war-specific package like PTSD. Critics wondered if the move didn't have more cultural and political meaning than diagnostic. [9]

The phenomenon of "flashback" was not formally recognized in PTSD's inaugural DSM inclusion, but the problem of disturbing memories, clearly implied in cases such as that reported by Sarah Halay, became critical to the battle for PTSD's confirmation in DSM. And, as with hysteria a century earlier and shell shock of the World War I years, culture and media technology would influence the outcome of that struggle, with flashbacks this time playing the central role in the story. In retrospect we can see that PTSD's original turf claim as a diagnostic category was not only its subject—the distraught Vietnam veteran—but the addition of flashbacks to the collection of symptoms it encompassed.

The battle line of that fight put followers of German psychiatrist Emil Kraepelin on one side and those of a neo-Freudian persuasion on the other. The Kraepelins understood mental disorders by analogy to physical illness and looked for the visible or bodily manifestations of mental problems that would have specifiable organic and biochemical origins. The neo-Freudian approach, on the other hand, weighed more heavily the verbal expressions of patients that revealed conflicts stemming from fantasies and personal relationships. The Kraepelin paradigm led to drug treatment of patients while the Freudian-influenced psychodynamic approach led to versions of the "talking cure." [10]

Writing in his 1995 book *The Harmony of Illusions*, medical anthropologist Allen Young says the American Psychiatric Association's board of trustees chose in 1974 the Columbia University psychiatrist Roger Spitzer to head a task force to rewrite the DSM. Spitzer was a Kraepelin and the APA allowed him to stack the task force with likeminded thinkers. The taskforce's work, according to Young, was published in 1980 as the *Diagnostic and Statistical*

Manual-III with the "purging of references to the unconscious." Stated in other words, Spitzer and his colleagues had displaced the Freudian tradition with a "medical model" that valued empirical observation over the interpretive approaches that valued meaning as much as measurement.[11]

The paradigmatic tensions that divided the authors of *DSM-III* continued into the process leading to the definition of PTSD. *DSM-I* which had come out in 1950 and *DSM-II*, published in 1968, had contained language on "gross stress reaction" and "transient situational disturbances," respectively, but no language specific to war-related disorders. In 1975, Spitzer acceded to requests by psychiatrists Shatan and Lifton to form a subcommittee on what was then called "post-Vietnam Syndrome." Kraepelins argued that the etiology of war trauma was vague because the identification of the events supposedly causing the trauma was dependent upon veterans' memories—memories that were themselves supposedly impaired by the event: in short, the evidences of *cause* could be intertwined with the effects.

In fact, the very notion of trauma was imprecise. In a 1996 essay, philosophy professor Ian Hacking recalled that prior to the nineteenth century "trauma" referred to the shock felt by the nervous system during surgery; it was an effect of surgery, not itself a cause of injury. It entered the lexicon of psychology through the encounter with "railway spine" and underwrote as it did "an anatomical theory of memory, that everything that happened was preserved in some little spot of the brain." It was a "strange transmutation," Hacking wrote, whereby "instead of remembering being what affected us, it was the forgetting." If a bad event was forgotten, it "was still there and could act on us in potent ways."[12]

That physical theory of memory, as Hacking called it, merged into the awkward blend of neurology and psychology that characterized American mental health practice. For a century, American doctors had mingled the French approach of privileging psychiatry while allowing neurology an independent existence, with the German approach of fusing the two into a single approach guided by a medical framework. In the United States, a neurological approach developed at Harvard in the late nineteenth century, while Bellevue Hospital in New York City moved along the German path that rolled neurology and psychiatry into one field. Despite efforts to reconcile the disparate approaches in the twentieth century, the distinction between psychiatric and neurological conditions remained difficult to define, according to neurologist Christopher Goetz.[13]

The neurology-psychiatry debate over war trauma carried high stakes. As seen by neurologists, war trauma was an organic effect with the corporeal properties of the brain having been actually disrupted by a wound to the head. For them, war trauma was a medical condition treatable by brain surgery, electric shock, or drug therapy—but hard to undo. Psychiatrists, on the other hand, were more likely to see emotional and psychic damage—harder to define and treat but ultimately reversible through less intrusive methods.[14]

The disparate understandings of war trauma carried into debates about what flashbacks were, how they should be treated, if at all, and how they could be used strategically by either the neurological camp or the psychiatry camp in debates over the legitimacy of what would eventually emerge as Post-Traumatic Stress Disorder. Ironically, given the vagueness of the original identity of "flashback," its gestation in cultural circles far from those of medical science, and its own complicated cause/effect relationship to trauma, it was the insinuation of supposed neurological properties in "flashback" that paved the way for PTSD into the DSM.

FLASHBACKS: FROM THE SCREENWRITER'S PEN TO THE DSM

The ostensible logic of the flashback is that something happened in the past that was so unpleasant or threatening that its occurrence became etched in memory deeply enough to become preoccupying, or that it had to be banished from consciousness. In either case, experience of a similar event in the future causes the subject to *re*experience the original trauma and respond as would have been appropriate for that situation. The etiology of "flashbacks," however, extends beyond the pages of PTSD's history, and reveals them to have a questionable relationship to actual memory. [15]

In a 1994 article, "The Concept of Flashbacks in Historical Perspective," psychiatrist Fred Frankel reported that "flashback" was first used in the medical literature to describe the consequence of drug use, and had nothing to do with war veterans and trauma. The use of hallucinogens like LSD seemed to have an aftereffect causing the user to reexperience something that occurred or was visualized during its use. Frankel was particularly interested in findings that flashback*ers*, as they were sometimes called in the medical literature, "absorbed themselves in imaginative activity more easily than drug users who did not experience flashbacks," an observation leading him to speculate that "drug flashbacks may represent, in part, imaginative role-playing and not the symptoms of psychotic decomposition." [16]

The first association of "flashback" with drug culture was made in 1969 but its lineage ran still deeper to its use as a story-telling device in film and literature; it was widely used that way in Vietnam War films to tell about the war from some later point in time. But the flashbacks in these films weren't of the usual sort: descriptions of earlier events spliced into a narrative. Rather, these flashbacks were in the minds of the on-screen veterans, vivid memories of traumatic events. Filmmakers thus virtually created the definition of a flashback as a trauma-induced, mental phenomenon. [17]

If flashbacks migrated from screenplays to psychiatry journals it is probably because they functioned similarly in both settings. Cinematic flashbacks created a blank space between the historical record of the war and the viewer that could be sketched in by the artist, whereas mental flashbacks filled a space between wartime experiences and the recall of them as memory. It was the term assigned by psychiatrists to some, but not all, memories about the war. Those memories that mental health professionals wanted to treat as symptoms of trauma and associated with behavioral pathologies were labeled flashbacks.

Flashbacks were not blank slates for psychiatrists to write on in quite the same way that they were for filmmakers, but the *meaning* of "flashback" *was* something created out of the interaction between psychiatrist and patient. The flashbacks put mental distance between memory and experience, allowing the veteran to reinterpret and even reimage what had actually happened to him. In conjunction with psychiatric intervention, popular culture, and the additional difficulties of life in post-Vietnam America, flashbacks functioned to reconfigure memory for individual veterans, just as they had functioned through film to rewrite the history of the war.

The term "flashback" would not find its way formally into the medical literature on PTSD until 1987 with the publication of DSM-III-R. Presented in that volume as an essential criterion for the diagnosis of PTSD, flashback was described there as "a sudden acting or feeling as if the traumatic event were recurring." But "flashback" had crept into mental health usage before 1987, usually without evidence that the events supposedly causing the trauma actually occurred. Contrary to the impressions created in the media, wrote Dr. Robert Fleming for an article in the journal *Psychiatry*, "Legitimate dramatic flashbacks are virtually nonexistent."[18]

In a 1982 article for the journal *Social Casework*, M. Keith Langley recounted a patient's story that he had been left behind by his unit to guard a downed helicopter in Vietnam. He remembered

Viet Cong soldiers emerging from a nearby tree line and firing on him. Some years later, while working in a textile factory, he "began to visualize the long lines of fellow workers behind their textile machines, as the Vietcong soldiers. . . . He found himself reliving the [Vietnam] experience over and over and finally lost his job.[19] Commenting on the article, Frankel said it was difficult to sort out the presence in it of illusion and imagination from dissociation, and the influence of all of those three from what he called "veridical memory." With reference to that article, Frankel concluded that the content of flashbacks is "at least as likely to be the product of imagination as of memory."[20]

Frankel's assessment of "flashback" was delivered as a critique of colleagues who "had reified it as fact in the trauma literature" despite its having what he called "an imprecise nature." There were four implications to that conceptual imprecision, all of which are even more evident now than when he wrote in 1994.

The Trauma-Flashback-Trauma Circularity

One problem with the notion of "flashback," was that it allowed "therapists with a special interest in trauma victims to assert that the accuracy of a patient's delayed recall is affirmed by the content of his or her flashbacks." The problem was the circularity implicit in that reasoning: since "delay" was definitional to flashbacks, the presence of the delay validates the authenticity of the delay. By extension, with the element of delay integral to "flashback," the flashback itself validates the subject's claim to a traumatic experience responsible for the delay, even though Frankel noted several times, "appropriate verification" of the events is typically absent from the literature.[21]

In short form, "flashback" could be both the symptom of trauma and the evidence for the combat experience that caused the trauma: in effect a "purple heart" that authenticates the combat experience.

Frankel's suggestion that flashbacks could be a form of "imagina-tive role-paying," hit another target dead-center.

Rambo Contamination

By the mid-1970s the veterans' memories of the war were being influenced and even revised by the renderings given it by news media and popular culture; complicating matters still further, the thinking of the professional people and activists pursuing the legiti-mation of PTSD was itself entangled with war and post-war stories spinning from bar stools and film studios. If as suggested by histo-rian Martin Stone (chapter 4) doctors facing World War I veterans were overwhelmed by the influences of public and popular culture on their practice, their later-century counterparts immersed in an even more intense media environment would have a still harder time discerning the boundaries of political sentiment, art, and sci-ence.

While the medical community debated the need for new nomen-clature, Hollywood was twisting the representations of veterans into images of derangement and despair. Andy in *Deathdreams* (1972) was the ultimate "Other": the offspring of Cesare from *The Cabinet of Dr. Caligari*, Andy died in Vietnam, and has come home as a zombie. Like Cesare, Andy is a metaphor for the way a society deals with a generation of men returning without victory. Just as *Caligari* did for Germany after World War I, *Deathdreams* mirrored for America the horror that the boundary between life and death was not the ultimate boundary. Andy was the incarnation of death, the "living" proof that the reality of Vietnam was going to stalk America long after the war's end.[22] Brahmin in *Motor Psycho* (1965) came home physically whole but carrying the war's damage as psychological trauma on the inside. He and his biker pals terror-ize two couples before he's killed by the husband of one of the raped women. In the scenes leading to his demise, Brahmin lapses into delirious recollections about fighting the Viet Cong, scenes that anticipated by several years the linking of "flashbacks" with Vietnam veterans.

Incubated in film culture, it isn't clear when the notion of flashbacks crossed over into the imaginations of diagnosticians but Scott recalled being told by Chaim Shatan that psychiatrist Leonard Neff reported the following incident to the 1975 annual meeting of the American Psychiatric Association:

> A vet escaped from the Brentwood [California] VA and laid siege to some police cars. The vet was armed and took over a patrol car. Neff rushed to the scene and determined the vet was having a flashback. So Neff called out to him, "Attention! This is Captain Neff. The mission is accomplished. You don't have to fight anymore. Lay down your arms." The vet surrendered peacefully.[23]

This being Scott's account of something he was told by Shatan about a story told by Neff to an APA panel qualifies it as a friend-of-a-friend story—a kind of hearsay; as a window on the interpenetrating influences of entertainment, the science of mental health, and the historical memory of diagnostic terminology comes into being, it's invaluable. Six years before Scott's interview with Shatan, Sylvester Stallone's character, the Vietnam veteran John Rambo, had gone on a rampage in the movie *First Blood*. Surrounded by police, his former commander Colonel Trautman talks him down: "The mission is over, Rambo. . . . It's over Johnny, it's over."

The Brentwood incident really did happen, and the *Los Angeles Times* reported that Dr. Neff had assisted the police in subduing Mark Gabron, the troubled veteran. But the newspaper said Gabron had left the hospital on a weekend pass (not "escaped") and made no mention of the commandeered patrol car, or Neff's delivery of Trautman's movie-ready lines. Gabron was upset, according to the story, because agreements made with him had not been kept. Those "agreements" were not specified for readers, and Neff, quoted at some length in the story, never used the word "flashbacks."[24] Those discrepencies don't mean that the Neff-Shatan-Scott version of the incident was not true but it does mean that the release of *First Blood* between 1974 and the publication of Scott's 1988 interview with Shatan could have loaded some "Hollywood" into the psychiatric history of PTSD—and looking further upstream, that films like *Motor Psycho* could have flowed into the professional minds striving to imagine new and better treatments for troubled veterans.[25]

PTSD: From Diagnosis to Credential

By the time social scientists and mental health professionals began looking into the condition of Vietnam veterans in the mid-1970s, the image of the unanchored vet at odds with mainstream society was already firmly established in the culture; except for a few films with political veterans in minor roles, the images of veterans coming out of the film factories were almost universally disparaging. The "archetypal 'crazy vet' movie" was *Black Sunday* (1977) starring Bruce Dern as Michael Lander, a seriously deranged returnee who joins a Palestinian plot to arm the Goodyear Blimp and fly it over the Orange Bowl on Superbowl Sunday.[26]

The "crazy vet" movies like *Black Sunday* were fictional creations with the power to overshadow the reality that most soldiers had come home from Vietnam and reentered the workplace, rejoined their families, and begun schooling in unremarkable fashion; thousands of others came back ready to join the anti-war movement. By 1975 when psychiatrists began deliberating the need for new language applicable to war veterans, the image of veterans marching arm-in-arm with pacifists to end the war was already fading. The "damaged goods" image of veterans that was coming into focus was sympathetic enough, but it allowed their criticism of the war and the society that had sent them to fight to be spun by politicians and pundits as "alienation" and "catharsis"—more evidence of their mental and emotional needs.

The issuing of the DSM-III in 1980 with the inclusion of PTSD changed the narrative. While the sweep of the new category was so large that more veterans than ever could find something on its list of symptoms to claim as their own, war trauma's newly acquired legitimacy imparted to those veterans who claimed it, a status upgrade from "just crazy" to "wounded." In turn, "the invisible wound" could be accepted as a kind of Purple Heart, evidence of combat experience: the veteran with a PTSD diagnosis was now *ipso facto*, a *combat* veteran, a hero even.[27]

The change in the story line can be seen between the 1978 film *Coming Home* and the 1982 film *First Blood*. In *Coming Home*, Col. Bob Hyde (Bruce Dern) has come home wounded and paranoid. Bob sleeps with a handgun under his pillow; he drinks too much, is abusive to his wife Sally (Jane Fonda), and acts threateningly toward another veteran, Luke (Jon Voight). At the end of the film, Bob commits suicide. The character Bob, brought to life by screenwriter Waldo Salt, may have drawn sympathy from some theater goers; he was, after all, a walking case of human wreckage home from war. But it would be two more years before psychiatrists would coin PTSD, leaving with us the figure cut by Bob of just another crazy vet—not a hero.

John Rambo in *First Blood*, on the other hand, came to the screen two years *after* the DSM-III came out—good timing. Rambo, played by Sylvester Stallone, has arrived in a small, rural, conservative town. He is harassed by the town cop and given a one-way ride to the city limits. When he turns around and walks back he is arrested and put in jail. Behind bars, Rambo has a flashback to the confinement and beatings he endured as a POW in Vietnam; his abuse by the local authorities reminds him of the civilian indifference to his agonizing months of captivity and the government that cost the military its victory. Declaring "there are no friendly civilians," Rambo goes on a tear against the local people. At the end of the film he remembers his homecoming experience: "I see all those maggots at the airport. Protesting me. Spitting. Calling me a baby killer, and all kinds of vile crap."[28]

Rambo was as good a candidate for the psychiatrist's office as Bob in *Coming Home*, but by the early 1980s, developments in political culture were harmonizing with the arrival of PTSD in the DSM-III to give war trauma a political face it hadn't had. With the home-front betrayal narrative gaining currency, stories about veterans mistreated by anti-war activists began to appear; and with PTSD understood to be about emotional and psychic trauma, some veterans would claim their homecomings to have been traumatic, so bad even that stories, like Rambo's, of having been spat on at airports constituted a kind of war story; the embarrassment felt for having lost the war was blamed on politicians who had forced them to "fight with one hand tied behind their backs." The *real* war, it came to be said, was the war at home; the *real* hurt was inflicted on the home front.

Whereas Bob's behavior was presented to us as pathological, an unmanly form of "acting out," Rambo's violence was valorized as vengeance for wrong done to him. Rambo's flashbacks were a way for the screenwriters to retell the Homerian tale of the warrior returned to home-life unsettled by the war; through his mental state we see both the inhumanity of the Vietnamese who had tortured him in prison and the damage wrought by a civilian culture that rejects the men it sends to war. Rambo's flashbacks work as a story-telling prop by which we know that he is the real deal: a combat veteran of Vietnam shamed by the spitters, an image that welds vigilante and avenger themes with populist resentment of incompetent government and the right's preoccupations with betrayal. Bob and Rambo are both figures of film-making imagination, the difference between them being which narrative is supported by their trauma—Bob the loser or Rambo the hero?

The intermingling of diagnosis and credentialing in the representations of Vietnam veterans, be they on the screen or on the street, thickens the turbidity of their emergent post-war identity. The temptation to exaggerate accomplishments in war, seemingly universal among men, now yielded temptations to exaggerate the symptoms derived *from* the war. The presence of PTSD as wound in the war story inoculated it from questions that might have been hard to answer. In the first place, the "wound" itself authenticates the combat experience—'nough said. In the second place, who would risk inflicting further emotional damage by even implying that something about the story is suspicious? The veteran has suffered enough already; it would be disrespectful to him, and appear to *others* as being disrespectful, to be heard probing the truth of the story—just let it go.

The presentation of "flashback" could enhance the believability of the combat experience that was claimed. In a May 3, 2010 posting to *Slate.com* Lena H-Baltimore described waiting for a bus with a Vietnam veteran when a truck backfired. The veteran "hit the ground" and then explained that he had been in a "skirmish" in Vietnam only four days earlier and was still shook up. Medical anthropologist Allan Young observed case workers screening veterans for PTSD and described a patient who "held his wife and kid hostage because he said he saw enemy soldiers in a tree line across the street from his house." According to Young, the case workers believed the story. Another veteran observed by Young claimed a flashback in which he was "sitting at the bottom of a hill and a clump of earth rolled down. He thought [imagined] it was a grenade, and jumped into a ditch and put his hands over this head" (the brackets in the original). [29]

Vietnam War films at the close of the century continued themes established before Rambo. Stories about veterans returned home would displace the war itself; the war, when it was portrayed, would continue to be filtered through veteran memories, and im-

ages of anti-war veterans would remain mostly AWOL. As before
Rambo, there were few healthy veterans portrayed, the difference
being their derangements likely to be scripted as character development, warrior traits we should lionize. Stories about spat on veterans proliferated in the 1990s despite there being no evidence that
those incidents happened and only a thin record of stories like them
having been reported during the coming-home years. That hundreds of Vietnam veterans who suddenly remembered having been
spat on fifteen or twenty years earlier seemed implausible in itself
is a matter for study.

My own study of the spitting stories began with those told in
1990-91 during the months leading to the Persian Gulf War; I then
worked back through time to see when stories like these began to
be told and who told them. Going back to the late 1960s and early
1970s when the spitting incidents were said to have occurred, I not
only found no evidence that anyone was ever spat on, but no evidence either that anyone at the time said he had been spat on.
(Years later I would still have only one verifiable first-person *claim*
made during the war years, but even that one was uncorroborated.)
The gap of ten or more years between the time when the spittings
supposedly occurred, and the time when the stories began being
told, could have been due to suppressed memories that were later
recalled through therapy or experienced as flashbacks—or the delayed recall could be attributed, as psychiatrist Fred Frankel might
say, to imagination.

By the 1990s a virtual epidemic of war-related PTSD swamped
social workers, many of the cases wrapping together hard-to-be-
lieve war stories with claims of PTSD. Paul Solotaroff, writing
about homeless veterans in his 1995 book *House of Purple Hearts*
said, "Check the discharge papers on all those guys telling war
stories and you'll find that a third of them never got within twenty
klicks [kilometers] of a firefight and another third did their entire
tour in Dusseldorf or Fort Dix." Dallas businessman and Vietnam

veteran B. G. "Jug" Burkett used the Freedom of Information Act to glean information on seventeen hundred "troubled veterans" and exposed three-quarters of them as partial or total frauds. Some men in his study falsely claimed to have seen combat; others had come nowhere near Vietnam. Oftentimes, the stories combined exaggerated combat biographies with accounts of mistreatment upon return home. Solotaroff also saw the reaches being made for a diagnosis and noted the recognition in the PTSD literature to the new phenomenon of "facetious PTSD."

Solotaroff and Burkett are both committed to adequate care for war veterans and the respectful treatment of them in the media. Perhaps more than other writers, they would be loath to dismiss the impact of war on the minds and bodies of those who fight them. But they also see the confusion and distrust that false stories create, the "crying wolf" effect that could cause the real problems of other veterans to be ignored, and the honor due those who served with distinction be denied lest they be revealed to be impostors.

And the problem of authenticity in PTSD claims was a serious one. Doctors Landy Sparr and Loren Pankratz entitled their 1983 article for the *American Journal of Psychiatry* "Factitious Posttraumatic Stress Disorder" after reexamining five cases at a VA medical center whereupon men had presented "an array of symptoms that could be directly related to their stressful experiences in Vietnam." Three of the men said they were former prisoners of war. "In fact," the authors found, "none had been prisoners of war, four had never been in Vietnam, and two had never even been in the military."[30]

Hit the Deck!

Frankel developed his critique of "flashback" against neurological premises in the psychiatric treatment of trauma-related disorders. A key characteristic of that premise is that there is something persistent and enduring in the symptoms of war trauma that are physiological in nature. The "soft" version of that understands flashbacks to be unbidden and inappropriate reappearances in post-war situations of behavior that was made habitual through training and repeated occurrences of combat experiences. An example would be the veteran who was trained, through multiple repetitions of the exercise, to "hit the deck" when hearing a shot fired; in Vietnam he supposedly used that well-practiced skill so many times that the body came to do it reactively—the "body" being the veteran's neurotransmitters sending signals along familiar paths to tell the muscles what to do.

In his book *Lethal Warriors* reporter David Philipps describes what he says is the "reflexive fire" program that trains new soldiers to shoot their weapons without thinking. "Through repetition," he writes, "conscious thought is minimized . . . firing becomes a reflex." According to Philipps, the training program is "the same process Ivan Pavlov used to get a dog to salivate at the sound of a bell." "They drill it into you over and over," he quotes an Iraq war veteran saying, "until it's all muscle memory." Citing statistics from the Vietnam War, Philipps says it is an "extremely effective" training method.[31]

It was this muscle-memory theory of "flashback" that was in play in the story (above) of the veteran diving for cover when hearing a truck engine backfire, and in the story of Iraq War veteran Matthew Sepi recounted in chapter I. In fact, Philipp's source was Kenny Eastridge who had been charged with murder in Colorado and was employing a PTSD defense, like Sepi had (see chapter 1), when Philipps interviewed him. Eastridge is a central figure in Philipps's book, presented to readers as tragically victimized by the war in Iraq. Eastridge's captivating stories of combat and Philipps's account of his post-war condition resulting from that combat, larded with details of brain anatomy like the amygdalae and hippocampus, are engrossing—and that might be the problem. So compelling does the science of it all make it seem, that Philipps either didn't notice or think it was important to tell us that Eastridge was also immersed in a neo-Nazi movement that spread through the U.S. military in the early 2000s. That association doesn't invalidate the trauma theory for Eastridge's criminal behavior but it does cue up a political/cultural narrative as an alternative to the mental health narrative constructed by Philipps—thereby suggesting, also, that Eastridge and other veterans in his situation might not be getting help for the problems they really have.

On trial for murder, Eastridge obviously had a substantial personal interest in the muscle-memory explanation for post-combat violence. It's a theory, though, that doesn't stand up well under critical scrutiny. In the Vietnam era, which Philipps invokes, rifle training involved shooting at targets that popped up down-range at various distances and angles. Some of the targets had crudely shaped conical "hats" which trainees knew were supposed to "look Vietnamese"; but the total amount of time in actual shooting positions was probably less than an hour, the total broken up into blocks of minutes of which few involved repeated movements other than pulling the trigger. Bayonet practice was another "drill" sometimes given as an example of a Pavlovian attempt to inspire mindless action. The exercise entailed sticking the blade into a target made of shredded rubber two or three times, yelling "kill, kill" with each thrust, and then running past the target. That exercise was repeated one or two times on one day. But that was it for bayonets—which were issued only sometimes in Vietnam but seldom used, if ever.[32]

In other words, the assessment of David Philipps notwithstanding, there was virtually nothing in the Vietnam-era basic training routine that sustains the now popular belief that combat skills drilled into military recruits altered them in some basic way that could not then be undone in later civilian life.[33] In Vietnam, the guerrilla strategies employed by the Vietnamese, and the counterinsurgency measures used by the U.S. made tactical improvisation the order of day, and the idea of repeatable experiences almost oxymoronic. As Fleming put it in *Psychiatry*, "The only consistency in the war was its inconsistency." It is conceivable, of course, that a twig snapped by a footstep brought down a hail of hot lead on someone, sometime, someplace—and that a snapping twig on a family hike years later caused a husband and father of four to revert to his jungle self. But the idea that something like that could have occurred so many times in combat conditions, in similar enough circumstances, to automate the senses-to-brain-to-muscle flow of information is easier to imagine than demonstrate.[34]

Remarkably, no studies of the flashback phenomenon have noticed that the military activities in Vietnam combining the highest levels of danger with the most frequent occurrences *and* the postwar circumstances similar enough to trigger a relived experience would be those carried out by pilots. Even before the war was over, U.S. airlines were recruiting veteran fliers who had, more likely than an infantryman stepping on a twig, executed the same maneuvers over and over. So, just imagine a United Airlines flight in 1973 with an ex-Marine fighter pilot in the cockpit: descending into LaGuardia Airport, the controls in his hands now the same ones held on a bombing run just months ago; a shoreline approaching—the coast of Vietnam or Long Island? It's nighttime, the streaking lights ahead—cars on the expressway or tracer rounds? The mind panics. The body, been there before, knows what to do—and does it. The steep dive slams unbuckled passengers and crew members into the ceiling and suspends coffee cups and newspapers in midair.

This did not happen, of course, and that being the fact, makes the authenticity of many other flashback claims even easier to question.

FORMATIVE TRAUMA: NOT SO FAR FROM CHARCOT

A "harder" version of the neurological approach to "flashback" harkens back to the nineteenth-century attempts by neurologist Jean-Martin Charcot at Salpêtrière Hospital in Paris to find the brain lesions causing hysteria in his female patients. Freud tacked away from neurology as did Pierre Janet, another former student of Charcot's. Janet made the distinction between traumatic memory and narrative memory and coined the term "subconscious" referring to a "level" of memory in which unpleasant experiences could be stored away. Decades later, a new generation of neurologists led by Dr. Bessel van der Kolk imaged the subconscious physiologically, describing it as an altered condition of the brain.

Van der Kolk and colleagues applied Janet's notion of traumatic memory to the study of flashbacks and developed an alternative to the more commonly used narrative forms of memory. Van der Kolk thought that the locus coeruleus in the brain stem, when stimulated, released neurotransmitters to the cerebral cortex and limbic system which regulated the emotional responses to the situation. He also thought stressful events could stimulate the secretion of endorphins that produce numbing that accompanies trauma. Van der Kolk thought that with extreme stress, abnormal amounts of neurotransmitters could be released that could increase the size or potency of the locus coeruleus pathways to the limbic system. If these changes in the pathways were permanent, their altered state could support abnormal responses in the limbic system to stimuli associated with post-war re-experiences of war-time events. Such long-term augmentation constituted a neurobiological or traumatic memory that was "literal" and independent of the conventional sense of memory (or narrative memory) that he saw as mediated by social and cultural influences. [35]

However, the laboratory study of Vietnam veterans with PTSD failed to verify Van der Kolk's hypotheses. In a carefully designed experiment involving intravenous doses of drugs and placebos, comparison with a control group of normal veterans, and the exposure to clips from the Vietnam War movie *Platoon*, "the researchers found no significant differences in hormonal responses between the PTSD and the control group, nor did they find any significant differences in endorphin levels."[36]

Two years later, Frankel reported similar laboratory results. He began looking at findings from drug studies suggesting that the same "aftereffect" left by hallucinogens can appear as "the reenactments of a fixed memory," memories that can be viewed as "pristine rather than effected by psychosocial factors"—a distinction similar to that between traumatic and narrative memory. Like the accumulation of "kindling" eventually sufficient for a fire, he continued, bioelectric or biochemical change in the limbic system resulting from the repetition of stimulations (e.g. training for combat) could, theoretically, "fix" an image that would be recalled later through a flashback. If this model was correct, "flashbacks [would] represent an amalgam of abnormal neuronal firing . . . a neurophysiological happening."[37] The kind of "flashback" events described by the neurological model should, then, be demonstrable in electroencephalography (EEG) tracings, But, Frankel wrote, they were not, a nonfinding, he said, that left unconfirmed the "kindling focus" as a basis for flashbacks."[38]

Flashbacks, in themselves, were important for their content because they seemed to authenticate that the troubles of the veteran were war-based as opposed to some other trauma-inducing experience such as a car accident or child abuse. But research done at the Veterans Administration Medical Center in Augusta, Georgia, found that "parenting behaviors," especially of veterans' fathers, are more important than military variables in identifying which PTSD patients might commit suicide.[39]

Harkening forward, the reification of flashbacks as expressions of bodily disorders led in the early twenty-first century to another iteration of war trauma, Traumatic Brain Injury (TBI). As the "hard" version of neurological theory, TBI would reincarnate much of what had been buried years earlier as "shell shock" by suggesting a causal relationship between trauma and actual physiological or organic brain damage. The conceptual leap to TBI was made across both evidentiary and logical spaces, a distance that had been narrowed, somewhat, by the seldom recognized inclusion of age as a variable in the debate leading to PTSD's confirmation in the DSM.[40]

One of the presenters at the 1976 annual convention at the American Psychological Association in San Francisco, where deliberations were leading to the new diagnostic terminology (PTSD), was the social psychologist John Wilson. Wilson had a PhD but twelve years later he told author Wilbur Scott that his research interest had grown out of an undergraduate's interview project with Vietnam veterans. Subsequently, Wilson discovered "Department of Defense statistics showing the average American combat fatality in Vietnam was nineteen years old." Wilson then expanded the scope of that figure to read, in Scott's words, that the average age of *all* those who served in-country was nineteen. That young age, reasoned Wilson, encompassed the transition from adolescence to adulthood, making traumatic experience at that point *formative* of the adult identity to follow.[41]

Wilson's point was that the electro-chemical pathways of young brains are still developing and therefore only weakly patterned, a tentativeness leaving them vulnerable to disruptions. It was an idea that would gain currency with studies of how the fragmenting characteristic of Internet culture and "social media" would affect young minds in the twenty-first century.[42] But the problem with Wilson's use of it was that the figure "nineteen" was not even close to the real mean age of the American dead in Vietnam, making it virtually impossible for Wilson to have ever seen such a figure in a Defense Department source. In his 1998 book *Stolen Valor* B. J. Burkett claimed to be the first researcher to find the actual data on Vietnam

War dead, and he put the mean age at 22–23 years. Indeed, the "nineteen" figure as the mean age of casualties doesn't meet a common sense test. Men were not eligible for the draft until they were eighteen but even then, local draft boards took the oldest men in their pool first. Allowing for the time to be reclassified as draft-eligible, processed for induction, given eight weeks of basic training and four to eight more weeks for advanced training, and then processing and shipment to Vietnam after some leave time at home, almost everyone in Vietnam was at least nineteen; with nineteen being the near-*minimum* age to be in Vietnam, it would be statistically impossible for the mean age of the dead to be nineteen. By rank, moreover, officers were over-represented among the dead, with many shot-down pilots being over thirty.[43]

That Scott would uncritically reproduce Wilson's account in his book *The Politics of Readjustment*, when even a moment's reflection suggests its implausibility, could signal the willingness of PTSD's champions to suspend disbelief in data that did not support their cause. It could also have been that "nineteen" seemed right to them because the anti-war left had repeated it so often for so many years in an appeal to emotions that could end the war; the figure may also have had some appeal to Americans wanting to balance the good-versus-evil scale of war: the death of our "kids" by enemy hands shows how evil *they* are. Either of those sentiments, or some combination of them, may have been enough to make "nineteen" one of those things that "everyone knew to be true."

It's likely, though, that there was more to the dynamic that fixed "nineteen" in the public imagination of its war dead, a likelihood suggested by the British inclination to do the same thing after World War I. "Many British war memorials," writes Fiona Reid in her book *Broken Men: Shell Shock, Treatment, and Recovery,* "depict soldiers as boys rather than men." In this way, she writes, the soldiers are all victims of the war, rather than grown men who have been trained to kill as effectively as the enemy." Yet, she points out, the average age of the shell-shocked man was 26 years, hardly a 'boy' by any definition."[44]

Reid sees the British misrepresentation of its war dead as a machination in its effort to deal with the horribleness of a terrible and controversial war. Not so different from the British experience with World War I, some Americans had enthusiastically supported the war in Vietnam, but most were either ambivalent about it or opposed to it; when the war was over, few felt good about it, and many wanted emotional separation from it. Emotional separation of that type can be achieved by holding others responsible for the war, in effect projecting one's own responsibility for it (or for not helping to end it) onto "them." Eric Dean writing in *Shook over Hell*, his book about war trauma in the Civil War and Vietnam, said common portrayals of Vietnam veterans as poor, uneducated, and rural Southerners was a form of "otherizing" the conduct of the war—"they," those toothless hillbillies did it, not "us."

The year between nineteen and twenty demarcates teenagers from adults, kids from grownups, a boundary perfect for other-making. Adults regularly separate themselves from certain behaviors by otherizing those who do "those things" as "kids." A phrase like "boys will be boys" attributes unseemly behavior to youthfulness and excuses it from adult levels of accountability; simultaneously, that attribution to the youthful "other" excuses adults from holding their young responsible for their decisions to, say, join the military. Culturally, that dynamic broadens into the essentializing of war as a growing-up experience for boys, a rite-of-passage to manhood.[45]

That same cultural boundaring of kids and adults is what permitted the Krapelians in San Francisco to conceive that war trauma could have the organic, semi-enduring consequence on veterans that they wanted to leave town having established—never mind that the potency of the "nineteen" figure for that purpose was in its *cultural* properties, rather than anything demonstrably physiological about it. Going forward, the association made between age and the impact of trauma by the medical profession further reified the popular notion that "kids" did the fighting and dying in Vietnam, and moved onward from there into the emotional appeals during the Persian Gulf War to either support the troops (aka "our kids") who we've sent to fight—the propaganda of the pro-war community—or oppose the war because the troops (aka "our kids") are in harm's way—the propaganda of the anti-war community.

ON TO BAGHDAD AND A NEW AMERICAN IDENTITY

By the early 1980s the image of the traumatized, psychologically impaired Vietnam veteran had almost totally displaced that of the politically active, anti-war veteran in the American memory. Boys growing to military age during the late 1970s and 1980s were unlikely to have encountered any record of GI and veteran dissent from the Vietnam era, but saw powerful representations of soldiers damaged by war and heard the stories of veterans forgotten and spat on by an ungrateful public. Little surprise, then, that they went off to war in the Persian Gulf in 1990–1991 expecting the same, and returned "symptomatic" and feeling neglected.

In many ways, the Persian Gulf War was a continuation of the war in Vietnam. President George W. H. Bush said as much when he proclaimed that the "Vietnam Syndrome" would be exorcised in the Persian Gulf, a reference to the supposed reluctance the American people had for another war. Much of that "syndrome" derived from the nation's obsession with how "the boys" had been treated when they came home from Vietnam. The popular perception that Vietnam veterans had been neglected, even abused, spawned a yellow-ribbon campaign to support the troops in the Gulf, and parades to welcome them home in the spring of 1991.

And the Gulf War was a strange event. Although nominally a victory for the United States, it was fought entirely from the air by a small number of elite pilots who inflicted an obscene kill ratio on the Iraqis. Notwithstanding the patriotic "rah rah" that surrounded their mission, there was little that veterans of a hundred-day skirmish could take pride in. As veterans *qua* veterans, what were they supposed to feel? What could they ask their countrymen to feel for them? What identity could they derive from a war that was not really a war?

The absence of tangible military experience, much less of a war supposedly served *in*, prompted reaches for alternative credentials for which the post-Vietnam culture offered the viable option of the "unseen wound." Within months after the bombing stopped, men home from the Persian Gulf complained of mysterious ailments, and reported erratic behavior. One vet complained of fluorescent vomit, others of semen that burned or blistered their wives. Stories of birth defects in veterans' children proliferated. Newspapers reported high levels of cancer among soldiers home from the Gulf. The failure of epidemiological studies and other medical research to confirm the reality of the sicknesses didn't stop the rumor mill from churning out causes: nerve gas, secret drug experiments, deadly toxins, and PTSD.[46]

By December 2012, nearly half of the 700,000 veterans of the Gulf War had filed disability claims with the Department of Veterans Affairs and more than 85 percent have been granted benefits.[47]

In the same sense that the lost war in Vietnam presented an anomaly to cultural workers tasked with rendering its representations for public memory, so too did the-war-that-wasn't in the Persian Gulf confound those who would script its place in the country's identity—so they avoided it. Hollywood didn't take a stab at it until 1999 with *Three Kings*, an oddball forgettable movie about three U.S. soldiers who find a map leading to a stash of gold bullion in the Iraqi desert. With (Marky) Mark Wahlberg, then just out of his bubblegum boy-band stage, and the Gangsta Rapper Ice Cube in starring roles, nobody expected serious cinematiques from this number (much less something with insight into where the aftermath of the Gulf War would lead America)—and no one was disappointed.

Three Kings was made in the late 1990s when the Gulf War itself was perceived by the public as having been a kind of interregnum in end-of-history-America that had seen the last of twentieth-century-type warfare. For veterans of the Gulf, it confirmed, if anything, that their war would go into the books as a joke. The laughter ended with 9/11, and within months the vintners of motion picture fare began cultivating the lost-war storylines familiar to them: America at war with itself, wars lost on the home front, and a preference for stories about veterans *of* war over the wars themselves.[48]

Jarhead America

It's telling that popular culture mostly left the Persian Gulf War alone until the attacks of 9/11 put the prospect of *real* war back on the country's plate. Even then, the first major rendering of the Gulf War into popular culture didn't come until *Jarhead* in 2005, a film whose vintage-Vietnam themes and images confirmed that the country's preoccupations with its defeat in Southeast Asia would filter its experience with war in the millennial years. In it, we see Marines getting pumped for the Persian Gulf by watching *Apocalypse Now*, and later, as the platoon trudges through the sand toward the Iraqi border, an aircraft passes overhead, blasting the Doors' song *The End*, with which *Apocalypse Now* ended, prompting one Marine to wonder out loud, "Can't we even have our own music?"

By 2005 when *Jarhead* came out, the two-year-old invasion of Iraq was going badly, and the war in Afghanistan was in a kind of holding pattern. The instincts inherited by cultural workers from the generation ahead of them who had blotted out the failed mission in Southeast Asia with stories about national flaccidity and the despoliation of veterans was to do the same: change the subject— forget the war and write about the warriors. In retrospect, it is remarkable that it took four years after the September 11, 2001, attacks before something related to that event made it into theaters; and then it was a film that frog-leaped backwards over the 2003 invasion of Iraq to the desert dust-up of 1990–1991. It was two more years before movies explicitly themed by Iraq and Afghanistan were ready for the box office.

With surprising transparency, *Jarhead* repackaged Vietnam-film subjects like the brutality of boot camp from *Full Metal Jacket*, the sergeant out of *Hamburger Hill* with Nietzschean-themed reasons for preferring the war front to the home front, and even *Apocalypse Now*'s exhibition of primal darkness in a farewell rave with which the Marines depart the desert. Like its progenitors, *Jarhead* turned the war into a solipsistic affair about Americans: literally, the only Iraqis we saw were the "crispy critters" left smoldering on the desert floor by the boys with the Doors.

For its *finis*, *Jarhead* copped one last revisionist cliché molded in the culture of post-Vietnam America: the displacement of the historically grounded image of the veteran empowered and politicized by his Vietnam experience, by the strung-out, dysfunctional, and dangerous victim-veteran who brought the war home with him. That wigged-out stereotype makes a gratuitous reappearance in *Jarhead*, stepping onto a busload of Iraq-war returnees, as another cheap shot at the Vietnam generation of anti-war veterans who continue to work for peace and decent treatment of all veterans. There is no Siegfried Sassoon in this script, no lines for Donald Duncan or Charlie Clements. [49]

The presence given enemy Iraqis by *Jarhead*'s "crispy critters" was conspicuous compared with the Afghanis reduced to blinking cursors in *Lions for Lambs* (2007). In keeping with the motif established by Vietnam War films, this one began with the plot-line narcissism of Americans versus Americans (about what it means to be an American), continued through a story of Americans trying to save Americans (from the blinking cursors), and ended with an American contemplating his Americanism. The theme of war trauma remained implicit in this film, but its suggestibility just off screen far enough to keep away the alternative narrative with young men, as civilians or soldiers, imaged as anti-war activists.

In the Valley of Elah (2007) was the signal Hollywood offering on the war in Iraq, reprising in one package all the storylines that gave the films of war in Vietnam their *sui generis* character: the "war" removed to the home front; a film about *veterans* featuring *damaged* and *dangerous* veterans; conflict between veterans driven by a *betrayal* narrative that raises in viewers' minds *specters* of the unknown; religious hues (imparted by its title); and PTSD invoked as an alibi for murder. Most of what needs to be in this film is in *The Visitors* (1972) about Mike and Tony, veterans who have tracked down Bill to wreak vengeance on him for ratting them out for war crimes in Vietnam.

Girl with the Cong Skull

By 2007, though, filmmakers were no vanguard in the Vietnamization of the way Americans absorbed their new wars in Iraq and Afghanistan. The home-from-war-with-PTSD narrative achieved hegemonic status in the culture using "like Vietnam" as its coda. That rhetorical device worked most effectively to deliver collateral messages about the present wars through material that was ostensibly about Vietnam. And it wasn't just the news pages and programs that pressed PTSD into the public conversation. The cover page of the *New York Times* March 12, 2006, Sunday book review section, for example, featured a memoir by Danielle Trussoni, a Vietnam veteran's daughter who suffers the terrors he brought home with him.

Reviewed by one of the *Times*'s marquee critics, Kathryn Harrison, *Falling Through the Earth* appeared to be an unlikely candidate for hyping with her sizable reputation, and its front-page placement with large and bold block letters: THE WAR AT HOME. The book's premise, that war-born trauma of the Vietnam War years could be inherited by the next generation, pushed further the already ambitious boundaries of PTSD's claimable scope; when added to a fantasized anecdote that Trussoni grew up with the Viet Cong skull her father had brought home as a war souvenir, the review itself invited critical interest in what the editors were *really* trying to say with it. Exaggerations—one reader posting on amazon.com said the book was full of "tall tales" like those told on "bar stools"—are often symptoms of an author's doubt about the believability of her own story. The readers of Harrison's review might have wondered if, by repeating something so implausible as the Cong Skull, she was signaling her own skepticism of the narrative the *Times* wanted supported.

$$[(19 \times 4) + (20 \times 2) + 21 + (22 \times 4) + (24 \times 3) + 25 + (26 \times 3) + 30$$
$$+ (37 \times 2) + 41] / 22 = 19: \text{OR DOES IT?}$$

In 2007 the Pulitzer winning *Washington Post* reporter David Finkel was embedded with the Army's 2-16 Battalion in Iraq. Writing about that experience, Finkel said, "The average age in the battalion was nineteen." His account revolved around the fatalities taken by the 2-16: "so many of them were nineteen," he wrote. Apparently, though, Finkel didn't run the numbers on the soldiers' ages that he, himself, had provided in the book. He tells us about twenty-two deaths, each presented to us with names, ages, and other personal details. The ages, 19–41 are displayed in the subhead above, with the multipliers of how many of each age were killed. Of the twenty-two, only four were nineteen. The mean age of the dead was 24.7; the median was 23.

Phenomenologists study why people believe what they do; the Hans Christian Anderson fable of "The Emperor's New Clothes" presents the kind of anomaly that they are interested in. As the King parades naked through town, his subjects marvel at his beautiful new clothes. Since the empirical facts of the matter are not in doubt—the King *is* naked—the phenomenological inquiry turns on a different matter—how the minds of his subjects have dressed him.

In the matter of David Finkel, how did his mind manufacture an "average" of nineteen out of numbers—his own numbers, no less—whose average is not even close to nineteen? How could he write that many of the dead were nineteen when 82 percent were *older* than nineteen? Some readers might answer, "Well, it's obvious or common sense—let's not quibble about numbers, the nineteen-year-olds were, after all, boys whose lives will never be lived." But there were as many men over thirty (four) among the dead as there were under twenty. The oldest was 41-year-old Ralph Kauzlarich, a husband and father, and it's not so obvious why the voluntary presence of these older men in a war zone isn't as remarkable and worthy of a reporter's attention, or why the holes left in their families and communities by their deaths is so easily eclipsed by fascination with "nineteen."

The better answer is the one the narrator leads us to in the "The Emperor's New Clothes" which is that truth is constructed by the social relations of the society which has created the paradox. The Emperor's subjects were not lying when they testified to his faux finery; but they feared him, and it was that power dynamic defining the kingdom that led their minds to put clothes in places their eyes had not seen them. Finkel's mind worked in the same manner to create conformity with the dominant beliefs of the society out of measureable information (i.e. the actual ages of the dead) that said otherwise. It is fair enough to say he is wrong in the way he arrives at the "nineteen" figure and the way he uses it, but he isn't lying.

Rather, his knowledge of "nineteen" as the average age of the war dead has an existence independent of the data on which such a claim would have to be based—if, that is, empirical reality was the arbiter.[50]

In turn, the media coverage of a book like Finkel's feeds his claims back into popular culture in a way that bolsters the very misperceptions that mislead him. The *New York Times*, for example, devoted a major review to his book, likening it to Tim O'Brien's *Things They Carried*, a book about Vietnam with an established place in the post-war literary canon. That pompom proffered, the reviewer then states matter-of-factly that the book shows us the average of "these young soldiers . . . is nineteen."[51]

The "truth" of the figure "nineteen" uses dead nineteen-year-olds as a metaphor in the mythology of American innocence stolen away by violent enemies and betrayed at home by political incompetence and indifferent public opinion. The loss of "youth," moreover, has long-lasting consequences that form a scar on the society that will always be there—it is real, it is a wound. In the same sense that the "formative trauma" of the "kids" home from war shapes their adulthood, so too does the societal trauma left by war remake the collective sense of the national self. Belief in nineteen as the age of war dead provides grounding for the image of the victim-nation, a nation rent by trauma seeking to heal, seeking to restore an imagined wholeness.[52]

CHAPTER EPILOGUE: PISSING ON THE DEAD

In early January 2012 a video began circulation showing U.S. Marines urinating on the corpses of Taliban fighters. The story led the January 12 edition of the PBS *News Hour*, a normally cautious, even staid, news outlet. Moderated by *News Hour* regular Judy Woodruff, the segment featured Andrew Exum, a former Army Captain and now a Fellow at the Center for a New American Secur-

ity, and *Washington Post* reporter David Ignatius as guest commentators. Exum denounced the alleged acts, referring to the accused
Marines as eighteen- and nineteen-year-olds who had been dehumanized by the war. Ignatius followed with equally exculpatory
remarks, calling the Marines "young men at war . . . dehumanized."
Ignatius added that things like this have "always occurred in war
but that "now we have the Internet" that makes such acts more
visible.

The problem: almost nothing of what Exum and Ignatius said
made sense. To begin with, Woodruff herself had introduced the
segment identifying the Marines as "elite" and "highly trained,"
descriptions which, whatever their actual ages, was hard to reconcile with the images of American kids all shook up by war. Even at
the time of the PBS broadcast, news sources were identifying at
least some of the Marines as snipers—a military occupational specialty more likely to traumatize would-be targets than the shooters;
a specialty whose design to *take* human life could hardly be recali-
brated to make life-takers into victims.

Moreover, Exum and Ignatius evidently went on the air not
knowing the actual ages of the perpetrators—the next day's *New
York Times* coverage of the story said only one of the accused had
been identified by the military but even his name and age had not
been released. It's true that Marines in Afghanistan are often
younger than average ages of military personnel there, and it's
possible that when the actual ages become public information we'll
see that the PBS commentators were correct. But the fact remains
that, at the time, Exum and Ignatius had created the "eighteen- and
nineteen-" year-old figures out of their own imaginations.[53]

The most telling story within the PBS report, however, was Ignatius's remark that the Marines' behavior is the kind thing that
happens in war. Not quite a boys-will-be boys quip, his comment
nevertheless misses the disturbing underside of American society
that the incident revealed. Atrocities in war happen, for sure. But

their staging by troops for the purpose of photographic documentation is a perversity that makes no sense outside a cultural context in which war trauma has become an alibi for war crime, and the commitment of atrocities is conflated with martial accomplishment.

NOTES

1. Duncan appears forty years later in the documentary film *Sir! No Sir!* in which he recalls having left the Army not even knowing, at the time, that there was a movement against the war.

2. The best account of the U.S. covert war against North Vietnam is by Richard H. Shultz, Jr. (1999).

3. The early-nineteenth century theorist Henri St. Simon thought that social systems were essentially systems of *ideas*. His theory prioritized the role of intellectuals as either maintaining the status quo or being revolutionary vanguards. Ideas consistent with his make ruling elites, even two hundred years later, especially uncomfortable with intellectuals.

4. In World War II by contrast the 25th Infantry Division arrived on Guadalcanal in January 1943 and by July it had moved to other islands. By the end of the year it was in New Zealand for rest before retraining on New Caledonia in 1944. From there it shipped to the Philippines for a fight-and-move campaign that ran to the end of the war.

5. One of Bobby Darin's hits was *Dream Lover* (1959). The definitive filmography for Vietnam War films is Malo and Williams (1994). For this and the following paragraphs I have borrowed from my own chapter on film in *The Spitting Image* (1998).

6. Fleming (1985, pp. 123, 136). Although Fleming did not cite him, the sociologist Talcott Parsons developed the idea of the "sick child" as a "role" that serves the needs of both the child and the family—or as Fleming was using it, the veterans and the society.

7. Roth (2012, Chapter 5). Roth writes of the centrality of trauma to the dystopian sense of society that has displaced the utopianism characteristic of late-nineteenth-century America.

8. Whether the symptoms of shell shock disappeared during World War II or doctors' interest in identifying veterans' behaviors and ailments as such declined, the broad category called "war neuroses" is itself discussable. Contrary to some of the scholars cited here, for example, John V. H. Dippel makes a case in *War and Sex* (p. 233) that the psychiatric casualty rate was actually quite high, although Showalter made a distinction between psychiatric causalities and symptoms of hysteria.

9. See Paul Starr's review of Robert Jay Lifton's book (1973a).

10. Young (1995, Pp. 94-117) has a good account of this.

11. Young (1995, Pp. 99-100).

12. Hacking (1996, p. 76).

13. Goetz (2010).

14. The irony was that the Kraepelin approach was the original source of skepticism about what "war trauma" meant when there was no evidence of physical wounds—for example, shell shock without exposure to shells. And yet the assumptions of that approach would later undergird the formulation of Traumatic Brain Injury, the idea that war trauma is (or can be) neurological but caused by non-physical events. Before that irony played out, however, professional psychiatry would undergo a transition, trading its preference for talk therapy for drug therapy.

15. Repression of the event is more likely if the trauma resulted from fear of *self*, e.g. fear that a comrade died because the subject lacked the courage to do what he could have to save him.

16. Frankel (1994, p. 324). Frankel's article is a review of professional literature on flashbacks. He used a computer search for articles indexed under "flashbacks."

17. Frankel (1994, p. 322) wrote that the lineage of "flashback" ran from literature and film into the drug culture of Haight Ashbury and thence to the symptomology of PTSD.

18. Fleming (1985, p. 133).

19. Langley (1982, p. 596).

20. Frankel (1994, p. 321). Langley, in the same article (p. 595), wrote without attribution that "veterans report incidents of crowds of people spitting on them as they disembarked from their plane."

21. Frankel (1994, pp. 321, 331-332).

22. *Deathdreams* was a 1972 Canadian film also named *The Night Walk, The Veteran*, and in Great Britain, *Dead of Night*. A seldom recognized film, critic Tony Williams (Malo and Williams, 1994, p. 293) calls it "a rare inter-generic gem deserving further analysis."

23. Scott (1993, p. 60).

24. See Mosqueda and Meagher, n.d.

25. A version of the story close to the Neff-Shatan-Scott version made its way into an early draft-script for what became the 1978 film *Coming Home*, perhaps providing the prototype for Jon Voight's character "Luke" in that film. That the figure of a deranged Vietnam vet on the loose in Los Angeles somehow captured the attention of both screenwriters and mental health professionals goes to the core of the art-science nexus in matters of mental health diagnoses.

26. *Black Sunday* had an especially strong emotional impact because of its association with the massacre of Israeli athletes by the Palestinian Black September group in Munich, Germany, in 1972.

27. Lair (2011, P. 218) makes similar observations about the notion of veterans with "invisible wounds."

28. *First Blood*, 1982.

29. Urbina (2009) writes about the problem of fake heroes, from the war in Vietnam through the current wars in Iraq and Afghanistan, many involving false claims for disability due. Dishneau (2009) reports on Iraq War veterans using fake PTSD claims to bolster their combat identities. The circularity of claims in these stories is interesting: false claims to combat can leverage disability awards; in turn, a disability award can be cited as validation for the claims to combat. For variations on the theme, see Caywood (2009) who reported details in a particular case, and Brad Hamilton's *New York Post* 2010 report "One Arm Bandit: B'klyn bum fakes war wound for cash."

30. For "factitious PTSD" see Sparr and Pankratz (1983) and Lynn and Belza (1984). Hagopian (2009, p. 73) writes that Jack McCloskey, team leader of the San Francisco Waller Street vet center, funded by the Veterans Administration outreach program, refused to check the DD-214 discharge papers of new clients before counseling them. As a result, says Hagopian, "Some of the clients his staff saw turned out not to have been Vietnam veterans at all."

31. Philipps (2010, p. 25)

32. In the 2010 *HBO* special "War Torn: 1861–2010" about war trauma across the decades, a Vietnam veteran says he "was a mad dog" after the "kill, kill, kill" drill and that years later he still does not know how to get rid of it, a claim that strains credulity.

33. The idea that "reflexive responses" can be drilled into young men is a kind of folklore that found its way into the professional literature by the 1980s. With no citation or attribution for the claim, Langley (1982, p. 596) writes, "The fear of losing control and perhaps killing someone . . . is especially frightening to combat veterans because many have had special training in martial arts and hand-to-hand fighting."

34. There are lots of "hit the deck" stories. Langley (1982, p. 596) says, "Many veterans exhibit a pronounced startle response to sudden loud noises or flashes of light. An example of this reflex-like response is the veteran who immediately 'hits the ground' or runs for cover when a car backfires in the street." Langley provides no evidence for this actually having happened and, as far as I know, there is none—or, for that matter, any evidence that cars in the 1970s and 1980s still "backfired." I wrote about the hit-the-deck stories in "Fireworks and Flashbacks—and Cars that Backfire?" at *Counterpunch* in July 2013.

35. Leys (2000, pp. 257–258).

36. Leys (2000, pp. 257–258).

37. Frankel (1994, p. 330).

38. Frankel (1994, p.331).

39. Hyer, Lee et al. (1990, p. 718). PTSD's qualification as a "wound" required some physiological character, properties suggesting permanence, damage done to the body that could not be undone by counseling, meditation, or psychotherapy.

40. Like "flashback" had, TBI had a pre-PTSD life and was insinuated into diagnostic discourse through popular culture and the news media. That story will be told in the next chapter.

41. Wilson's work was seminal in the formulation of PTSD. An often cited article by M. Keith Langley (1982), for example, is framed by a reference to Wilson.

42. Nicolas Carr (2010) writes about the effect of social media on young brains.

43. By 1968 when I was drafted many draftees had been, like me, deferred for several years for educational or occupational reasons, making that cohort as a whole much older than nineteen. I was twenty-five.

44. Reid (2010, Pp. 85–86).

45. I wrote more about the "nineteen" fallacy in "The Problem of Soldiers' Ages," *National Catholic Reporter* (2007).

46. See Fumento (1997) for a good critique of what he called "Gulf Lore Syndrome." Showalter (1997) discusses Gulf War Syndrome as a form of hysteria.

47. Dao (2012). In the same report, Dao notes, "Many of those veterans have reported long-lasting problems . . . some of which had no clear causes. Many veterans insist that their problems are not the result of stress but have a biological basis"—an insistence recalling Elaine Showalter's (chapter 4) observation about shell shock and masculinity: "anything but psychological."

48. In a July 16, 2010, review of *Inception*, the *New York Times* critic A. O. Scott observed that "movies, more often than not these days, are made out of other movies."

49. The theme of going back for something essential that was left behind in the war was made a staple by the Vietnam POW rescue films. *Blackhawk Down* (2001) extended that theme into the era of the new wars. Not slapstickish like *Three Kings, Blackhawk Down*'s fictional rendition of a shootdown of a U.S. helicopter and loss of its crew in Mogadishu, Somali, in 1993, was gasoline for the flames of Islamaphobia fanned by Rightists wanting another go in the Gulf. Keeping faith with the standards of their Vietnam-era elders, the makers of *Blackhawk Down* brought the Battle for Mogadishu to the screen, but without the Somalis who had brought down the Blackhawk.

50. Described here as phenomenology, the same approach might be recognized as epistemology by philosophers, and sociology of knowledge of social scientists. Thomas Kuhn's *The Structure of Scientific Revolutions* is one of the modern classics of the field. In Kuhnian terms, the "nineteen" figure of war dead was a kind of paradigm that Finkel wanted to maintain belief in—so he ignored data that was inconsistent with it.

51. Kakutani (2009). On the day the *Times* review ran, October 6, the PBS *News Hour* scrolled the names, ages, and home towns of twelve recent U.S. war dead. The average age of the twelve—a tad over 27.

52. In *The Scar that Binds* (2000) Keith Beattie explains how the image of the scar works to mythologize the American experience in Vietnam. Hagopian (2009) shows how PTSD worked both as a way of stigmatizing veterans as "losers" for the loss of the war, and as evidence for the "mutual destruction" thesis that Vietnam and the United States suffered equally from the war.

53. The name and age of one Marine was released in December 2012. He was Staff Sgt. Joseph W. Chamblin, 35 years old (Fuentes 2012). Another facing trial in early 2013 was Staff Sgt. Edward W. Deptola, 27 years old (Gannon 2013).

Chapter Six

Traumatic Brain Injury: Making a "Signature Wound"

In a March 11, 2007, column, *New York Times* Public Editor Brian Calame responded to criticisms that the paper had been scooped by a February 18 *Washington Post* story exposing the poor treatment being given veterans of the war in Iraq at Walter Reed Army Medical Center. According to the *Post* story, veterans reporting symptoms of PTSD and Traumatic Brain Injury were being neglected; mice droppings, mold, dead cockroaches, and stained carpets were found in parts of Walter Reed. The *Post*'s report resulted in Walter Reed's Director Maj. Gen. George W. Weightman being fired, and an investigation of the Center begun by a bipartisan presidential commission. How had the *Times* missed all this?

Calame consulted *Times* executive editor Bill Keller for his response. Keller acknowledged being "slow" to pick up on the Walter Reed story, but offered in defense that ''we had done a lot of our own reporting on the plight of the wounded in Iraq . . . including a three-part series [in 2006] that explored . . . the devastating wounds of this war, particularly traumatic brain injury. ''

Keller's singling out of traumatic brain injury (TBI) was interesting because it underscores for us that by March 2007 the term carried the cachet he needed for saying the *Times* was *au courant* on the matter of veterans' health care. But was Keller right in suggesting that his paper might have been ahead of the curve in bringing TBI to public attention?

Actually, the *Times* 2006 series made *no* mention of TBI, a fact that makes the making of Keller's memory itself a candidate for study: how and why would he have remembered something that wasn't true and, regardless of whatever attention may have been given to TBI in 2006, how had TBI achieved such emblematic standing by then that he deigned to use it as shorthand for so much else? The *Times* did run several major stories on war-related PTSD during 2006 but none of them mentioned Traumatic Brain Injury. In fact, TBI was such a newcomer to the news about veterans that by mid-year 2005, two years into the invasion of Iraq, the *Times* had never linked war and TBI. [1]

THE MEDIA TRAJECTORY OF TBI

As a diagnostic category applicable to war veterans, Traumatic Brain Injury would gain media visibility at meteoric speed after 2007. Its origins, however, were humble, way off the front page, and unrelated to war. But as it was with shell shock and PTSD, economics, political context, and culture mediated the movement of TBI into the mainstream media where it established a public presence as a new diagnostic category.

The very first *New York Times* reference to Traumatic Brain Injury had come in 1983; between then and April 1989 there were only a half-dozen more references, usually carried in reports on treatment facilities and charity events related to head injuries. None of those early stories referred to veterans, even of the Vietnam era; nor did they provide a provenance for the term, a curious quality leaving its identity open and subject to future interventions. [2]

It wasn't as though the news media were just ignoring TBI. There were only scattered uses of the phrase "traumatic brain injury" in U.S. medical journals during the 1970s and early 1980s. In 1988, one of the first full-length articles appeared with Traumatic Brain Injury in its title. Its author C.T. Gualtieri began by noting that "the relevant research on TBI is so sparse" that he had had to extrapolate from the small assortment of patient groups to write his article. The presence of TBI in the professional literature grew when a new journal, *Brain Injury*, began publishing in 1988 but the number of articles featuring it the fields of psychology and psychiatry remained small.[3]

Public interest in TBI didn't come until May 21, 1989, when news broke about a 28 year old white investment banker who had been raped and beaten a month earlier while jogging in Central Park. The crime-story content of the report was quickly surpassed by the "urban legend" tinge of its randomness, and the identification of the arrested assailants as young male members of racial minority groups. The anonymity of the comatose victim, meanwhile, protected as it was by news media policies to not reveal the names of rape victims, enabled the scripting of her as "The Central Park Jogger," a figure soon "known to the world" as *New York Times* reporter Ronald Sullivan put it.[4]

Sullivan's hyperbole aside, the "any-woman" blankness of "the jogger" tag invited emotional identity of the could-have-been-me type that the *Times* fed with eighteen stories on her by December, many with TBI embedded in them. Tens of thousands of readers, including health-care professionals working in New York City, hooked on the drama of the celebrity-victim jogger, were thereby exposed, collaterally, to TBI—yet in its emergent stage. When in 2003 Trisha Meili revealed herself at the Spaulding Rehabilitation Hospital in Boston as "the jogger," and then coauthored an article with her doctor in the journal *Advances in Mind-Body Medicine*, the significance of the jogger–TBI interplay seemed apparent: her story was not for the criminologists or the sociologists of race/gender/class—it had become a mental health story.[5]

The Central Park Jogger had all but disappeared from the news between 1990 and 1995, and with her, Traumatic Brain Injury. The rise and fall of media interest in TBI, with the enchantment of its poster victim, encourages speculation that its emergence as a diagnostic concept was being led, as shell shock and PTSD had, by popular culture. While that speculation is hard to confirm, the number of journal articles featuring TBI had more than doubled by 1993, four years after the assault in Central Park and about the minimal number of years it takes for research and writing to get into print. Professional interest in TBI continued to grow after 1993 but never so dramatically as in that four-year span.

The *re*appearance of TBI in the news, however, did coincide with coverage of another highly popular topic—sports injuries. The first of those stories came on July 16, 1997, a year after head injuries to "high profile quarterbacks" Steve Young of the '49ers and Troy Aikman of the Cowboys had led the National Football League to begin a five-year study of players suffering concussions. The *Times* story, "NFL Embarks on Stepped-up Effort to Deal with Head Injuries," reported that the League would add neurological and psychological testing to its evaluation of players. The results of the NFL's five-year study were released in the journal *Neurology* in October 2003 and reported in the sports pages of the *Times*.[6]

With sports as a "hook" certain to draw attention from both healthcare-professional and lay audiences, the story put Traumatic Brain Injury back into the public conversation. By using TBI as a synonym for "concussion," however, the story highlighted the conceptual vagueness of the term: was "traumatic brain injury" just another way of saying "concussion"? Or was it a symptom *of* concussion? Could trauma be the *cause* of brain injury—is that the meaning of the word trauma in "Traumatic Brain Injury"? The word trauma used in this way recalled something like shell shock without the explosions from shells—was it supposed to be read that way? Or read as a qualifying term to "brain injury"—a certain kind of brain injury? The league's resort to *both* neurological and psychological testing only added to the sense of confusion surrounding TBI—did it refer to disorders of a physical and organic nature, or problems that were of a mental or emotional nature? Were there cultural matters at play in it? Where did injuries to the head, brain, mind, and emotions begin and end? And if they were related, in which direction did the lines of influence run?[7]

The cloudiness of TBI may have been a brake on its professional acceptance, foretelling its destiny as a concept with more cultural clout than diagnostic. By 2003, six years after the story of football concussion injuries made headlines (and more than enough time for research studies to be published), increased professional interest in TBI was measureable but not as dramatic as that following the jogger story and, notably, increased more slowly after the 2005 article in *Neurology*.[8]

The war in Iraq was already going badly when the National Football League's findings on Traumatic Brain Injury were released in the fall of 2003, but the sports-framing given TBI by the press held firm even when casualties mounted during the battle for Fallujah a year later. Traumatic Brain Injury's incursion into the war-injury discourse came, when it did, from an unexpected quarter: an August 21, 2005, Sunday Magazine Q & A segment when reporter Deborah Solomon asked author Kayla Williams about her new book, *I Love My Rifle More Than You*.

Williams had used her experience as a soldier in Iraq to expose the difficulties faced by women in the Army. Citing her "chick-lit sensibilities," Solomon asked Williams about Brian, the man she was about to marry. Brian, also a veteran, had shrapnel lodged in his brain, said Williams, before adding that he suffered from Traumatic Brain Injury, as well. Solomon did not follow up on the reference to TBI, and it was another year before the *Times* would again put veterans and TBI in the same story.

The reference to Traumatic Brain Injury in the interview was off-topic enough—the "topic" being a campy exploitation of a girls-with-guns fetish that was gaining popularity at the time—to be dismissible as an incidental, "oh, by-the-way." The seminal power of popular culture to trigger associations—like those between war and its physical and emotional wounds, in this case—make it hard to conclude that it was Williams's comment that inspired Solomon to write the 2008 series on crime, veterans, and PTSD used in chapter 1. The fact remains, however, that the very first link made between Traumatic Brain Injury and war veterans (of *any* war) by the *New York Times* came in an interview with a pop-culture author that appeared way off the news pages.[9]

But other developments with the potential to drill Traumatic Brain Injury into the home-from-war-and-hurt narrative, tasked with distracting Americans from the war itself, would move TBI into wider view. Some of those were already underway: the openness of TBI's meaning was a space waiting to be filled by lawyers and marketers working for pharmaceutical companies. By May 2005 the drug company Avanir was running clinical trials for Neurodex for use in treating Pseudobulbar Effect, a bundle of symptoms that included TBI. The chief ingredient in Neurodex was dextormethorphan, a common cough suppressant found in products like Robitussin-DM. Dr. Gerald J. Yakatan, a leader in pharmaceutical science, compared the development of Neurodex to the way drug companies made erectile dysfunction and attention deficit hyperactivity disorder well-known terms. "Before there were drugs, these conditions didn't exist," he said.[10]

The early 2000s also consolidated the place of computer-imaged brain scans in diagnostic practice. The ability to imagine *visually* the properties of TBI extended the gendered logic of trauma diagnoses begun during the Railway Spine outbreak of the early nineteenth century that reached into the treatment of war trauma as shell shock after World War I, and then the formulation of PTSD following the war in Vietnam. Psychological explanations—thought to be unmanly—were avoided in favor of events occurring external to the soldier that could account for mental or emotional damage—or, in effect "wounds." Each phase of diagnostic development, moreover, had associated with it a new medium by which the disorder *du jour* could be represented: the camera, silent movies, film with sound track, and for the TBI of the twenty-first-century, wars— magnetic resonance imaging or MRI.

The efforts to "see" the brain began in the early twentieth century but it wasn't until the late 1940s, when magnetic resonance was discovered, that variations in brain tissue could be visualized and measured. Advances in computer technology in the 1980s made more detailed imaging of the brain possible through CT and CAT scans; functional MRIs, known as fMRIs, followed in the 1990s. Premised on the ideas that specific human traits and activities could be associated with certain areas of the brain, and that the detection of blood molecules flowing through the brain could identify brain damage, fMRIs were ridiculed by critics as a new form "phrenology," the junk science popularized by the German anatomist Franz Joseph Gall in the 1700s. It's devotees, reported Sandra Blakeslee for the *New York Times* in 2000, were "dazzled" and "thrilled" with the "tool that can peer inside the thinking, feeling human brain," even seeing the "spot that lights up when a man is sexually aroused."[11]

The blood flows lighting up the computer screen also lighted researchers imaginations that they were actually seeing the brain *think*, a connection that may have been accurate—or a connection as spurious as the facial distortions captured in women's faces by Londe's camera at Salpêtrière, faces in which Jean Martin Charcot thought he saw hysteria. As late as 2013, however, searches for something physical that could be associated with PTSD were still coming up empty handed. "There has been minimal progress in identifying [biomarkers] for PTSD or depression," wrote James

Dao for the *New York Times*, "and many mental health experts believe the search is futile."[12]

The futility of the search for PTSD bio-markers seems a given; it is, after all, an assemblage of disorders like depression, none of which themselves have known bodily causes—how could the package have a bio-marker if nothing in the package does? The "brain injury" part of TBI, however, raises new possibilities. Brain matters are physiological and injuries to the brain imply external events having occurred *to* the victim/patient—like those exploding shells causing shell shock. But how can something as definitionally physical like "brain injury" be made to look and sound like it belongs in a collection of purely psychological and emotional categories? *Voila*—the discursive conjunction formed by adding the word "traumatic" to "brain injury." With "traumatic brain injury" mixed in, the PTSD package now becomes nominally biological, relieving it of its otherwise "only psychological" stigma.

With more time, we'll know if the invisibility of the PTSD/TBI wound is brought into view by the availability of tools to "see" it, and drugs to treat it. What is clear now, though, is that the arrival of a "face" for those hidden injuries, a figure with media appeal even higher than the jogger's, was a godsend for the popularization of TBI. With drop-dead good looks, Cary Grant charisma, and the market leverage of a television news anchor—because he was one—ABC newsman Bob Woodruff was the poster boy who could move TBI onto the evening news and maybe into the diagnostic manuals.[13]

BOB WOODRUFF: WOUNDS WITH CELEBRITY

Woodruff, forty-five years old at the time, was traveling as an embedded reporter with the 4th Infantry Division 12 miles north of Baghdad on January 30, 2006, when the Iraqi personnel vehicle carrying him and photographer Doug Vogt was hit by a roadside improvised explosive device (IED). Standing with his head above the hatch, Woodruff was struck in the face by stones and shrapnel from the explosion. At a U.S. Air Force hospital in Iraq, surgeons removed a piece of his skull to relieve the pressure from swelling; he was then evacuated to the Army Medical Command hospital in Landstuhl, Germany, before being moved to Bethesda Naval Hospital in Maryland on January 31.

Only weeks earlier, Woodruff had been named co-anchor of ABC's *World News Tonight* after his predecessor, Peter Jennings, announced he had lung cancer. Jennings died at sixty-seven on August 7 of 2005 after being at ABC for forty years; he was very popular with news viewers, facts which, when combined with his death, gave Woodruff's ascension into the chair on December 1 a prominence it would not have had under more normal circumstances. For Woodruff to have been wounded on a military convoy when he was still in the national spotlight as Jennings's successor almost insured that his *wounds* would be conferred celebrity standing; that the wounds would be to his head at the very time when PTSD and Traumatic Brain Injury were consolidating their hold on the country's imagination made it certain that the story of his survival and recovery would galvanize the public's emotions about war trauma.

News organizations were understandably riveted by the wounding of one of their own and spared no effort to bring the story to their readers and viewers. The Woodruff story got front-page coverage in the *New York Times* on January 30; there were two other related stories in the *Times* that day and nine more in the next five days. The *Washington Post* devoted comparable coverage to it while providing glimpses of some controversies that would trail the story going forward. Had ABC been reckless in putting journalists at risk in a war zone in the pursuit of ratings? On January 31, the *Post* echoed a *Times* subhead from the day before that read, "Field Reports Were a Ratings Strategy." The implication of that specula-

tion was that ABC had put its bottom line ahead of the journalists'
safety, an implication that was rebuffed by ABC and criticized by
media personality Barbara Walters. It nevertheless resonated, if
discordantly, with speculation that Woodruff and Vogt had been
"hotdogging" by standing up in a lightly armored vehicle when
they could have been tucked more safely in a U.S. Humvee. The
Post's report that same day that Woodruff had walked to the medical aid chopper seemed to imply that his wounds were not serious,
thereby placing an asterisk on the drama surrounding his recovery
that would build in the following days. [14]

TBI in the Woodruff Story

What did not "build" was the TBI story. For a full year, none of the
news stories on Woodruff's medical condition mentioned Traumatic Brain Injury. That changed on February 27, 2007, thirteen
months after the explosion, when a press conference promoted the
ABC documentary "To Iraq and Back" to be shown that evening.
The program would be based on a new book, *In an Instant: A
Family ' s Journey of Love and Healing*, written by Woodruff and
his wife Lee. The press conference featured Woodruff talking about
his recovery; surprisingly, given the absence of TBI in the yearlong press attention to his condition, he now headlined it as the
disorder he struggled to overcome. The *Times* report on the news
conference mentioned TBI four times but didn't inquire into how
that term had found its way into Woodruff's story. In fact, that was
a story in itself: the story of the trauma narrative that incubated in
the writing of the Woodruffs' book. As well, that incubation can be
read as a chapter in how TBI got written into the American discourse about its new wars and those who fight them. [15]

The story of Woodruff's recovery and return to work, as written
by him and his wife Lee, can be read for its interplay between the
ongoing social construction of Traumatic Brain Injury (the diagnostic category), and the efforts to portray his condition as repre-

sentative of that diagnosis. Writing in their coauthored memoir, Lee recalled being told on the day he arrived at Bethesda that "he did *not* have a penetrating brain injury" (the emphasis hers). His "intercranial pressure" had remained normal, she wrote, but "there had been a discrete injury to the speech and language part of his brain." She didn't say what that discrete injury was but added, "The blast had a concussive effect, shaking the whole brain."[16]

In the absence of a penetrating injury or even any claim (in the Woodruffs' version of the diagnosis) of organic damage to the brain, phrases like "discrete injury" and "concussive effect" become elastic terms. In Woodruffs' case the concussive effect would gain stature in the story as the TBI narrative took shape during his Bethesda stay and the year it took to write the book. But the mold for its shaping was formed on that first day when Lee Woodruff says she was told by a doctor that even being near a blast had an effect on the brain that could be permanent.[17] Handed that element, she discarded the need for organic brain damage in the story, writing later that by February 12 as much as possible had been done "surgically for Bob's brain"—even though readers had been given no reason to believe there ever was brain damage needing surgical repair.[18]

With groundwork thereby laid for a switch in the narrative being developed—from the physical/brain wound to the trauma/mind wound—Lee Woodruff introduced Traumatic Brain Injury to the story. From that point about halfway through the book, almost one-fourth of the remaining pages dealing with Bob Woodruff's recovery use the language of TBI and PTSD to develop his "walking wounded" image, with the "wounds" being the unseen ones associated with trauma.[19]

Bob Woodruff did have serious damage caused by a small rock that ripped into the left side of his throat and entered his lower jaw, threatening the vocal cords and nerves of the tongue and voice box. It is those injuries that weave in and out of the trauma narrative, mingling the physicality they bring to mind with the more elusive imagery suggested by TBI's thread of hypothetical causality connecting mind, brain, and body. Recalling February 13, for example, Lee referred to "get[ting] the rock out of Bob's head" ten lines before speculating that "his mind had left us." A rock lodged in the jaw, having entered from the throat even further below, may be in the "head" but it would be a stretch to, therewith, associate it with a brain injury. But that is the almost deniable effect of her word choices and syntax—with the loop completed through her subsequent allusion to his injured mind. The next six pages, comprising one of the longest vignettes of the book, continue in that vein to comingle Bob's physical injuries to the throat and jaw, with brain injury (that stays unspecified throughout the book), and the effects of trauma. Those elements of the narrative are woven so tightly that one has to reread to confirm that no brain surgery is ever actually done.[20]

Fifty-six pages later it is March 1, 2006, when Bob Woodruff is one month into his recovery. He has come out of his drug-induced coma and has spoken his first words since the roadside attack in Iraq. Fully committed to the TBI narrative, his wife Lee writes through the voice of the doctor, compiling the signature characteristics of PTSD that she says come with "a blast injury": impaired judgment; personality differences (profound on the "inside" but unnoticeable to others); aphasia; forgetfulness; depression; nightmares; flashbacks; seizures. The litany, with as many qualifiers—sometimes, always, often, might—continues on for four pages at which point its length, and drama with which she presents it, compels the reader's acquiescence: her husband *has* PTSD/TBI.[21]

What Bob Woodruff did *not* have was four inches of skull that had been intentionally removed by doctors in Iraq to relieve pressure on his brain. It is presumably a sensitive medical procedure but one that had become routine by that time for doctors working in the war zone. While the Woodruffs' account would lead us to think it is a treatment *for* brain injury, it is in fact a procedure done to *prevent* brain injury, and does not in any way equate *to* brain injury. And yet, other than that excision and the aforementioned "blast injury," there does not seem to be a causal basis for Bob Woodruff suffering Traumatic Brain Injury. If overreaching is suggestive of weakness in one's case, Lee Woodruff's reference, a few pages before the end of *In an Instant*, to her husband's "traumatic brain injury dealt by a roadside bomb powerful enough to blow open his skull" would draw the eyes of skeptics.

Woodruff's skull had not been blown open by an IED and, notwithstanding the book's effort, a critical reading of *In an Instant* gives us no reason to think he suffered a brain injury—except for the possible concussive effect of the blast itself, or the possibility that trauma can cause brain injury. With the shadow of doubt cast over the blast/concussive effect by the historical studies of shell shock, and the confusion about the meaning of the word "trauma" in TBI, the Woodruff case brilliantly illuminates the constructionist properties of the TBI/PTSD formulations, and underscores the weight of their narrative value relative to their diagnostic value.

The News, A Book, and Prime-time

The narrative value of Traumatic Brain Injury can be weighed by comparing the number of TBI stories in the news before and after the press conference: in the month leading up to it, there were two *Times* stories about TBI, both of them about football injuries; in the month after, eleven stories covered TBI, with nine of those connecting the diagnosis with war veterans. The most important of the nine was Paul D. Eaton's March 6 op-ed entitled "Casualties of the Budget Wars." Eaton was a retired Army major general, whose opinion piece was a virtual sequel to the 1972 *Times* op-ed written by psychiatrist Chaim Shatan about PTSD. Just as Shatan's observations on Vietnam veterans came with political implications—the medicalizing of their dissent—Eaton used TBI (and PTSD) to leverage criticism of the Walter Reed Army Hospital then under the command of President George W. Bush.[22]

The political waters that Eaton stuck his oar into had been roiled by casualty figures reported on the ABC program about the Woodruffs' book. According to the Department of Defense the number of wounded in Iraq and Afghanistan was about 23,000 while the Department of Veterans Affairs recorded treating more than 200,000 veterans of those two wars. That discrepancy, said Paul Sullivan from the advocacy group Veterans for America, was due to the keeping of "two sets of books": the larger number, said R. James Nicholson, the Secretary of Veterans Affairs, included 73,000 mental disorders and 61,000 nervous diseases that the Defense Department's figures did not include.

Eaton's article gained traction with democrats who were looking to impugn the Bush administration for its failure to care for the veterans with the same enthusiasm it had in sending them off to war—an "enthusiasm gap" the democrats hoped to exploit for the 2008 presidential campaign season just getting underway. But the discrepant numbers also unveiled the campaign to gain recognition for TBI as a diagnostic category and status as a cultural term resonant enough with PTSD to extend that Vietnam-vintage nomenclature into the new century. Those who championed PTSD had claimed that 30-50 percent of Vietnam veterans "had" PTSD, when only 15 percent of the soldiers in Vietnam had seen combat. A similar gap appeared in the figures for the new wars reported on the ABC program: even if all the 23,000 veterans counted as wounded by the Department of Defense suffered some sort of trauma—an implausible 100 percent ratio—that would leave 111,000 trauma cases unrelated to some other injury. Even Woodruff, the face and voice of TBI's legitimating, acknowledged on the program that "those are huge numbers beyond the 23,000."[23]

The gap between the number of soldiers who plausibly could have seen combat and the numbers associated with war trauma led to the discrediting of shell shock as a physiological ailment after World War I. After the war in Vietnam, the high number of suicides among veterans set off alarm bells that abetted the adoption of PTSD as a diagnostic category before it was recognized that the suicide rate among veterans who had never been to Vietnam was the same as those who had. Eric Dean wrote that the idea that as many veterans had committed suicide as died in Vietnam "appears to be a rumor that turned into a myth that has now become a legend and is being quoted as the truth."[24] Suspected suicides among soldiers and veterans of the Iraq and Afghanistan wars were readily attributed to combat trauma until data on eighteen suicides at Fort Campbell in 2009 revealed that most of those soldiers had never been deployed. Among the alternative explanations for those lifetakings, according to the *New York Times*, were divorces and parenting issues.[25]

Nevertheless, just as Shatan's 1972 article in the *New York Times* made PTSD the centerpiece of America's home-from-Vietnam story, thence propelling it into medical and popular discourse, Eaton now declared TBI to be "the signature malady of this [Iraq] war"—the signature malady despite having almost *no* association with war veterans prior to the ABC program. On March 12, Susan Sontag and Debora Alvarez moved "the signature malady" phrase off the opinion pages and into mainstream news, writing as a matter of fact that "TBI *has become* a signature wound of this war" (italics mine). In their 2,796-word story, "For War's Gravely Injured," the reporters used "Traumatic Brain Injury" five times. By the end of April, TBI would be connected to veterans in eleven more *Times* stories, several of them about *In an Instant* that was flying out of the bookstores onto the *Times* best seller list (where it bumped Barak Obama's autobiography *The Audacity of Hope* from the #1 spot on March 18). The *Times* listing that day appended a descriptor to the book's title that read, "the aftermath of the ABC coanchor's traumatic brain injury in Iraq," acknowledging thereby that

TBI had become what the Woodruff story was about: a process having created its own wave that it was now riding for commercial success.

A month after the Sontag and Alvarez article, The *Washington Post* joined the pack reporting on TBI with a large article by Ronald Glasser in which he declared Improvised Explosive Devices to be "the signature weapon" of the war. The IEDs, he wrote, had caused "wounds and *even deaths* among troops who have no external signs of trauma but whose brains have been severely damaged" (italics added). According to Glasser, "Iraq has brought back one of the worst afflictions of World War I trench warfare: shell shock. The brain of the soldiers is shocked, truly."

Glasser continued, detailing the mechanics of brain-shock, and drawing a distinction between what he called "blast-related brain injuries" and "other severe head traumas." The standard care for a highway accident, he said, involves using "calcium channel blockers to protect damaged nerve cells, intravenous diuretics to control brain swelling, and removal of some skull to allow swelling." But "TBIs from Iraq are different," he quotes neurologist P. Steven Macedo as saying. Glasser continues, saying that "something else in Iraq is going on," and then quotes Macedo again: "When the sound wave moves through the brain, it seems to cause little gas bubbles to form . . . when they pop, it leaves a cavity. So you are littering people's brains with these little holes."

Even a gentle parsing of Glasser's words—"TBIs from Iraq are different"—points to the meaning of TBI being at least as much derived from the socio-cultural context of the war as from anything diagnostic—as if the same event happening in Indiana would *not* cause TBI, or a different kind of TBI. Glasser makes it hard *not* to think that, just as care takers and culture makers needed a war-specific label, PTSD, to set Vietnam veterans apart from other patients with depression or anxiety, now too the medical and media

workers constructing how we view Iraq War veterans are determined to assign to them a "signature wound."

The suggestion that Traumatic Brain Injury is as much a cultural
as diagnostic category is objectionable to many listeners because,
to them, it seems to convey insensitivity to the needs of those
claiming the injury, and even disloyalty to them and their service.
While the cultural approach to understanding where the TBI diagnosis comes from might appear to deny the reality of brain injuries,
the response to the criticism is that the realities of TBI, like those of
PTSD, extend beyond the physiological assumptions of positivist
science. That response received considerable support in July 2010
when the Department of Veterans Affairs dropped the requirement
that claims to PTSD be supported by documentation of the battlefield events that caused the trauma. Speaking for Veterans for
Common Sense, one of the organizations who supported the
change, Paul Sullivan said, "PTSD is associated with deployment
[as opposed to exposure to combat]. It's a cultural thing."

If PTSD/TBI is a "cultural thing" then the frequency of its appearance should vary by cultural context. In fact, that seems to be
the case. Writing for the Ochberg Society for Trauma Journalism in
November 2012, Lori Grinker noted the UK's Royal Society report
that PTSD rates for UK veterans of the war in Afghanistan were
lower than those for the American veterans. According to the Royal
Society, she wrote, "PTSD might not be a 'universal stress reaction' arising in all societies, across all time." "Instead," she continued, "evidence suggests that the communication of stress is culturally determined. Whereas British soldiers may be expected to don
a stiff upper lip and 'get on with it,' American soldiers largely
return home to a society that expects them to be psychologically
wounded."[26] Beyond the "culture of expectations" identified by
Grinker, there is also the differing national cultures that bear on
health-care availability. In 2010 the British medical journal *The
Lancet* reported that British veterans with exposure to combat equal

to Americans had rates of PTSD that were about 25 percent of the American rates. Dr. Simon Wessely who headed the study attributed some of the difference to the British health care system covering all citizens, veterans or not, for their lifetimes, whereas American veterans have to win a claim for a service-connected disability (like PTSD) in order to receive lifetime benefits. [27]

The implication of PTSD/TBI being a cultural thing, as Paul Sullivan of Veterans for Common sense put it, is that trauma *qua* trauma—even the trauma of being deployed, sans combat—can be the cause of brain injury. Thereby, the gap between veterans who saw combat and those who did not, as discussed in chapter 3, is basically dissolved. [28]

But not everyone was buying the kind of physiological association with TBI that the *Washington Post*'s Glasser was making. In the first place, the analogy to World War I shell shock doesn't work the way he meant it to. Historian Ben Shephard recalls that Berlin neurologist Hermann Oppenheim was the main proponent of the "microscopic lesions" theory of war neurosis, and that his ideas were "comprehensively routed" by critics even before the war was over. Shortly after the war, the British "Report of the War Office Committee of Inquiry into 'Shell Shock'" called shell shock a "gross and costly misnomer" and expressed "unanimity of opinion . . . that the term be eliminated from our nomenclature." Anyone pursuing an analogy to shell shock as Glasser did, in an effort to establish the bona fides of TBI, would undercut their own case. [29]

Nor were twenty-first-century medical professionals buying it. Looking back even from a few years hence, it is almost unbelievable that with the media wave of Traumatic Brain Injury interest and imagery sweeping through the nation after the Woodruff's book, TBI was still a virtual blank page in the medical literature on war injuries. With the caveat that finding nothing doesn't mean that something unfound isn't there, it is notable that a computerized search of medical journals for articles on veterans with Traumatic

Brain Injury found only one published prior to 2008 and the data for it was almost entirely drawn from Vietnam veterans. Professional interest exploded after the Woodruff media blitz with twelve articles in 2008, twelve in 2009, ten in 2010, and fifteen through the first ten months of 2011.[30] And some of that interest was critical. In a 2009 *New England Journal of Medicine* article, for example, Dr. Charles Hoge and colleagues noted the vagueness of the criteria used for classifying TBI, saying the attribution of "nonspecific symptoms to concussion/mild TBI is subjective." In words that could have come from the historians of shell shock, Hoge and associates wrote, "Psychological factors, compensation and litigation, and patients' expectations are strong predictors of the persistence of symptoms." Traumatic Brain Injury, they noted, correlates more strongly with PTSD than with concussion, a finding suggestive of PTSD patients' need for some event external to themselves that validates their malady—anything but psychological.[31]

Predictably, given the decades-old pattern of media-led trends in the diagnosis of war trauma, the number of TBI cases reported from Iraq and Afghanistan rocketed along with interest in Woodruff's story, increasing 150 percent from about 1,200 in 2006 to nearly 3,000 in 2007. American deaths in those war zones, meanwhile, increased only 11 percent, making it unlikely that soaring incidence of trauma was due to increased combat.[32]

Clearly, the Woodruffs' book, ABC, and the press, not medical science, were emerging as the difference makers in the legitimating of Traumatic Brain Injury. But that difference was not being made in a vacuum. The legacy of PTSD was that Americans expected their soldiers to come home damaged. All parties to that narrative were on the same page: the Americans sent to war felt obliged to meet that expectation; health-care professionals were prepared to find the damage they were looking for; journalists were ready to report the damage found and write the stories their readers expected to see. A story not fitting that narrative would likely be, well, barely a story.

One could disagree with this analysis and point out that Woodruff's celebrity status alone was enough to account for the attention given his wounds, and that even if he had, say, lost a leg in the explosion, his story would still have made prime-time and his book about it been a best seller. A counterfactual argument like that is plausible, of course, but in this case we don't have to deal in hypotheticals. When CBS reporter Kimberly Dozier was wounded by a car bomb in Iraq on Memorial Day 2006, we had a case for comparison that matched, almost point for point, Woodruff's case, the exceptions being: A) that she actually had serious head wounds and yet, B) did not use PTSD/TBI to frame her condition the way he had done, and C) was a woman.

KIMBERLY DOZIER: CELEBRITY WITH THE WRONG WOUNDS

Dozier, a forty-year-old graduate of Wellesley College with a masters degree in foreign affairs from the University of Virginia and a list of awards for journalism, was on a foot patrol in Baghdad with a unit of the Fourth Infantry Division on May 29, 2006, when they walked into a car bomb ambush. Army Capt. James Funkhouser and his Iraqi translator, Sam, were killed immediately as were CBS cameraman Paul Douglas and soundman James Brolan. The explosion injured six other soldiers.

Dozier regained consciousness in Landsthul Medical Center in Germany about 48 hours later. The doctors had opened her skull to remove shrapnel and then riveted it closed with titanium screws. Her face and body bore red and black cuts from shrapnel. Both legs were broken. Jagged, burning chunks of shrapnel had done major damage to the quadriceps of the right leg, she later recalled; her broken femur bone was exposed, forcing doctors to consider amputating the leg. In the end, both legs were saved and realigned with their hip joints with titanium rods hammered into them. The pain was "soul-wrenching, excruciating" she later recalled, and the epidurals and morphine drips used to relieved it came with their own risks of added complications. Shrapnel had pierced her right temple requiring neurosurgery to remove it.[33]

Dozier was at Landsthul for a week before being shipped to Bethesda Naval Hospital in Baltimore, much longer than the usual 24–48 hours. Stateside, she faced two weeks of daily surgeries and procedures, huge doses of pain killer that gave her terrifying hallucinations, tube feeding, and the prospect of serious disfigurement and impaired mobility. The final operation to close the wound to her right leg on June 12 involved harvesting skin off her back and moving it to the leg—an eleven-hour operation that left 2,000 stitches. Modern medicine, she learned, has no answer for screaming, mind-thrashing, skin pain, and when the bandages covering her skin grafts failed she was left with huge, raw, constantly weeping patches across her back that exposed the nerves to air. Later she would recall, "The smallest breath of air feeling like a gale-force sandstorm ripping across my back." Her fortieth birthday on July 6 was marked by such pain that words and sentences were hard for her to form.[34]

Emotional pain slammed into Dozier during her third and fourth weeks at Bethesda, much of it stemming from feelings about her dead and wounded colleagues. At some point, though, while working through those emotions, the narrative of her injury and recovery would tack away from Woodruff's. That point came midway through her hospitalization when she took her psychiatrist's advice to let her father sign her pre-op consent forms lest they distress her. That was a mistake, she later realized, because it cast her as needy and emotionally impaired in the eyes of family members and care takers—a trauma victim and candidate for drug therapy. She wanted to *talk out* her feelings, not mask them; psychototropic drugs and antidepressants only hide the pain she recalled telling the psychiatric team. "No Prozac Nation. . . . That's not for me," she told them.

Nor was she going to be a wounded-woman-war-reporter-poster-child, at least not for those championing the diagnostic value of Traumatic Brain Injury. Whether the collective intuition of the journalism community took that as a "read" on her personality, or perhaps leaks from Bethesda about her treatment signaled her incompatibility with the PTSD/TBI narrative that was building in popular culture and medical circles, press interest in her recovery dropped like a rock after a few days.

Dozier's wounding *had been* news. It happened on Memorial Day, after all, a time when feelings about war casualties were already running high; and she was a journalist, making her, like Woodruff, a subject of special interest to newsmakers. With the gender theme, her case added to the growing body of media coverage of war injuries—how many *women* journalists have been wounded in action?—it was no surprise that the story got major coverage. The *New York Times* ran four items on it in its May 30 edition and two more the next day. But it faded fast. Frank Rich mentioned her in his June 8 column, and a June 16 sports section report on the visit of the U.S. soccer team to Ramstein airbase in Germany dropped her and Woodruff into the story. Then nothing until an August 1 story about CBS news anchor Katie Couric's refusal to go to Iraq ("too dangerous") mentioned Dozier in passing, and the August 4 "Performing Arts/Weekend Desk" sandwiched her release from Bethesda between paragraphs about Mel Gibson's anti-Semitic tirade and Madonna's mock crucifixion scene in her "Confessions" tour. It would be seven months before Dozier's next incidental mention in a *Times* story.

Woodruff's recovery, too, had faded as a news item during 2006, although not as quickly and completely as Dozier's did. His reappearance in the news came with the release of his book in

February 2007. Would a book about her wounding and recovery do the same for her? Dozier's book *Breathing the Fire: Fighting to Report—and Survive—the War in Iraq* came out on May 13, 2008, over a year after Woodruff's book had been on the market. Even if she had championed Traumatic Brain Injury, her book might not have achieved best-seller standing—the country had its "face" and he didn't need a companion. In any case, her book didn't follow that script; if anything, she cast herself in it as the *anti*-victim.

Dozier: The Anti-Woodruff

She had come back from "near death," Dozier wrote in the book's introduction, and "faced the horror of two lost colleagues . . . and a yearlong fight to learn to walk and live on my own again." "The bomb," she wrote, "changed me." Then she staked out her narrative terrain:

> One thing I know I'm not: a victim. That's what anyone is called when he or she suffers major trauma: assault victim, car crash victim, Baghdad car bomb victim. But "victims" have no independence. Family, friends, and colleagues, all with good will, coddle you. They tend to you when you first need it, but they don't know how or when to let you out of your cotton-cushioned cocoon.
>
> It's almost as hard to prove you're not a victim as it is to recover. You have to teach those around you that when the "victim" overcomes the trauma—learning from it, changing from it, and moving beyond it—she becomes a survivor, physically, mentally, and spiritually.
> I survived. This is a survivor's tale.

Just as self-consciously as the Woodruffs framed his recovery story to valorize Traumatic Brain Injury, Dozier framed hers as a counternarrative to the cultural imperative of the victim role ascribed to persons like her wounded in war. Her first mention of

Post Traumatic Stress Disorder comes on page 25 whereupon she prioritizes *avoiding* the symptoms of PTSD over passively identifying them so they can be treated. The next and last appearance made by PTSD in her book comes 165 pages later—and it has nothing to do with her recovery. Rather, she recalls there the stressful months in Baghdad before the explosion when a doctor prescribed pills for insomnia and a counselor tried to treat her for PTSD. Dozier rejected both remedies and led the CBS Baghdad staff in a successful campaign to get resources from the company for safer housing. Besides the invocation of Traumatic Brain Injury by her neuropsychiatrist (noted above), which she spurned, there are only two mentions of TBI in Dozier's book and neither is directly related to her wounds and recovery.[35]

Media interest in *Breathing the Fire* was minimal. The *New York Times* all but ignored the book, only covering the controversy arising from an interview Dozier did with Howard Kurtz for CNN's *Reliable Sources* program Sunday May 25. The interview had been arranged by Sheri Annis who was Kurtz's wife and the publicist for Dozier's book, an arrangement that some critics thought violated journalism ethics.[36] The *Washington Post* only posted calendar notes about reading and signing events scheduled for it when it was released. While some of those were quality events—the National Press Club on May 19 and a reading at Politics and Prose Bookstore on May 28—they were a far cry from the prime-time reception given Woodruff's book. There was no bestseller list for Dozier.

It's a sociological principle that the importance of societal norms can be measured by the severity of the punishments meted out to those who break them. The cold shoulder given Dozier's book by the media might have been expected for it having challenged the broken-warrior literary genre then dominating the market; and disappointing though a marketing flop is, writers understand the vicissitudes of the publishing game and cope with its downside when they find themselves on it. What came next, though, suggested something of a witch hunt, an effort to not only kill the book's sales but to embarrass Dozier and use her public humiliation as a stake in the heart of her ideas.

Ironically, given the taint of nepotism in her CNN interview with Kurtz, it was he who hung the "loser" label on her. In the interview he reminded her, "You had some trouble selling this book. You wound up with a small publisher, Meredith Books." For any writer, that was a cringe-and-look-away moment, not something you want to see; for any publisher, the "end of the line . . . Meredith Books" inference was a stigma hung on the book and its editors. It was an ugly moment prolonged by Dozier who said she had "taken it to five or six places," meaning other publishers, before winding up where she did—at Meredith Books in Des Moines, Iowa.

The Woodruffs Strike Back

Clearly Dozier was paying the price for following her own script; the market was withholding its dollars and the press was taking its pound of flesh. Six months after the Kurtz interview, the media world took its biggest bite out of her allowing Lee Woodruff to interview her for the CSPAN program *Book TV*. The drama of competing narratives emerging from the Woodruff and Dozier books could only be heightened by a cat-fight pitting the stand-by-her-man woman against the tougher-than-your-man woman. The structure of the interview was flawed by both its asymmetry—why is the *wife* of one wounded journalist interviewing the other wounded journalist?—and conflict of interest—Lee Woodruff was the coauthor of the competing book/narrative, and yet privileged as the interview*er*. Perhaps attempting to mask or compensate for the program's built-in bias, Woodruff adopted a patronizing posture toward Dozier that only made matters worse.[37]

In her opening remarks, Woodruff tries to establish equivalence between herself and Dozier, saying "you went through a horrifying experience . . . and, of course, I was on the sidelines watching *my* husband Bob . . . which [gives] us a real connection." A short time later, she reiterates the been-through-this-together theme, saying "there is a real bond between us."[38] From there, she asks, appropriately enough, for Dozier to give an overview of *Breathing the Fire* so that viewers will know what the book is about. Dozier briefly recounts the details of the ambush and then pays tribute to the medical workers who saved her life. Then, she segues to what the book is really about: the difficulty of dealing with well-meaning people trying to take care of you but holding you back with their preconceived notions of people who have been through traumatic experiences. There is a crossroad, she says, at which point some people, like her, want to get back to what they were doing as quickly as possible; others, she says, "whether because of their injuries or *where they were when it happened* want to use it as a turning point to move on to something else." Her message to care takers, she emphasized, was "don't keep us in the injury box."

Anyone having followed the evolution of the Woodruff and Dozier stories since their respective woundings over two years earlier, and read the books, would not have missed the digs taken at the Woodruffs and the champions of the PTSD/TBI labels by those words. Dozier's inference that some trauma patients would "use" their condition to leverage a change-of-life status (because of *where they were* in their lives prior to being injured) invited viewers to consider that that was exactly how the Woodruffs were using his condition. Lee Woodruff's bid to change the subject was a clear indication that she heard it that way too—and she wasn't going to let Dozier develop the point.[39]

Woodruff diverted Dozier from the PTSD/TBI cultural subtext by saying "let's go back" to Iraq and take a look at the "scrappy spunky Kimberley" on that dusty road that day. Woodruff's language was infantilizing but Dozier rolled with the punch and, after sketching her class background and youthful aspirations, got the interview back on message: the independence of her life to that point had prepared her to direct her own recovery. But the *not-victim* portrait wasn't what Woodruff wanted painted so: let's go back (again)—this time to the crew members who were killed and the survivor's guilt that Dozier *must* be suffering.[40]

Dozier nibbled politely at the bait but didn't take it. After another "back again," this time to the wonders of medical science and Dozier's skin transplants, Woodruff turned to the subject of PTSD, assigning Dozier an identity that was clearly inappropriate and unwanted: "Kimberly, can you talk a little bit about your knowledge of PTSD and how you became a poster-child for it." Dozier could have short-handed her response by saying, "Me? Poster-child for *what*? PTSD? Ah, that would be your husband, not me." That wasn't her response, of course, but what she said came close.

Dozier said the hardest thing was dealing with people who just assume she must be having nightmares. (Like Woodruff had just done.) "People just assume, because of what they see on television or Hollywood movies that anyone coming back from a war zone is mentally scarred for life. You got to educate people, including troops, diplomats, and journalists, that the effects of trauma aren't something you need to be tarred with for life." From there, Woodruff and Dozier bobbed and weaved their way through a series of assertions and counter-assertions, "buts" and "yeah buts" about the inevitability of trauma symptoms after service in a war zone and validity of PTSD as a diagnosis.[41]

Not surprisingly, given the importance of PTSD in the backstory of TBI and the echo of Vietnam that Americans hear in both terms, the interview ended with a reprise of the historical context giving rise to them and the political tensions they embed. Dozier began it, observing that she hears from a lot of angry Vietnam veterans whose attachment to the PTSD identity seems threatened by her book. Then, with tonality and body language that belie the sincerity of her words, Woodruff offers an assurance to viewers that there is no anti-troop/veteran animus in Dozier's message—but reminds us that troops returning from Vietnam had rocks thrown at them and we shouldn't let that happen again.[42]

••••

The CSPAN interview aired in November 2008, several months after the Woodruffs' book had reaffirmed the place of Post-Traumatic Stress Disorder (PTSD) in the American post-war story and established Traumatic Brain Injury (TBI) as a new element of that narrative. There is little doubt that when *Times* editor Bill Keller mistakenly "remembered" his paper having covered TBI during 2006, he was reflecting the power of the press to shape, and even *re*shape, our past—in his case, the presence of TBI in the coverage and conversation about returning troops became so dominating so fast with the Woodruffs' book release as to overwhelm his sense that TBI had not always been a player.

But the establishment of TBI as the "signature wound" of the new wars begs the questions about what that means. That a wound "signs" something implies that it has cultural or social meaning separate from its more literal meaning. Calling TBI a "signature wound" makes it a kind of simulacrum, a quality that invites further inquiry into what is being "signed." If the "signature wound" was, say, amputation, that inquiry would be redundant; but the ethereal properties of TBI (as identified earlier in this chapter) make the inquiry more interpretive and open to the interventions of commercial and political interests and the mavens of popular and medical culture.

For one thing, "trauma" works in the signature to help construct the enemy-other as "terrorism," itself a category lacking the materiality that a nation-state or political-economic system might present as an enemy. For another, the mind and emotion components of the wound extend understandings that the war in Vietnam was for "hearts and minds," with *our* hearts and minds contested terrain as much as *theirs*. But as the CSPAN dialogue between Lee Woodruff and Kimberly Dozier illustrates, a wound to the "heart" or "mind" is subjective, even metaphorical.

Traumatic Brain Injury as "signature wound" also reproduces the blurring of the line between the home front and war front. On the one hand, the expectation of traumatic homecomings woven into the betrayal narrative for the lost war in Vietnam licenses comments like Woodruff's about rocks being thrown at veterans that discredit anti-war activism; on the other hand, Dozier's focus on the imperial presence of PTSD/TBI in American post-war culture casts light on a society that *needs* its soldiers to come home damaged—and if they're not, put them in that box until they agree they are.[43]

NOTES

1. The *Washington Post*'s first mention of TBI was in 1985. Over the next 17 years the *Post* ran more than 50 stories with some mention of the disorder but the first to connect TBI with war came on July 21, 2003 (Jones and Hull).

2. An August 8, 1995, *Washington Post* story reported Traumatic Brain Injury resulting from bicycle and in-line skating accidents, swimming and diving mishaps, and playground injuries. No mention was made of war wounds.

3. A Medline search for English language articles about humans with "Traumatic Brain Injury" in their titles in psychiatry and psychology journals found only eleven articles prior to 1988.

4. Sociologist Egon Mayer noted at the time that the jogger's race, class, gender, and occupational identities drew a disproportionate amount of interest to her plight, thereby threatening to obscure the thousands of other victims of violence and rape, many of them racial or ethnic minorities. See Woff (1989) for the *Times* story on the April 21, 1989, assault. Altman (1989) wrote TBI into the *Times* coverage. Mayer's comment is in his letter to the *Times*, June 17, 1989.

5. Meili, Trisha and J. Kabat-Zinn (2004). The convictions of the young men were vacated in 2002 but the TBI/mental-health narrative had so totally eclipsed the legal story that few people noticed. A sociologist friend learned of that legal

development in April 2013 watching *The Central Park Five* produced for public television by Ken Burns.

6. See Damon Hack (2003). A May 12, 2000, *Times* story (McKinley, Jr. 2000) "Invisible Injury" noted that "no position in sports is more associated with concussions than quarterbacks." Given that quarterbacks are the best protected and least hit players in football, their strong "association" with concussion might have derived from their status as the sport's elite and highest paid white players. In short, the association might have been, as it was for "the jogger," as much sociological as anything else, an artifact of their attractiveness to the public and health-care professionals.

7. The distinction between neurology and psychology was explored further in chapter 5.

8. The same MedLine search described in note 2 found an increase in articles after 2005 but not even a doubling of the number by 2012. The number actually decreased from 2010 to 2011 and appears to be decreasing even more dramatically in 2012.

9. My efforts to reach Solomon for comment have not been successful.

10. Andrew Pollack, "Marketing a Disease and also a Drug to Treat it." NYT May 9, 2005.

11. There is a skeptical tone to Blakeslee's report that I've tried to retain here.

12. Dao, 2013.

13. Goldin and Merrick express their reservations about fMRI in a 2012 article, "Neuroscience or Neurobabble?: What's this thing called fMRI?"

14. Kurtz, 2006.

15. A Lexis-Nexus search for "traumatic brain injury" turned up thirteen stories on TBI during that year but none of them mentioned Woodruff. See Stanley (2007) for the *Times* coverage of the press conference. The *Washington Post* (Kurtz, 2007) covered the same press conference but made only one reference to TBI, indirectly connecting it to Woodruff. There are shades of difference in the *Times* and *Post* reportage on Woodruff's TBI, suggesting some hesitancy on the part of the *Post*.

16. Woodruff and Woodruff, 2007, p. 90.

17. Woodruff and Woodruff, 2007, p. 118.

18. Woodruff and Woodruff, 2007, p. 133.

19. *In an Instant* is a smoothly written memoir that intersperses vignettes from Bob and Lee Woodruff's life before and after his wounding in Iraq, some of them written by him, some by her. While always writing from the temporal "present" of the explosion and medical recovery that followed, the Woodruffs sift the past into that present using a "flashback" technique that gives the book and their biographies great depth in a very readable fashion. It is thus that only 83 of the book's last 148 pages deal with Bob's recovery; at least nineteen of those pages construct the TBI/PTSD framing for his condition.

20. Woodruff and Woodruff, Pp. 146-53.

21. Woodruff and Woodruff, Pp. 212-16. Some of what the Woodruffs wrote fit the caricature of PTSD. Lee Woodruff claimed the doctor told her to not use

the word *helmet* lest it trigger an emotional response. Call it a *hat*, the doctor supposedly advised. According to Woodruff (p. 218) the doctor said, "'A lot of these guys hit people and throw punches; they can become very violent. When they start biting, that's when I really get worried about their long term prognosis. You can take comfort in the fact that Bob has not been violent. He hasn't bitten anyone. That's a good sign."

22. The Woodruffs' book was the difference maker; within a week it was #1 on the *New York Times* best-seller list.

23. In early 2007, there were about one million veterans of the war in Iraq. The ratio of combat to noncombat in Iraq was about the same as that in Vietnam, 15 percent, meaning 150,000 Iraq War veterans would have seen combat by that time; using the Veterans Affairs numbers cited on the Woodruff program, an unlikely 89 percent of them would be suffering some sort of trauma. Any interpretation of these numbers should also take into account the finding of World War I shell shock cases that veterans actually wounded were *less* likely to present symptoms of shell shock.

24. Hyer et al., reviewing other research findings for their article in *Journal of Clinical Psychology* (1990, p. 714), reported the suicide rate for Vietnam veterans to be "not excessive," that there were "no differences in proportion of death due to suicide between Vietnam veterans and non-Vietnam veterans." Dean (1997, p. 19).

25. See Robertson and Rivera (2009) for the Fort Campbell story. Note that the reporters refer to the eighteen deaths as "confirmed *or* suspected" suicides (my italics), the kind of elasticity that can seriously distort the picture. Reporting on the same spate of deaths for *USA Today*, Alan Gomez (2009) noted that it can take months to confirm suicide as the cause of death. Writing for the *Associated Press*, Pauline Jelinek (2009) reported the same suicide story without a single mention of PTSD. In 2012 in-service suicides reportedly soared again. The Associated Press story (Burns 2012) associated the increase with combat exposure and PTSD but said "a substantial proportion of Army suicides are committed by soldiers who never deployed"—without defining what was meant by "substantial proportion." The talking point on veteran suicides is that, just because a soldier or veteran commits suicide does not mean the individual committed suicide *because* he or she is a veteran, much less because of war trauma.

26. Grinker, Lori (2012). While PTSD might not be a universal affliction, the *universalizing* of American notions of mental illness, including PTSD, is a real and troublesome development. For an excellent inquiry into that issue, see Ethan Watters's *New York Times* Sunday Magazine article, January 10, 2010.

27. *The Lancet* study was reported in the *New York Times* (Carey 2010). The report quoted Dr. Wessely as saying he suggested to U.S. military leaders, "why not switch to nationalized health care [in order to lower the claims for PTSD]?" the Doctor said, "It went over like a cup of cold spit."

An inquiry posted for me by anthropologist Diane Fox on a Vietnam Study Group about Vietnamese veterans of the war and PTSD returned comments of the type: "they have moved on," "PTSD doesn't have the meaning there that it does for Americans," "all of life is hard for them." Australian author Keith Beattie (*The Scar that Binds: American Culture and the Vietnam War*, 2000) responded to my inquiry about PTSD and Australian veterans of the war in Vietnam with a set of links to government and veteran-interest groups. There, interest has risen in recent years but the "moved on" spirit is very strong. Australian military history and commemoration is dominated by the losses it took at Gallipoli in World War I.

28. See Dao (2010) for the change in VA regulations.

29. In her 2011 article "The Paradox of PTSD," Katherine Boone states matter-of-factly that shell shock was "quickly discredited" after WWI. She then acknowledges that "the term lingers on."

30. The computer search done by student researcher Kati Chorbanian used Google Scholar Search, a search engine that aggregates links to other search engines such as PubMed and APA PsycNet as well as direct links to journals such as the *New England Journal of Medicine*. A Medline search *ala* note 3 (above), but refined to "veterans" but not psychology and psychiatry journals, confirmed the Google Scholar results: 2005 = 0; 2006 = 0; 2007 = 8; 2008 = 14; 2009 = 28; 2010 = 14; 2011 = 15.

31. The "compensation and litigation" phrase in Hoge's observation is especially ominous because it raises the specter of patients' intentional misrepresentation of their conditions for financial gain. And "faking impairment," writes Dr. Albert M. Drukteimis, "may not be that difficult." In one study he wrote, " Children were instructed to 'fake bad' on comprehensive neuropsychological testing with minimal guidance on how to do it. Of 42 clinical neuropsychologists who reviewed these cases, 93 percent diagnosed abnormality, 87 percent of those said it was because of brain dysfunction; no clinician detected malingering. When specific tests for malingering or exaggeration are not administered, the likelihood of missing deliberate distortion is even higher. "

32. The TBI numbers are from the Department of Defense as reported by *USA Today* (Zoroya 2012). The death figures are from iCasualties.org (May 4, 2012). According to iCasualties.org, 117 deaths in 2007 were due to Improvised Explosive Devices (IEDs), the weapons most often associated with TBI. Pairing numbers from these two sources, that would mean that there were 25 TBI injuries claimed for every TBI death—an almost impossibly high ratio given that Humvees were the often-hit targets of IEDs and the standard crew size of those vehicles was four.

33. Dozier, 2008, pp. 77-79; 87-89.

34. Dozier, 2008, pp. 147-49; 153-57; 202.

35. The subject of one TBI reference (p. 43) is the soldiers she was with that day; the other (p. 74) reference is in notes taken by her sister that Dozier quotes.

36. See Steinberg 2008.

37. CSPN *Book TV* November 2, 20008.

38. Woodruff's intonation of *my* husband provides a momentary distraction from the reality of the program's asymmetry—as if to say to viewers that, "Kim-

berly Dozier will be talking about *her* husband, and together we will be talking about *our* husbands." It's an insidious rhetorical device that decenters the focus.

39. Dozier is alluding to a form of "the devil made me do it" alibi for something the person doesn't want to take responsibility for. A veteran may have felt locked into a bad marriage before the war but avoided the difficulty of confronting that. After being wounded, he can attribute the erratic, even violent, behavior that threatens the marriage to his medical condition. He can now seek a divorce without having to deal with the fact that he made the wrong decision by ever getting married. That's what Dozier's words mean when she says, "where they were in their lives prior to their injury."

40. Repeatedly, Woodruff framed the interview with her husband's experience as a way of coercing Dozier's complicity with the PTSD/TBI narrative she wanted confirmed. Here, she said doctors "did not want Bob to hear of his colleague's death" lest he suffer survivor's guilt.

41. With there being not a hint that Dozier is aware of the dynamic between art and culture and the construction of diagnostic categories, as presented in chapters 4 and 5, her understanding, derived as it is from her own experience, is itself a kind of data supporting the constructionist analysis of PTSD.

42. Woodruff was using a form of rhetoric known as apophasis or praeteritio which is to imply something negative about a person (Dozier in this case) while seeming to say something positive.

43. Recall Dr. Robert Fleming's words in chapter 5 that some "elements in our society really do not want to see the Vietnam veteran 'come home'," noting that "some veterans take on the role of the 'sick child in the family,'" thereby meeting a societal need. Dozier's deviation from that script sets in stark relief the presence of that very dynamic between American society and the veterans of wars in Iraq and Afghanistan.

Chapter Seven

Mt. Rushmore: Ready for War's New Face?

By 2008, PTSD packed a lot of synergy. As a diagnostic category, it helped bring mental and physical health services to war veterans who needed them; simultaneously, it cast the stigma of "damaged" over everyone who returned from war. That discrediting, in turn, became yet another source of trauma, adding to the damage and extending the war into the coming home experience.[1]

The inglorious nature of the wars from Vietnam through Iraq and Afghanistan, meanwhile, left veterans and many other Americans searching for meaning in those conflicts and finding it in their own losses and sacrifices. With the nation's expansionist plans having been frustrated by failed and stalemated military ventures abroad, people mined the anger and angst left by defeat in search of a new identity and some sense of a future—an endeavor that mustered the creativity of entertainers, media entrepreneurs, and artists.

SEEING AND SELLING THE ZEITGEIST

We live in a commercial culture. That doesn't mean that everything we see and hear, or eat and wear, is available to us only at the mall or shop.com. And it doesn't mean that everything with meaning is exchanged through cash. We still make our own music at religious services, eat from the garden, and wear shawls knitted by grandmothers. But those are exceptions. So exceptional, that their value lays precisely in their quality of being outside the marketplace that we know to otherwise dominate our lives.

Commercial culture is also a window through which we can see what it is that masses of people value enough to pay money for. Neil Postman began his 1985 book *Amusing Ourselves to Death* observing that deeply seeded societal traits can reveal themselves through cultural and commercial expressions. Las Vegas, he said, is a metaphor for the nexus of dollar-driven entertainment that forms the new soul of America. In effect, what people are willing to pay for, and be entertained by, is a window into who and what they are—be that slot machines and chorus girls, or the dollars spent for television advertising and theater tickets in the nearest big city.

The market magnetism of ABC correspondent Bob Woodruff's book about his wounding in Iraq and subsequent diagnosis of Traumatic Brain Injury is surely a league away from the seduction of casino sex and gambling, but the fact that it made it into the mix of cultural commerce at all, much less the level of a number one bestseller, is remarkable. It was the "sensing" of popular mood that told book publishers, advertisers, and sellers that "the market" would like Bob Woodruff's story about Traumatic Brain Injury but not Kimberley Dozier's counter-narrative about war trauma and the social construction of victim identity—even though Dozier was more seriously injured and, as a female war correspondent, the more compelling figure. The country needed to know that the men and women it sends off to war come home damaged and Woodruff's story provided assurance that the wounds were there even if unseen. As it turned out, Woodruff's place at the top of the bestseller list was only an indicator of the public's demand for trauma-themed material.

The promotion of TBI through the commercial medium of Woodruff's book sales took the synergy of medical and commercial cultures to levels way beyond Charcot's marketing of the photographs taken of his patients, but there was still room for growth. The legacy of Vietnam carried into the new wars was that "the wound" credentialed the warrior. The nature of the conflicts in Iraq and Afghanistan was even more ambiguous, making combat even harder to define, to say nothing of what valor meant in those endeavors. The vagueness of the wars themselves added to the public need for some tangible sense that the fighting mattered and "heroes home" were tangible. With wounds making heroes, and invisible wounds countable, everyone who deployed could have a hero-eligible story, and the nation's foundational sense of itself as a besieged people sacrificing for the defense of Good could be affirmed. The individual and collective demand for wounded warriors, in other words, was fertile ground for growth and the market did not miss its cue.[2]

THE NEW MARLBORO MAN

The tangling of PTSD's commercial, medical, and political messages became even more evident on March 13, 2006, when ABC's *Nightline* ran a lengthy segment on James Blake Miller, a Marine veteran of Iraq. The story opened with the familiar factoid—one-third of veterans of Iraq and Afghanistan seek treatment for PTSD. And, "It's not just those who are weak," intoned the narrator Martin Bashir as a photograph of Miller with a cigarette dangling from his lips and a helmet on his head appeared on the screen. The photograph had been taken by a Los Angeles *Times* photographer and appeared in newspapers around the world. For many Americans, said Bashir, Miller had become "a symbol of strength and resolve," the country's new "Marlboro Man." Now, the voiceover said, he was "the symbol for PTSD."[3]

Miller, from a holler in Eastern Kentucky, had been a radio operator in Falluja during the tough fighting of November 2004. He describes having "called in tank fire" on Iraqi militants and tells the interviewer that "he lost friends there." His pack-a-day cigarette habit exploded to six-plus packs a day while in Iraq, we're told. After leaving, Miller said he had a vision of a dead Iraqi, and would pull his trigger finger while sleeping at night. Once on a navy ship, a sailor made a whistling sound "like a mortar round." Miller, apparently having a flashback, attacked the sailor before blacking out.[4]

On one level, *Nightline's* use of Miller's nicotine addiction in this way seemed a tacky reach for something sensational that would draw and hold viewers. Even beyond that, the exploitation of his Marlboro Man status in order to "sell" its viewing public on the home-from-war narrative that the link with PTSD helps construct, seemed callous and opportunistic. Without the "Marlboro Man" packaging, the story reported, *qua* war story, didn't have much weight, and could have left some viewers wondering what was so traumatic about Miller's experience. The implausibility of his smoking almost 200 cigarettes a day, meanwhile, raised questions about what the *Nightline* producers hoped to cover up with such an outsized claim.[5]

On another level, though, the use made by ABC of Miller's story and the photograph was brilliant: the story was about PTSD; by labeling the photograph "The Icon," as they did, the producers told us (in case we missed it) that it represented strength, and power, and masculinity. The fusion of the two made manifest the expression of loss, defeat, and damage through the iconography of strength and honor that the country had been fumbling for since its evacuation of Saigon in 1975. Miller was the real deal—the photograph said so and so did his PTSD: the message that *real* men return from war with PTSD dallied just at the edge of collective consciousness.[6]

With the wars in Iraq and Afghanistan frustrating Americans, and John Kerry's presidential campaign certain to have voters making links between past wars and present wars, it's easy to imagine major news organizations looking for alternative storylines. Coming just weeks after Bob Woodruff's wounding in Iraq, moreover, it was a propitious time to amplify the medical discourse of PTSD in the American conversation; the producers, editors, and writers who held the keys of access to a wide swath of American thinking about wars and their legacies did not miss their cues.

SEE THE INVISIBLE WOUNDS: (ON PAY-PER-VIEW TELEVISION)

The advertisements had the ring of the carnival barker: "Step right up boys. See the unseen. In the tent, the freak of nature. Step right up. See what you've never imagined. For 50 cents . . ."

The magnet for the half-dollars in those dusty county fairgrounds of yesteryear was the allure of the unknown, the attraction of the never seen that flowed more from the emotions and imaginations of the kids with the coins than from the stage hung with the orange and red bunting with the words "World's Only Hermaphrodite." And so it was with the advertisements for the Home Box Office (HBO) special "War Torn: 1861–2010" that aired on Veterans Day, 2010. . . . Step right up, key in your credit card number and we'll show you the unseen, the wounds. . . .

The promotion of "War Torn" dispelled any doubt about the commercial viability of unseen wounds. A full page *New York Times* advertisement ran in the paper's front section on November 11, the day of broadcast. Beneath four large military-style stars that constituted its review and endorsement by *Bloomberg News*, the ad used the gauzy image of a soldier with his bowed head in hand and a faded American flag in the background. The dismal graphic was overlaid with block letters promising a show that would be "Heart-breaking" and "Powerful." "In every war, there are invisible wounds," read the ad's come-on, wounds that would be revealed at 9:00 p.m.—"only on HBO." Step right up . . .

Costing tens of thousands of dollars, that ad alone signaled HBO's expectations of high revenue from subscriptions to the program and downstream revenues from first-time viewers who might get hooked on the pay-per-view concept.[7] The *Times*'s own immeasurably valuable endorsement for the program—perhaps the marketing *quid pro quo* for HBO's advertising dollars—was encoded in an op-ed piece that ran the same day on the back side of the advertisement. Written by Ronald D. Castille, a lawyer and Vietnam veteran, the article entitled "A Special Court for Veterans: An Alternative to Jail for Veterans with PTSD" argued for the codification of preferential treatment for veterans in the legal justice system, the kind of preference seemingly given Matthew Sepi whose case was described in chapter 1. Although Castille did not refer his readers to that evening's HBO broadcast and the *Times*, as it always does, would surely have disavowed any connection between the advertising dollars it was paid by HBO and the editorial decision to run Castille's article and marquee it with the PTSD acronym, the commercial-cultural interplay seems undeniable.[8]

That HBO was plying the commercial potential of PTSD programming was evinced as well in the person of *War Torn*'s Executive Producer, James Gandolfini. Gandolfini had recently finished a long run as Tony Soprano in HBO's hit series *The Sopranos*. The show had won numerous Emmy and Golden Globe awards and entertainment weekly had recently named him #42 on its list of all-time greatest TV icons. Gandolfini also appeared in *War Torn* as the interviewer of veterans and military authorities. But of all the occupational credentials that viewers might expect someone in that role to have—doctor, psychologist, lawyer (since some the veterans featured in the film were in legal troubles related to their PTSD), or even an experienced news interviewer—an actor closely identified with the role he played as a New Jersey mobster would least likely come up in minds seriously interested in war trauma. Reviews of *War Torn* in the *Los Angeles Times* and *New York Times* on the day of its showing made the Gandolfini-Soprano connection thereby flagging for still other eyes the entertainment-market value of the broadcast.[9]

The *War Torn* special itself was long on emotional appeal and short on science or even information suitable for cognition. Its hidden-horrors-of-war motif was established with the letters of Civil War veteran Angelo Crapsey who committed suicide despite having no apparent physical wounds. A segment on World War II featured six veterans testifying to the nightmares they still have, while images and references to World War I reminded viewers of that era's "shell shock." The Vietnam segment made peculiar use of a veteran identified as "a combat illustrator" who spoke of the terrors brought home by that generation; no mention was made of GI and veteran opposition to the war in Vietnam. The invisible wounds brought home from the current wars were "shown" to us through four vignettes: Noah Pierce and Jason Scheurmann who committed suicide, Nathan Damigo who went "into combat mode" during a taxi stick-up and was subsequently sentenced to prison for six years, and Billy Frass who we see unnerved by a trip to Walmart.[10]

War Torn was applauded by critics across the Left-Right political spectrum, a reception indicative of the ideological mash-up wreaked by PTSD in the post-Vietnam War decades. Amy Goodman, whose radio and television show *Democracy Now* is as close to being the "voice of the left" that Americans have, gave it her imprimatur, interviewing the filmmakers and parents of Damigo and Scheurmann for her show the day before Veterans Day. Goodman's ovation was consistent with the view of the anti-war left that the "cost of war" as measured in human casualties is routinely denied by the military and covered up by Washington and the news media—*War Torn* would be a stick in the eye to the military-political-media complex, and ignite the outrage sufficient to end the war.[11]

But *War Torn*'s exposure of war's unseen terrors was embraced just as enthusiastically by the very powers alleged by the left to keep a "top secret" classification on their existence. Commercial cable television, represented by HBO in that complex, had obviously seen the market potential of PTSD—war trauma as a commodity, so to speak. The day after the broadcast, a panel of military leaders effused its approval of the film with Army Vice Chief of Staff Gen. Pete Carelli calling it "the most powerful hour of TV that I've ever seen." Then, retired Air force Lt. Col. Greg Harbin testified to himself being one of the "best of the best" as a fighter pilot, while yet needing counseling for PTSD. Following Harbin, retired Army Capt. Paul "Buddy" Bucha, awarded the Medal of Honor for his service in the 101st Airborne in Vietnam, said that it took him forty years to come to terms with PTSD. Disagreeing with claims that 30 percent of veterans need help, Bucha said, "I can tell you it's 100 percent." "Four stars or no stripes," he said, waving his hand toward the audience filled with uniformed men, "You have this problem."

Putting the brass on-board the *War Torn* train could have been just a Pentagon–White House public relations maneuver to humanize its image in the face of growing concern about the rising number of casualties. But Bucha's declaration that we're *all* traumatized would only multiply those numbers, potentially adding to the anguish felt by the country about its losses. Looking at it differently, what if the primary emotion evoked by the costs was not anguish but admiration? What if the professions by Harbin and Bucha to being wounded warriors were heard as expressions of pride more than public acknowledgements of their medical conditions? What if, in the spirit of Protestantism that makes sacrifice a virtue, the costs of war are revalorized from the horrific to the honorific, the trauma carried by these and other veterans tallied as the triumph of their disciplined spirits over the indulgence of civilian life? What if the invisible wounds, now testified to, validate the warrior in the man rather than consign the man to the status of needy victim? What if, in other words, the damages on the inside of the warrior and ineligible for Purple Hearts are set in relief and displayed as badges of honor?

And what of the unthinkable: that the horrors of war had morphed during the post-Vietnam War decades from being a barrier *to* war into an incentive *for* war? In fact, the anomaly of bemedaled heroes like Bucha taking on the identity of traumatized warriors can only be explained that way. It is an anomaly, moreover with the added twist that PTSD's ascension to hegemony in America's post-war narrative comes not from Washington and Pentagon insiders but from liberal and left cultural circles normally associated with the anti-war movement. That those who would be expected to tally war trauma as an unacceptable cost of war would rewrite its meaning into something embraceable as a credential for heroism makes it a cultural phenomenon.

FROM THE WOODRUFFS AND *WAR TORN* TO MTV

Since Bob Woodruff was a television star before his wounding while covering the war in Iraq for ABC News, it should not have been a surprise that the story of his recovery and the launch of his book about the bombing, coauthored with his wife Lee, would play out through television with a patina of entertainment value added. What looked then like mutual titillation between medical and marketing cultures, went full-bloom in 2008 when MTV produced a special on PTSD hosted by Kanye West.

With a father who was a Black Panther and a long resume of anti-racist rap music that he had written and performed, West's credentials as a progressive artist were in order. The hour-long

MTV show consisted of him and his sidekick Sway swooping un-announced, Home Makeover style, into the homes of three Iraq War veterans who, we are told, suffer from PTSD. In each segment we see the featured veteran shocked to see the celebrity rapper is at his or her door. We then hear about the veteran's struggle with post-war trauma, and see West and Sway present them with a pack-age of benefits that include tickets and backstage passes to a West concert.

The first veteran we see is Tiram. As narrator, Sway tells us that Tiram returned from Iraq "with no visible wounds," and yet he is anxious and paranoid and "still ducks for cover as if he was at war." Tiram has been diagnosed with PTSD and has been unable to keep a job. West promises to pay off his bills and help him go to school. Backstage at the evening concert, Tiram is introduced to music stars Rihanna and Pharrell who tells Tiram, "You are our hero." Lorenzo wants to be a rapper so the stars outfit him with a home studio to produce his music; Shameeka has a child for whom they promise a college fund. The segments are separated by com-mercials for Taco Bell, Clearasil, Target, Wendy's, iphone, Dr. Pepper, and other products. Upcoming MTV shows like the Music Video Awards are promoted as are other films like *Tropic Thunder* just then coming to theaters. [12]

That the hyper-commercial television venue MTV would ven-ture to draw its teens-through-twenties viewers to market for brand-name advertisers, using a mental disorder as the lure, speaks vol-umes about the cultural complexity of PTSD. On one level, it was but another example of PTSD being used, as it has since the war in Vietnam, to displace interest in the war itself by drawing attention to the men and women who fought the war—thereby depoliticizing the war-related discourse. That discourse also reified the victim-veteran image for veterans themselves and many anti-war activists watching the show, pushing further off screen any sense of veterans having been empowered and politicized by their military experience.

On another level, the show highlighted the aura surrounding PTSD that carries connotations broader than diagnostic. We're told nothing about Tiram other than that he has PTSD so that when Pharrell proclaims him "our hero" the use made of trauma to validate valor is unmistakably clear. Besides the cues provided for the general audience by the hurt-and-heroic connection made there, veterans get some clues to what is or may be expected from them. In June 2012 singer Timothy Michael Poe wooed the judges on NBC's *America's Got Talent* show with his story that he had suffered TBI while taking a grenade blast to save some buddies in Iraq. But the story was not true. On another occasion, he told a news source he had been wounded by a roadside bomb. That wasn't true either.[13]

The MTV/Kanye West collaboration boosted PTSD's place in American commercial culture way beyond the level achieved by the Woodruffs' book, and did that by plying the low end of the youth and pop culture markets. Playwrights and artists, meanwhile, went the other direction, mainstreaming the cachet of war trauma through New York theaters and galleries.

BEASTS: ON THE STAGE AND ART GALLERY WALLS

While PTSD was collecting market share for cable television, the stage play *Beast* was going into rehearsal in the East Village. Riffing on Irwin Shaw's post–World War I use of zombies to warn that the soldiers killed in unpopular wars will haunt the nations that sent them to their graves, *Beast* opens in a hospital ward in Germany where PFC Jimmy Cato talks to the coffin holding his friend Benjamin Voychevsky (Voych). Just as the coffin is about to be removed for transport home, Voych sits up and begins talking, then joins Cato in filling the coffin with random items from the supply room to approximate his weight. They close it and exit for a night on the town, confident that the coffin full of junk will soon board for the states.[14]

At a beer hall in the German city, Voych and Cato meet renegade Army Capt. Adler with whom they hope to arrange for fake documents that will allow Voych to get home. In the course of the negotiations, we learn that Adler is thoroughly corrupt, making lots of money on illicit deals in weaponry and women—he will only help Voych and Cato if there is something big in it for him. We also learn that Voych wears a hat pulled down to cover the top of his head. He has on dark sunglasses and has a bandana covering the bottom of his face; Adler won't make any deal with them until he sees the face.

Adler turns his back while Voych uncovers his face, telling them (and the audience) that his (Adler's) San Francisco associates have sold a new reality series, "Suburban Zombie," and calls the German hospital town "a career gateway for the talent they want." When he turns back and sees Voych uncovered, he freezes, uttering "Dear God—I must have died and gone to heaven. You have no idea how big this could be. With the right marketing we might create a new look, Zombie Chic."

The playwright Michael Weller may well have let "zombie chic" stand as the metaphor for the post-empire zeitgeist that he channeled through his character Adler. The idea that disfigurement from war could have market draw with the Wow! value of underground arms sales and prostitution, Adler's usual pursuits, was a recognition by Weller of the commercial viability in something so unspeakably dark that it could only be brought to light through theater. What Weller knew is that the American public was ready to embrace the denouement of its humanity as evidence for greatness, its willingness to *bestialize* its own in pursuit of its primal Self. Only hinted at in the German bar, the insight in his "zombie chic" line is confirmed before the play's end.

Voych is married to Bonnie-Ann who delivered their baby soon after he deployed. She had been informed of his death in Iraq and has buried the coffin she thought contained his body. Now, Voych is nervous about his homecoming. He killed Adler in Germany and is traveling on the Captain's papers, and he knows Bonnie thinks he's dead. Delaying the homecoming, he and Cato do some stateside touring. At a Motel Six in Kansas they negotiate with Victor for sex with the prostitutes Camilla and Sherine. Victor offers special girls for veterans like Voych with special needs—the girls are blind.

When they finally arrive at Voych's home, they find Bonnie-Ann living with another Iraq War veteran, Smalldom. An argument ensues about who should leave and Smalldom stabs Voych in the throat. Voych doesn't bleed and grabs Smalldom, snapping his neck. As they exit the scene, Voych says, "Jimmy (Cato), I think something's wrong with me."

Voych and Cato return to the road. Hitchhiking, they stop for the night with a trucker in Mount Rushmore National Park. Voych has killed Adler and Smalldom, and Cato admonishes him, "We're home now, it's different rules. We gotta fucking *adjust* or something."

But now it's Cato's PTSD that kicks in:

Cato: Listen to them folks across the road? Enjoying their portable TVs. Their propane grills. Relishing nature, enjoying what we made possible, Voych. You think they'd even care if they knew we spent an hour securing the perimeter around this campground before we thought about sleep? Fat fucking chance. . . Take things for granted. I'm sick of keeping everyone safe and no one gives a shit. (yells) IT'S TIME YOU GAVE A SHIT, PEOPLE.

Voych: Easy, soldier. They don't know any better.

Later that night, the presidents on the mountain come to life. Speaking as a chorus, they tell Voych that he and Cato are more than heroes, more even than legacies of the war: "You *are* America, mighty and beautiful." Go to President Bush's ranch in Crawford, Texas, they tell Voych, and demand to be sculpted into Mt. Rushmore. The two wounded warriors follow the command of the stone faces and hitch to Texas where they confront the president. "Put my face on Mount Rushmore with the four great men," Voych tells him, "and warriors will line up to serve till the war is won!!!"

The president scoffs at the suggestion he'd be "intimidated by two fucking lunatics . . . threatening harm if I don't promise to get the head of a misshapen, psychotic escapee, from whatever asylum couldn't hold you, up on Mount Rushmore."[15] Voych's hideous face on the mountain—what a crazy idea. "Like any of this will ever fucking happen," he shouts at the veterans. "What's wrong with you pinheads? Where in your twisted brain did you work it out that a disfigured face on Mount Rushmore would inspire anything but revulsion and outrage?"

Indeed, who would even imagine a culture in which disfigurement from war would conjure heroics and national greatness? Much less, who would image a time and place where the unsightly facial appearance of Voych's could conceivably inspire others to be like him? The genius in Michael Weller's *Beast* was not so much that *he* imagined the distended grandiosity of Voych and Cato's Rushmore fantasy, but that he recognized those sentiments lurking in the American cultural subtext and put them under his stage lights.

ART AND PURPLE HEARTS

Weller's *Beast* opened in September 2008 in a small off-off-Broadway theater, hardly a venture with the commercial significance of HBO and MTV specials. But the same cultural vein that those venues mined commercially, Weller tapped into artistically: if Kanye West and James Gandolfini could commodify war wounds for mass culture, performing and visual artists could make them, well, art—and as art, move their acceptance as signifiers of American post-empire identity to more elite levels of cultural mediation, levels even where art is a serious commercial interest.

Beast's opening was accompanied by a post-performance talk-back with the photographer-artist Nina Berman. Berman had turned heads with her 2004 book *Purple Hearts*, a collection of her photographs of twenty Iraq War veterans with amputations, serious facial disfigurations, and paralysis. Described that way, it was a book that might have gained anti-war acclaim as a twenty-first century *Johnny Got His Gun*, a work of literary genius that would surely kill the appetite for war. Or, astheticized as it was by Trolly Books, its war-porn affectation could have evoked enough revulsion to cost Berman and the publisher their professional respectability. But it didn't. If anti-war activists noticed the book, they kept it to themselves while Berman's career headed uptown.[16]

In August 2007 the Jen Bekman Gallery in Manhatten's SoHo district mounted an exhibit of Berman's photographs with the inclusion of "Marine Wedding," a studio portrait she took of Ty Ziegel and his bride Renee Kline. Kline was dressed in a traditional white gown holding a bouquet of flowers and Ziegel in his Marine uniform decorated with medals that included a purple heart. The *New York Times* story covering the Bekman opening described Ziegel:

> His dead-white face is all but featureless, with no nose and no chin, as blank as a pullover mask.

> Two years earlier in Iraq as a Marine Corps reservist, Mr. Ziegel had been trapped in a burning truck after a suicide bomber attack. The heat melted the flesh from his face. At Brooke Army Medical Center in Texas he underwent 19 rounds of surgery.

His shattered skull was replaced by a plastic dome and a face was constructed more or less from scratch with salvaged tissue, holes left where his ears and nose had been.

As a visual image, it's easy to think that Zeigel was Michael Weller's Beast. Less evident is the cultural nuance captured in the texts that Berman provided with her photographs—words drawn from interviews she did with the veterans—that carried into Weller's construction of his characters. Asked again—where would a screwy idea like putting Voych's face on Mr. Rushmore come from?—the answer is that it was laying latently in the words of Berman 's subjects, words that were in turn channeling an extant American mood.

Only two of the twenty veterans in *Purple Hearts* expressed opposition to the war and disenchantment with the military. But the words of another half-dozen display an emotional flatness with no or little political sensitivity—the words as dead-white and featureless as Zeigel's new face.[17] More revealing were the ten who flashed prideful identification with their disabilities:

Spc. Jose Martinez (massive burns to his face and body)

- I want to stay in the Army. It's just something I got addicted to and I like it. I'm this great Army soldier. I'm this great picture of the Army.

Spc. Sam Ross (blind with leg amputation)

- I don't have any regrets. No, not at all. It was the best experience of my life.

Sgt. John Quincy Adams (brain damaged)

- I joined the Guard for the money and I liked putting on the uniform.

Pfc. Tristan Wyatt (leg amputation)

- I just fell in love with it. I think about it every day. . . . Nothing will compare . . . I want to go back to the military. I want my old job back. I was a combat engineer. We blew things up. I felt like my heart was in the right place over there.

Pfc. Randall Chunen (disfigured from shrapnel in the face)

- I liked it. The excitement. The adrenaline . . . . I was doing what I wanted. I did something with my life instead of sitting around and doing nothing . . . now it's nothing. You just watch the news or you watch the war movies on TV. *Full Metal Jacket*, there's a couple of other ones. I want to find *Hamburger Hill*, that's a good one about the 101st.

Sgt. Josh Olson (leg amputation)

- My personal opinion, I think we should have finished the job in Vietnam. When the president came in December, that's when I got my Purple Heart. It was pretty cool. I was real fortunate to live my life's dream.[18]

Cpl. Alex Presman (leg amputation)

- It's just pride. The brotherhood. The way of life. Being in the military and being the few, the proud. Once a marine, always a marine.

Sgt. Erick Castro (leg amputation)

- I miss the military, the lifestyle, the whole chain of command. I get bored. Retired at twenty-three.

Sgt. Jeremy Feldbusch (brain damaged and blind)

- I don't have any regrets. I had some fun over there. I don't want to talk about the military anymore.

Sgt. Adam Zaremba (leg amputation)

- ... you get to wear a cool uniform. ... The Purple Heart, that's a good award.

Dalton Trumbo would have found few lines for his *Johnny* in the words of Berman's veterans.

CODA: THE PURPLE HEART, A GOOD AWARD

The apprehending of Berman's photography as "art," and the widespread acclaim it received as such—in 2010 items from her Purple Heart collection won acceptance to the Whitney Art Museum's biennial show, a venue considered the pinnacle of artistic accomplishment—are testimonies to her having touched a nerve. Her snapshots caught a collective emotion so tortured by loss and defeat that it could find self-valorization in the wounds she photographed.

Perhaps Berman knew, if only intuitively, that the same people who might have lynched a photographer of the World War II generation daring to artsy-up the horror of war would now celebrate her aesthetic courage. In any case, the real brilliance of her lens-work was manifested in the societal embrace of the wretchedness—their own—that Americans saw represented in her photographs.

Beast wasn't the only wounds-to-the-stage endeavor in the years following the 2003 invasion of Iraq. In June 2009, the Ensemble Studio Theater in Manhattan staged Tommy Smith's *PTSD* as part of its annual marathon of one-act plays. The play's central character, Riles, is back from Iraq and presenting himself to family and friends as traumatized, even though his actual combat experience doesn't seem to account for that. Smith's challenge to the authenticity of men's war stories nuances the usual celebratory connections between the "hidden injuries" and veterans' social standing, while yet reaffirming through the roles he scripted for Riles's family and girlfriend, to say nothing of the title he gave the play, that PTSD is the cultural mediator of soldiers' homecomings.

Beast and *PTSD*, as well as Nina Berman's photographs extend the post-Vietnam legacy of wars remembered through the wounds of veterans. It's a quintessentially colonialist legacy that displaces the Vietnamese and now Iraqis and Afghanis from those memories, leaving Americans as the only visible victims, indeed the only visible figures in the story. The domination of medical discourse in that narrative, moreover, bequeathed to the present by its Vietnam edition, virtually inoculated returnees from the "new wars" against a more political interpretation of their own experience. Playwright and screenwriter imagination, also debilitated by the costs-of-war idiom was, meanwhile, unable to find in that experience the images and storylines for a more empowering message. Weller's Voych and Cato, and Smith's Riles, all return with some upset about their time in Iraq but showing no hint of raised consciousness.

NOTES

1. The Veterans Day edition of the PBS *News Hour*, airing November 11, 2011, reported that 46 percent of human relations specialists fear that PTSD is a factor in the workplace performance of veterans.

2. Boyer (1992), Faludi (2007), and Strong (1999) are good introductions to the early American identity as a besieged and captive people.

3. The "old" Marlboro Man was the cowboy pictured in advertisements for Marlboro cigarettes from the 1950s into the 1990s. The image associated traits of ruggedness with smoking Marlboros and spawned tropes like "Marlboro Country" usually referring to rough-and-tumble occupations like ranching. Three men who modeled in the Marlboro ads died of lung cancer. The *Wikipedia* entry for "Marlboro Man" in September of 2010 led with a reference to James Blake Miller.

4. This kind of flashback story is stock Hollywood imagery.

5. Not being a smoker, I consulted a colleague who is. He said even the most dedicated chain smokers burn only three or so packs of cigarettes a day, about half of what *Nightline* claimed for Miller. The fact that Miller never says, on camera, how much he smoked leaves open the possibility that the six-plus packs a day was an invention of the news people and that Miller just went along with it. Miller does, however, channel a Pat Tillman type story, telling the ABC interviewer that the Marines offered him an early departure from Iraq lest "something happen to the [Marlboro Man] identity that Americans now linked to." Pat Till-

man was the U.S. Army ranger and former NFL football player killed by friendly fire in Afghanistan in April 2004.

6. The association of tobacco smoking with masculinity and strength reaches back well beyond the Marlboro Man era. In the 1920s advertising for cigarettes made claims for virility.

7. The cost of *New York Times* advertisements is negotiable and therefore known only to those who work out the deals. But controversies over how much the anti-war group MoveOn.Org paid for an ad critical of General Petraeus are recorded on the Internet, indicating that prices run from $60,000 to $140,000 for a full page.

8. The old and over-stated adage that newspaper "news" is the backside of its "ads" is called to mind by this example. The commercial value in an op-ed like this one is enhanced by its collateral nature: advertising works best when it is not read or heard as such. Regular news stories work even better in that way and, on the same day as the advertisement and the op-ed, which as noted was also Veterans Day, the *Times* ran a regular news story telling how Vietnam veterans felt scarred by their war and homecoming, many of whom came home "to no one" according to the report.

9. Remarking on the film's mission to have PTSD taken seriously, The *New York Times* reviewer (Hale 2010) might have betrayed some unspeakable doubt about its shaky status as a diagnostic category.

10. Damigo's and Frass's cases are easily associated with storylines derived from popular culture and other news accounts. That characteristic doesn't in itself impugn their authenticity but does provide a starting point for the pursuit of some source other than their war-time experience for the narratives they construct. One of my students commented, "It's almost like those guys were acting," an observation not inconsistent with the identification made by anthropologists of the element of performance in the presentation of symptoms, an idea that makes the identity of the patient, qua patient, something that is "performed."

11. A sector of the anti-war community seems to believe that if "the people only knew the truth" about the real cost of war they would rise up and put a stop to the fighting. I expressed my skepticism of that view in a May 25, 2007, opinion piece for the *National Catholic Reporter*.

12. Tiram's case is the most representative of PTSD's popular image. He can't sleep unless his door is locked and he lost one job as a telemarketer because the headphones he had to wear caused him to have a flashback in which he reached for his weapon. In none of the three cases is the link between the veteran's PTSD and their duties in Iraq made clear.

13. Karnowski and Forliti (2012).

14. This and the following paragraphs are drawn from the script of *Beast* made available to me by Michael Weller.

15. Weller (2008, pp. 48, 53).

16. The "war porn" comment about *Purple Hearts* was made to me by another artist, although without the inflection of disdain usually accompanying the word "porn."

17. The contrast with the boldly political stance taken by veterans wounded in Vietnam is striking. The protests of the 1972 Republican Party convention in Miami Beach, for example, was led by chair-bound veterans like Ron Kovic whose story was later made into the film *Born on the Fourth of July*.

18. Olson's comment and Chunen's above it testify to how strongly the war in Vietnam continues to play in their imaginations.

Chapter Eight

Embrace The Horror

Horror has a face and you must make a friend of horror.
Horror and moral terror are your friends.
If they are not, then they are enemies to be feared.
—Colonel Walter Kurtz

In the 1978 film *Apocalypse Now*, U.S. Special Forces Captain Benjamin Willard (Martin Sheen) is dispatched from the war zone in Vietnam to hunt down and assassinate the renegade Colonel Walter Kurtz (Marlon Brando) who is operating out of a secret base camp in Cambodia with his own army of defectors. The film tells us that Kurtz has gone insane, driven mad by the horror of war.

Willard finds Kurtz and prior to killing him, the Colonel tells Willard about the time he helped a commando team inoculate some Vietnamese children for polio. Later, some enemy soldiers had come and chopped off the inoculated arms and thrown them into a pile. Kurtz was struck by the political brilliance of that act:

> The genius. The will to do that. Perfect. Genuine, complete, crystalline, pure. Then I could understand that they were strong-er than we were. They were not monsters but trained cadres who fought with their hearts, who have families, who have children, who are filled with love, men who are moral who at the same

time are able to utilize their primordial instincts to kill without feeling, without passion, without judgment.

Thirty years later, it appears that the important subtext of *Apocalypse Now* was not its excursion into the dark side of the human heart, that critics at the time attributed to it, so much as its signaling of a postwar American culture that was beginning to form. Kurtz had to be assassinated not because he was crazy or because he had lost his morality but because he had defected from the softness of Washington liberalism and the feminization of the nation's culture. He had made himself the enemy of an immoral U.S. policy that would send men to kill without knowing why they were killing, or worse, knowing what the purpose was and not believing in it. Kurtz hadn't lost his morality; he had *found* it—in the hearts of the people he had been sent to kill.

Kurtz's turn to primitivism and embrace of horror as the ultimate expression of love for family and country appears in retrospect to have been an eerie harbinger of the militia movement that rode into Oklahoma City's Federal Plaza, the soft-core nihilism of Pink Floyd's *The Wall*—that deteriorated into Nine Inch Nails' dystopian *Year Zero*—the shattered-window look stylized for retailing hard-shell fashion to the young warriors on America's urban frontier, and the noir-themed images from Francis Ford Coppola to Mel Gibson projected into suburban multiplexes. By the early twenty-first century, apocalypticism had leaped from the book of Revelation to a best-selling series about unbelievers left behind in the Biblical rapture and the rendering of Iraq-war horror into art. [1] The collapse of reason into revelation, so graphically represented in post-Vietnam film and literature, was but one more symptom of modernism's fatigue manifested in the American defeat in Vietnam. [2] Attempts to understand and explain the loss imploded into solipsisms that made America the victim of the war it had perpetrated, and the means of war, the soldiers themselves, became the ends of the war they had fought. In its postwar renderings, the experience became an all-American affair fought and lost on the home front, the bi-focused American soldier remembered through one lens as an effete and dovish returnee rejected by all but the peacenik left; through the other lens the born-again Kurtzes whose commissions of My Lai-like atrocities authenticated the horror they themselves had been dealt and the light that what they did had brought them to. Going into the 1980s those two images merged, but asymmetrically: the politicized veteran empowered by his time in combat morphed into a troubled figure whose protest of the war was cathartic, a symptomatic expression distinguishable in form only from that of the twitchy, trigger-happy, and sexually deranged basket cases that flooded veteran self-help centers and Hollywood scripts. [3]

By 1982 when Sylvester Stallone portrayed John Rambo and his rampage through the rural Northwest, the Kurtzian character had already been codified in public memory, the morality of his violence established by the immorality of the government that sent him to fight a war it would not let him win and the Nietzschean impotence of the small-town Americans incapable of joining him. *Rambo*, in films, lionized "the-fucked-up" because it represented the free-range schizoid "Other" to modernism's confinement of the Self. Rambo, the bust-out rebel, had no cause; it wasn't culture or intellect that linked him, through Kurtz, to the primordial—it was his "half-Indian" blood. [4]

That the American film market and postwar culture was sufficiently ready to valorize the images of what otherwise would have been condemned as deviant, obscene even, testified to the bankruptcy of the conventional discourse within which to process the war. The war had been lost, eliding the possibility of a future built on the postwar present. The nation had to circle back on itself, postponing its arrival as the "city on the hill." [5] Its new identity would be built on loss, its new heroes the Ron Kovics of paraplegia, not the Audie Murphys of Anzio; its prophets not those with

confidence in an imagined future but those who had seen the horror, and the modernist delusions of strength, beauty, and reason it
mirrored. Distrusting the place of cognition in matters so essential,
the nation's late-century neo-militarism sought the restoration of its
will-to-war in something more basic: the truth of war was in the
body.[6]

The image of the wounded and disparaged veteran was rede-
ployed for duty in the Persian Gulf almost before its iconic status in
America's "great betrayal" narrative was secured. Twirling through
its index of politically saleable reasons for the airlift of a half-
million troops to Saudi Arabia in the late summer and fall of 1990,
President George H.W. Bush and his spokesmen tried and rejected
"national defense," "Saddam Hussein," "oil," and "jobs" before
abandoning the appeal to reason and simply saying, "We've sent
the troops—support them."[7] It was a rhetorical strategy that en-
listed, not the hero GI Joes who had taken Guadalcanal or liberated
Buchenwald; this time it was the image of broken and defeated
stretcher-laden rejectees who stirred the emotions for the new war.
It wasn't "Remember Normandy" or some other jingo-worthy moment in U.S. military history that motivated some let's-do-it-again
sentiment for Desert Storm but rather an impulse to *re*do something
that wasn't done right or finish something left undone. The Gulf
War was about the last war, the war lost on Morningside Heights in
Manhattan's West Side and Sproul Plaza at UC Berkeley. The
"Vietnam syndrome" that President Bush wanted kicked was the
psychological corrosion eating at the nation's sense of self.[8]

The cues for how the Gulf War generation should come home
were just as Vietnam War–framed as were the reasons it went to
war. One role was the politically enabled veteran who took his
dissent to the streets and returned his combat medals won in a war
that he later found unconscionable, the warrior turned peacemaker
who lobbied for an end to military funding; the other role called for
the disabled veteran, the wounded warrior whose damage could be

used to balance the accounts of American and enemy losses in the war, and then credentialing the authenticity of the experience—an encounter with horror and the scars to show for it.

But Gulf War veterans, and those following them home from Iraq and Afghanistan, were not choosing the scripts. The yellow ribbon hoopla that sent "the boys" off to the Gulf, and the support-the-troops rallies that blunted popular opposition to the invasion of Iraq, both put the means of war, the soldiers themselves, center stage and kept politics and economics in the wings. The reality of the wars themselves remained beyond measurement, beyond the mind even, something that registered *on* the body as wounds that were mere simulacrum for the horror *em*bodied.

The American embrace of war's elemental nature was galvanized by the attacks of September 11, 2001. Its own war of terror began days later with the bombing of Afghans who had no air-defense systems followed by commando operations using tactics so off the books that they were assigned to warlords with the same sense of morality to which Colonel Kurtz had defected.[9] The war was extended to Iraq with an air assault that targeted the Baghdad infrastructure but whose "shock and awe" marquee encoded its micro-political strategy of breaking the mind-body synapses in millions of Iraqis. Brilliant, pure, crystalline—and it was followed by the overthrow of the Arab world's most modern regime, the occupying authorities' indifference to the looting of civilization's most treasured artifacts, and their authorship of psychic violence on the prisoners of Abu Ghraib.

The negative synergy of America's retreat from modernity also pulled down the firewalls that could have retarded its advance to the past. With sense-making precluded, it was no surprise that the discourses of emotion and bodily representation shoved everything else off the front pages and evening news schedules.

From the day President George W. Bush's first fighters returned home, it was clear that the only countable evidence for their service was somatic—the childish "what did you *do* in the war, Daddy?" (a quaint reminder that wars once had a purpose)—refashioned to read through their battered bodies, "What *happened* to you in the war, Daddy?" By 2008 every major news organization in the country had done its obligatory special on bedridden and chair-bound patriots, each of them replete with gut-wrenching visuals and texts loaded with references to *traumatic* brain injury to make sure we knew that the real story was on the inside.

Years into the Huxlian convergence of news and entertainment, hope that "the news"— war is hell—would work as anything but a magnet for advertising dollars, catnip for military recruits, and more carnage to avenge the carnage was naïve. The persistence of "the kids," in the American vernacular for the men and women— closer to twenty-nine than nineteen—that it sent off to war, signaling less a people who could not count than a collective subconscious *wanting to believe* it is strong enough to feed its young into a killing machine.

Like the infant stumps in Kurtz's story, the appendage-emptied spaces on the bodies back from war and the chairs at the dinner table vacated by bodies that would never be there were mere devices bespeaking the unspeakable, the aestheticized acceptance for America's new friend.

Brilliant, pure, crystalline. As strong as they are.

NOTES

1. Nine Inch Nails's *Year Zero* was marketed with a companion video game in which America has been reborn as a Christian fundamentalist theocracy. See also the references to Nina Berman's work in chapter 7.

2. Modern warfare is characterized by fixed-place tactics (e.g.. trenches, permanent bases, positioned artillery), high-tech weaponry (i.e. machines and explosives), and hierarchical command structures. Pre-modern warfare is characterized by guerilla tactics (e.g. hit and run maneuvers), low-tech weaponry (e.g. hand-carved punji sticks and tripwires vs. modern landmines; homemade bombs (known in Vietnam as satchel charges, in Iraq today as Improvised Explosive

Devices) vs. mass-produced, factory-made bombs), informal and uniformed citizen-soldiers whose identities blur the military-nonmilitary boundaries.

The defeat of the world's most modern military—the U.S.—by the pre-modern, even primitive, tactics and techniques of the Vietnamese raised serious questions in the minds of social theorists (e.g. Foucault) about modernism's claims to superiority and even viability. In short, it was the American defeat in Vietnam that set the conditions for a post-modern consideration that "the *pre-modern*" might have been superior.

3. In March, 1968, soldiers of the U.S. American Division attacked the hamlet of My Lai in South Vietnam killing up to 500 men, women, and children, most of whom were civilians. Lt. Williiam Calley was the only soldier convicted for murder for the deaths.

4. *Rambo*, the film, was all about the character's mythic primitiveness, the mythic *being* about blood-lines, race, genetics—not his cultural traits. Stallone was chosen (and dressed in the headband) because of the *body* he brought to the part and the white-racist stereotype that it evoked. In "Thirst Blood" for the *Los Angeles Times* (February 3, 2008), film critic Peter Rainer reiterates these points and speaks to the attraction of *Rambo* for Americans in the post-9/11 years.

5. John Winthrop was a seventeenth-century Puritan leader who charged the Massachusetts Bay Colony with establishing a model of Puritan Christianity, a "City on the Hill" for the entire world to see.

6. Ron Kovic is a Marine who suffered a spinal cord wound in Vietnam in 1968. He later opposed the war and told his story in *Born on the 4th of July* which Oliver Stone made into the film by the same title. Audie Murphy (1924-1971) was the most decorated soldier in U.S. history for his Army service in World War II. Anzio, Italy, was the site of a beach landing where U.S. forces took heavy losses in 1944. Murphy's memoir *To Hell and Back* was made into a film and Murphy became a film star after the war.

7. I detailed the elements of this strategy in chapter 2 of *The Spitting Image: Myth, Memory, and the Legacy of Vietnam* (1998). Norman Solomon makes a similar point in his 2006 book *War Made Easy: How Presidents and Pundits Keep Spinning us to Death*.

8. Sproul Plaza is a central gathering point for students at the Berkeley campus of the University of California and the site for key events related to the 1964 Free Speech Movement and protests of the war in Vietnam. Morningside Heights is the upper West Side neighborhood of Manhattan in New York City on which Columbia University is situated. In one of the signature events of the anti-war movement, Columbia students struck and occupied buildings in protest of racism and the war in Vietnam. See Mark Rudd's 2009 memoir *Underground* about his role in the Columbia events.

9. The U.S. proxy in its post-9/11 campaign in Afghanistan was the Northern Alliance, comprised of Tajik and Uzbek warlords (also known for Islamist militancy as the Mujahideen) that had originally been cobbled together to fight the Soviets. Unlike al Qaeda that is known to have an internationalist agenda, the

Northern Alliance is a throwback to a feudalistic form of local/regional organization that pre-existed the modern state.

Bibliography

Ahmed, Azam. 2013. "In Afghan Transition, U.S. Forces Take a Step Back." *New York Times*, May 26.

Altman, Lawrence K. 1989. "Medical Advances Brighten Jogger's Prognosis." *New York Times*, May 21.

Anderson, Charles et al. (1944). "Psychiatric Casualties From the Normandy Beach-Head," *Lancet* pp. 218–221, August 12.

Anderson, John R. 2010. "New Era for Coffee Houses Rooted in Anti-war Tradition." *Army Times*, March 7.

Beattie, Keith. 2000. *The Scar that Binds: American Culture and the Vietnam War*. New York: New York University Press.

Bender, Bryan. 2007. "Accidental Deaths in Iraq Plaguing U.S." *Boston Globe*, May 3.

Berman, Nina. 2004. *Purple Hearts: Back From Iraq*. Great Britain: Trolley Ltd.

Blakeslee, Sandra. 2000. "Just What's Going on Inside that Brain of Yours?" *New York Times*, March 14.

Boone, Katherine N. "The Paradox of PTSD." *Wilson Quarterly* Autumn 2011.

Bourne, Peter. 1972. "Military Psychiatry and the Vietnam Veteran Experience," in *The Vietnam Veteran in Contemporary Society*, Veterans Administration.

Bowling, Brian. 2005. "Stress of Battle Haunts Soldiers." *Pittsburgh Tribune-Review*, February 23.

Boyer, Paul. 1992. *When Time Shall be No More: Prophecy Belief in Modern American Culture*. Cambridge: Harvard University Press.

Brogdon, William. 1953. "From Here to Eternity." *Variety Magazine*, July 29.

Browne, Janet. 1985. "Darwin and the Face of Madness" Pp. 151–165 in Bynum, Porter, and Shepherd (Vol. 1) 1985.

Brown, Kathryn Amy. 2008. "Baghdad Bound: Forced Labor and Third-country Nationals in Iraq." *Rutgers Law Review*. Vol. 60:3 pp. 737–767.

Burkett, B.J. 1998. *Stolen Valor: How the Vietnam Generation was Robbed of its Heroes and History*. Dallas: Verity Press.

Burns, Robert. 2012. "US Troop suicides surging once more." *Worcester Telegram & Gazette*, June 8.

Bynum, Russ. 2003a. "In 'Unprecedented' effort, military prepares to screen soldiers for war illnesses." Associated Press. June 3.

Bynum, Russ. 2003b. "Families Cheer as 3rd Infantry Soldiers Return Home to Georgia." Associated Press. July 5.

Bynum, Russ. 2003c. "After Grueling Deployment, 3rd Infantry Soldiers get longer stay in Iraq." Associate Press. July 14.

Cain, Susan. 2011. "Shyness: Evolutionary Tactic?" *New York Times*, June 26, Sunday Review p. 4.

Carr, Nicholas. 2010. *The Shallows: What the Internet is doing to Our Brains*. New York: W.W. Norton.

Carey, Benedict. 2009. "Army will train soldiers to cope with emotions." *New York Times*, August 18, p. A1.

Carey, Benedict. 2010. "U.S. Troops Suffer More Stress Than Britons, Study Says." *New York Times*, May 17, p. A10.

Carey, Benedict. 2011. "Antipsychotic Use Is Questioned for Combat Stress." *New York Times*, August 3, p. A13.

Caruth, Cathy. 1996. *Unclaimed Experience: Trauma, Narrative, and History*. Baltimore: The John Hopkins University Press.

Caywood, Thomas. 2009. "Tangled Web: Military, engineering background fabricated." *Worcester Telegram and Gazette*, August 2.

Chandrasekaran, Rajiv. 2013. "Plan to shut military supermarkets shows difficulty of cutting defense spending." *Washington Post*, June 1.

Clark, Constance. 2008. *God — or Gorilla: Images of Evolution in the Jazz Age*. Baltimore: Johns Hopkins University Press.

Clements, Charles. 1985. *Witness to War*. Boston: Beacon Press.

Coleman, Horace. 2012. "Meeting Lamont B. Steptoe, Warrior Writer." *The Veteran*, Spring, p. 20.

Conrad, Peter and J.W. Schneider. 1992. *Deviance and Medicalization: From Badness to Sickness*. Philadelphia: Temple University Press.

Dao, James and Dan Frosch. 2009. "Military Confidentiality Rules Raise Counseling Questions." *New York Times*, p. A10.

Dao, James. 2010. "Rule to Ease Veterans'' Mental Health Claims Doesn't Go Far Enough, Groups Say." *New York Times*, July 13.

Dao, James. 2012. "Paper Links Nerve Agents in '91 Gulf War and Ailments." *New York Times*, December 14, p. A18.

Dao, James. 2013. "Study Seeks Biomarkers for Invisible War Scars." *New York Times*, Februray 7, p. A17.

Dao, James and A. W. Lehren. 2013. "Baffling Rise in Suicides Plagues U.S. Military." *New York Times*, May 16, p. A1.

Daudet, Leon. 1894/2012. *Les Morticoles*. France: Ulan Press.

Dean, Eric. 1999. *Shook Over Hell: Post-Traumatic Stress, Vietnam, and the Civil War*. Cambridge, MA: Harvard University Press.

DiDi-Huberman, Georges. 2004. *The Invention of Hysteria: Charcot and the Photographic Iconography of Salpêtrière*. Cambridge: MIT Press.

Dipple, John V.H. 2010. *War and Sex: A Brief History of Men's Urge for Battle*. Amherst, NY: Prometheus Books.

Dishneau, David. 2009. "Marine charged with faking war wounds for gain." *Associated Press*, September 23.

Dowd, Maureen. 2020. "Wishes as Lies." *New York Times*, May 22.

Dozier, Kimberly. 2008. *Breathing the Fire: Fighting to Report and Survive the War in Iraq*. Des Moines: Meredith Books.

Drukteinis, Albert M. 2012. "A Head Injury is not a Brain Injury." *New England Psychodiagnostics On-line Library*.

Duke, Lynne. 2004. "Under Fire: Haunted by Memories of War, A Soldier Battles the Army." *Washington Post*. November 1.

Dunn, J.C. 1987. *The War the Infantry Knew, 1914-1919*. London: Janes Publishing.

Eaton, Paul D. 2007. "Casualties of the Budget Wars." *New York Times*, March 6.

Erichsen, John Eric. 1867. *Railway and other Injuries of the Nervous System*. Philadelphia: Henry C. Lea.

Farragher, Thomas and W.V. Robinson. 2000. "B'nai B'rith award now under review: A veteran's story of World War II exploits under review." *Boston Globe*, October 12, p. A01.

Faludi, Susan. 2008. "Think the Gender War is Over? Think Again." *New York Times*. June 15.

Faludi, Susan. 2007. *The Terror Dream: Fear and Fantasy in Post-9/11 America*. New York: Metropolitan Books.

Finkel, David. 2009. *The Good Soldiers*. New York: Farrar, Straus and Giroux.

Fleming, Robert H. 1985. "Post Vietnam Syndrome: Neurosis or Sociosis?" *Psychiatry* 48 (May): 122–139.

Frank, Thomas. 2007. "Non-combat Deaths in Iraq Drop. *USA Today*. July 24.

Frankel, Fred H. 1994. "The Concept of Flashbacks in Historical Perspective." *International Journal of Clinical and Experimental Hypnosis* 42:321–336.

Frederick, Jim. 2010. *Black Hearts: One Platoon's Descent into Madness in Iraq's Triangle of Death*. New York: Harmony Books.

Friel, Howard and R. Falk. 2007. *The Record of the Paper: How the* New York Times *Misreports US Foreign Policy*. London: Verso.

Frosch, Dan. 2011. "Fighting for the Right to Tell Lies: A Law Against Bogus Military Claims is Challenged." *New York Times*, May 21, p. A 10.

Fuentes, Gieget. 2012. "Staff NCO to lose rank in urination video." *Marine Times*. December 20.

Fumento, Michael. 1997. "Gulf Lore Syndrome." *Reason*, March 22-23.

Gannon, Tim. 2013. "Southold marine enters guilty plea at Court Martial." *The Suffolk Times*, January 16.

Gibson, James William. 1996. *Warrior Dreams: Violence and Manhood in Post-Vietnam America*. New York: Hill and Wang.

Gieryn, Thomas F. 1991. *Cultural Boundaries of Science: Credibility on the Line*. Chicago: University of Chicago Press.

Gillani, Waqar and Jane Perlez. 2009. "Pakistan says 5 Americans Sought to Fight U.S." *New York Times*, December 11:A1.

Gilman, Sander L. 1982. *Seeing the Insane*. Lincoln, Nebraska: University of Nebraska Press.

Gilman, Sander L. 2004. *ISI-Repertory*. Vol. 95, No. 4.

Gimbel, Cynthia and Alan Booth. 1994. "Why Does Military Combat Experience Adversely Affect Marital Relations?" *Journal of Marriage and the Family* 56:691–703.

Glasser, Ronald. 2007. "A Shock Wave of Brain Injuries." *Washington Post*. April 8, p. B01.

Goetz, Christopher. 2010. *Neurology for the Non-Neurologist*. New York: Lippicott, Williams & Wilkins.

Goldin, Rebecca, and Cindy Merrick. 2012. "Neuroscience or Neurobabble?: What's this thing called fMRI?" STATS (George Mason University) July 16.

Goode, Erica. 2009. "When Minds Snap." *New York Times*, November 8, wk p. 1.

Gomez, Alan. 2009. "Military focuses on 'internal insurgents' in Suicides." *USA Today*.

Gualtieri, C.T. 1988. "Pharmacotherapy and the Neurobehavioral Sequelae of Traumatic Brain Injury." *Brain Injury*, Vol. 2 No. 2 Apr–Jun.

Great Britain, War Office. 1922. *Report of the War Office Committee of Enquiry into " Shell- Shock. "* London: His Majesty's Stationary Office.

Hack, Damon. 2003. "Inside Pro Football: Clearing the Fog that Surrounds Concussions." *New York Times*, October 17.

Hacking, Ian. 1996. "Memory Sciences, Memory Politics" in Paul Antze and M. Lambek (eds.) *Tense Past: Cultural Essays in Trauma and Memory*. London: Routledge.

Hagopian, Patrick. 2009. *The Vietnam War in American Memory: Veterans, Memorials, and the Politics of Healing*. Amherst, MA: University of Massachusetts Press.

Hale, Mike. 2010. "A Searching Look at Combat Wounds to the Spirit." *New York Times*, November 10.

Hamilton, Brad. 2010. "One Arm Bandit: B'klyn bum fakes war wound for cash." *New York Post*, October 10, p. 1.

Harrington, Anne. 2008. *The Cure Within: A History of Mind-Body Medicine*. New York: W.W. Norton.

Harrison, Kathryn. 2006. "Falling Through the Earth." *New York Times* Book Review. March 12

Haynes, Samuel. 2009. *The Soldiers' Tale: Bearing Witness to Modern War*. New York: Penguin.

Hennessey-Fiske, Molly. 2007. "U.S. Soldiers Face Battle of the Bulge." *Los Angeles Times*, July 10.

Hoffman, Jan. 2009. "War's Other Enduring Videos: Surprise visits home by soldiers are being caught on camera." *New York Times*, November 29.

Hoge, Charles W., Herb Goldberg, and Carl Castro. 2009. "Care of War Veterans with Mild Traumatic Brain Injury—Flawed Perspectives." *New England Journal of Medicine*. Pp. 1588–1591.

Hyer, Lee, et al. 1990. "Suicidal Behavior Among Chronic Vietnam Theatre Veterans with PTSD." *Journal of Clinical Psychology*. Vol. 46, No. 6 November.

Isherwood, Charles. 2008. "Creature of Iraq War; Seeking Revenge on His Maker." *New York Times*, Septermber 16, p. B3.

Jelinek, Pauline. 2009. "Military suicides at record numbers." *Associated Press*. January 30.

Jones, Tamara, and Anne Hall. 2003. "The War after the War." *Washington Post*. July 21. P. A01.

Johnson, Chalmers. 2005. *The Sorrows of Empire: Militarism, Secrecy, and the End of the Republic*. New York: Henry Holt.

Kakutani, Michiko. 2009. "Ground War: The Iraq Surge Grunts Knew." *New York Times*, October 6.

Kaes, Anton. 2011. *Shell Shock Cinema: Weimar Culture and the Wounds of War*. Princeton: Princeton University Press.

Katzman, Jason. 1993. "From Outcast to Cliché: How Film Shaped, Warped, and Developed the Image of the Vietnam Veteran, 1969-1990. *Journal of American Culture* 16 (spring):7–24.

Karnowski, Steve and Amy Forliti. 2012. "More doubts cast on Singer's war injury claims." Associated Press June 9.

Kerr, Peter. 1992. "Treatment of Severe Head Injuries is Profitable, but not for Patients." March 16.

Klein, Naomi. 2007. *Shock Doctrine: The Rise of Disaster Capitalism*. New York: Metropolitan Books.

Kovik, Ron. 1976. *Born on the Fourth of July*. New York: Simon and Schuster.

Kracauer, Siegfried. 1947. *From Caligari to Hitler: A Psychological History of the German Film*. Princeton: Princeton University Press.

Kristoff, Nicholas. 2012. "War Wounds." *New York Times*, August 10.

Kulik, Gary. 2009. *War Stories: False Atrocity Tales, Swift Boaters, and Winter Soldiers — What Really Happened in Vietnam*. Washington DC: Potomac Books.

Kuhn, Thomas. 1996. *The Structure of Scientific Revolutions*. Routledge.

Kurtz, Howard. 2006. "Wounded Newsmen Show Slow Recovery." *Washington Post*, January 30.

Kurtz, Howard. 2007. "A Firsthand Report on the Wounds of War; Bob Woodruff Indicts Military for its Response to Veterans." *Washington Post*. February 27.

Lair, Meredith H. 2011. *Armed with Abundance: Consumerism & Soldiering in the Vietnam War*. Chapel Hill: University of North Carolina Press.

LaHaye, Tim and Jerry Jenkins. 2003. *Left Behind*. Carol Stream, IL: Tyndale House

Langley, M. Keith. 1982. "Post-Traumatic Stress Disorders among Vietnam Combat Veterans." *Social Casework: The Journal of Contemporary Social Work*. Pp 593–598.

Leed, Eric. 1979. *No Man's Land: Combat and Identity in World War I*. New York: Cambridge University Press.

Leys, Ruth. 2000. *Trauma: A Genealogy*. Chicago: University of Chicago Press.

Lembcke, Jerry. 1998. *The Spitting Image: Myth, Memory, and the Legacy of Vietnam*. New York: NYU Press.

Lembcke, Jerry. 2007. "The Facts about Soldiers' Ages." *National Catholic Reporter*. May 25.

Lembcke, Jerry. 2013. "Flashbacks, Fireworks . . . and Cars that Backfire?" www.counterpunch.org. July 11.

Lerner, Paul. 2001. "From Traumatic Neurosis to Male Hysteria: The Decline and Fall of Hermann Oppenheim, 1889–1919" in Mark Micale and P. Lerner *Traumatic Pasts: History, Psychiatry, and Trauma in the Modern Age, 1870–1930*. Cambridge: Cambridge University Press.

Lifton, Robert J. 1973. *Home from the War: Vietnam Veterans, Neither Victims nor Executioners*. New York: Simon and Schuster.

Lynn, Edward J., and Mark Belza. 1984. "Factitious Posttraumatic Stress Disorder: The Veteran Who Never Got to Vietnam." *Hospital and Community Psychiatry* 35:697–701.

Malo, Jean-Jacques, and Tony Williams. 1994. *Vietnam War Films*. Jefferson, NC: McFarland.

Marchione, Marilynn. 2007. "Thousands of GIs Cope with Brain Damage." Associated Press. September 2007.

Martini, Edwin. 2012. *Agent Orange: History, Science, and the Politics of Uncertainty*. Amherst, MA: University of Massachusetts Press.

Martini, Edwin. 2007. *Invisible Enemies: The American War on Vietnam, 1975-2000*. Amherst, MA: University of Massachusetts Press.

McKelvey, Tara (ed.). 2007. *One of the Guys: Women as Aggressors and Torturers*. Emeryville, CA: Seal Press.

McKinley, James C. Jr., and James Dao. 2009. "After Years of Growing Tensions, 7 Minutes of Bloodshed: Hasan Bought Gun Days after Arrival at Fort Hood." *New York Times*, p. A1.

McPeak, Merrill A. 2010. "Don't Ask, Don't Tell, Don't Change." *New York Times*. March 5, p. A21.

Meyer, Carlton. 2010. "The Myth of Low Military Pay." www.truthout.org. February 27.

Micale, Mark S., and Paul Lerner. 2001. *Traumatic Pasts: History, Psychiatry, and Trauma in the Modern Age, 1870 – 1930*. Cambridge: Cambridge University Press.

Micale, Mark S. 2001. "Jean-Martin Charcot and *les nevroses traumatiques:* From Medicine to Culture in French Trauma Theory of the Late Nineteenth Century. In Micale and Lerner, p. 115–139.

Meili, Trisha, and J. Kabat-Zinn. 2004. "The Power of the Human Heart: A Story of Trauma and Recovery and its Implications for Rehabilitation and Healing." *Advances in Mind-Body Medicine.* Vol. 20 No. 1, 2004.

Mills, C. Wright. 1967. *The Sociological Imagination.* New York: Oxford University Press.

Mishra, Raja. 2004. "Mental Toll on Troops Detailed Strains Shown in 17% of US Combat Troops." *Boston Globe*, July 1.

Mnookin, Seth. 2011 *The Panic Virus: The True Story Behind the Vaccine–Autism Controversy.* New York: Simon & Schuster.

Mosqueda, John, and Ed Meagher. n.d. "Viet Veteran Holds 3 at Gunpoint in Park before Surrendering." *Los Angeles Times.*

Nordheimer, Jon. 1971. "From Dak to Detroit: Death of a Troubled Vietnam Hero." *New York Times*, May 26:A1.

Musheno, Michael Craig, and Susan M. Ross. 2008. *How Reservists Bear the Burden of Iraq.* Ann Arbor: University of Michigan Press.

Olsen, Patricia R. 2006. "A Tangible Thank-you for Wartime Sacrifice." *New York Times*, November 13.

Oppenheim, Hermann, in Micale, Mark E., and Paul Lerner *Traumatic Pasts: History, Psychiatry, and Trauma in the Modern Age, 1870 – 1930.* Cambridge UK: Cambridge University Press.

Parsons, Talcott. 1975. "The Sick Role and the Role of the Physician Reconsidered." *Health and Society*, Summer.

Pendygraft, John. 2003. "Return of the 365th; Squadron Dismissed." *St. Petersburg Times*, June 29.

Postman, Neil. 1985. *Amusing Ourselves to Death.* New York: Penguin Books.

Philipps, David. 2010. *Lethal Warriors: When the New Band of Brothers Came Home — Uncovering the Tragic Reality of PTSD.* 2010. New York: Palgrave Macmillan.

Rajiva, Lila. 2007. "The Military Made Me Do It: Double Standards and Psychic Injuries at Abu Ghraib" Pp. 217–228 in McKelvey (ed.) 2007.

Reid, Fiona. 2010. *Broken Men: Shell Shock, Treatment and Recovery in Britain 1914 – 1930.* New York: Continuum Books.

Rich, Frank. 2006. *The Greatest Story Ever Sold: The Decline and fall of Truth from 9/11 to Katrina.* New York: The Penguin Press.

Ricks, Thomas. 2006. "A Different Operation for U.S. Doctors in Iraq." *Washington Post.* February 1.

Roberts, Joel. 2005. "G.I.s Enjoy a Taste of Home: Pizza, Subway, or Burger King? U.S. Soldiers Have it Their Way." *CBS News.* February 7.

Robertson, Joe. 2003. "The Homecomings are a Mixture of happiness and anxiety." *Kansas City Star.* July 3.

Robertson, Campbell, and Ray Rivera. 2009. "For Soldiers, Strain Met With Resolve." *New York Times*, December 2, p. A14.

Roig-Franzia, Manuel. 2003. "On-and-Off Rotations leave families boiling." Associated Press. July 31.

Roth, Michael S. 2012. *Memory, Trauma, and History: Essays on Living with the Past*. New York: Columbia University Press.

Rudd, Mark. 2009. *Underground: My Life with SDS and the Weathermen*. New York: Haper.

Satel, Sally. 2006. "For Some, the War Won't End." *New York Times*, March 1: op-ed.

Schutz, Alfred. 1944. "The Stranger: An Essay in Social Psychology." *American Journal of Sociology* Vol. 49 No. 6 (499:507).

Scott, A.O. 2010. "This Time the Dream's on Me." *New York Times*, July 16, 2010: C1.

Scott, Wilbur Jr. 1993. *The Politics of Readjustment: Vietnam Veterans since the War*. New York: Aldine de Gruyter.

Shane, Scott. 2009. "The Call of Extremism, Echoing at Home." *New York Times*, December 12: A1.

Shatan, Chaim. 1972. "Post-Vietnam Syndrome." *New York Times*, May 6.

Shephard, Ben. 2001. *A War of Nerves: Soldiers and Psychiatrists in the Twentieth Century*. Cambridge: Harvard University Press.

Showalter, Elaine. 1997. *Hystories: Hysterical Epidemics and Modern Media*. New York: Columbia University Press.

Shultz, Richard H., Jr. *The Secret War Against Hanoi: Kennedy and Johnson's use of Spies, Saboteurs, and Covert Warriors in North Vietnam*. New York: Harper Collins, 1999.

Smith, G. Elliot (M.D.), and T.H. Pear. 1917. *Shell Shock and its Lessons*. London: Longmans, Green & Co.

Smith, Timothy. 1997. "Pro Football Embarks on Stepped-up Effort to Deal with Head Injuries." *New York Times*, July 16.

Solomon, Deborah. 2005. "A Soldier's Story: Questions for Kayla Williams." *New York Times* Sunday Magazine), August 21.

Sontag, Deborah. 2008. "An Iraq Veteran's Descent, A Prosecutor's Choice." *New York Times,* January 20.

Sontag, Deborah, and Lizette Alvarez. 2008. "Across America, Deadly Echoes of Foreign Combat." *New York Times,* January 13.

Solomon, Norman. 2006. *War Made Easy: How Presidents and Pundits Keep spinning us to Death*. New York: Wiley.

Solotaroff, Paul. 1995. *House of Purple Hearts*. New York: HarperCollins.

Sparr, Landy, and Loren D. Pankratz. 1983. "Factitio Posttraumatic Stress Disorder." *American Journal of Psychiatry* 140:1016–19.

Stanley, Alessandra. 2007. "One Man's Survival Story Becomes a Rallying Cry." *New York Times*, February 27.

Starr, Paul. 1973. *The Discarded Army: Veterans after Vietnam*. New York: Charter House.

Starr, Paul. 1973a. "Home from the War: Vietnam Veterans—Neither Victims nor Executioners." *Worldview*, October, 53–55.

Steinberg, Jacques. 2008. "*CNN*'s Reporter Raises Ethical Questions." May, 29, p. 3.

Stone, Martin. 1985. "Shellshock and the Psychologists" pp. 242–271 in W. F. Bynum, Roy Porter, and Michael Shepherd *The Anatomy of Madness*. Cambridge: Tavistock Publications.

Strong, Pauline Turner. 1999. *Captive Selves, Captivating Others: The Politics and Poetics of Colonial American Captivity Narratives*. Boulder, CO: Westview Press.

Sullivan, Ronald. 1989. "Jogger Returns to Limited Work at Salomon." November 30.

Trudeau, G.B. 2005. *The Long Road Home: One Step at a Time*. Kansas City: Andrews McMeel Publishing.

Trudeau, G.B. 2010. *Signature Wound: Rocking TBI*. Kansas City: Andrews McMeel Publishing.

Turse, Nick. 2013. *Kill Anything that Moves*. New York: Metropolitan Books.

Tyson, Ann Scott. 2003. "The Other Battle: Coming Home." *Christian Science Monitor*, July 9.

Urbina, Ian. 2009. "In Ranks of Heroes, Finding the Fakes." *New York Times*, August 2.

United States Senate. 1972. "Oversight of Medical Care of Veterans Wounded in Vietnam." Pp. III–21 to III–36 in Veterans Administration, *The Vietnam Veteran in Contemporary Society*, U.S. Senate.

Verrengia, Joseph B. 2003. "Some Iraq veterans find forgetting the hardest part about killing." Associated Press. April 18.

Watters, Ethan. 2010. "The Americanization of Mental Illness." *New York Times* (Sunday Magazine). January 10.

Wehman, P.H. et al. 1990. "Return to Work for Persons with Traumatic Brain Injury: A Supported Approach." *Archives of Physical Medicine and Rehabilitation Studies*. Vol. 71, No. 13. December.

Weller, Michael. 2008. *Beast*. New York: Michael Weller. December 7 (post-performance draft).

Wells, Tom. 1994. *The War Within: America's Battle over Vietnam*. Berkeley: University of California Press.

Williams, Kayla. 2006. *I Love My Rifle More Than You*. New York: W.W. Norton.

Wilson, John P. 1977. "Identity, Ideology and Crisis: The Vietnam Veterans in Transition, part I." Research Report. Cleveland: Cleveland State University.

Wingo, Hal. 1969. "From GIs in Vietnam, Unexpected Cheers." *Life*, October 24, p. 36.

Wolff, Craig. 1989. "Youths Rape and Beat Central Park Jogger." *New York Times*, April 21.

Woodruff, Lee & Bob. 2007. *In an Instant: A Family's Journey of Love and Healing*. New York: Random House.

Young, Allan. 1997. *The Harmony of Illusions: Inventing Post-traumatic Stress Disorder*. Princeton, NJ: Princeton University Press.

Zoroya, Gregg. 2007. "Veteran stress cases up sharply: Mental Illness is now No. 2 injury." *USA Today*. October 19-21. P. 1.

Zoroya, Gregg. 2009. "Review: GIs at risk by fitness policies." *USA Today*. March 23. P. 1.

Zoroya, Gregg. 2009. "Officials: Troops hurt by brain-injury focus." *USA Today*. April 17.

Zoroya, Gregg. 2012. "Troop brain injuries hit record." *USA Today*. April 12. P. 1.

Filmography

The Activist. 1969. Regional Films.
All Quiet on the Western Front. 1930. U.S.A. Universal.
Alice 's Restaurant. 1969. MGM.
Apocalypse Now. 1979. U.S.A. United Artists-Zoetrope.
The Best Year of Our Lives. 1946. U.S.A. Samuel Goldwyn Company.
Black Sunday. 1977. U.S.A. Paramount.
Blackhawk Down. 2001. U.S.A. Revolution Studios.
Born on the Fourth of July. 1989. U.S.A. Ixtian.
Bus Riley 's Back in Town. 1971. U.S.A. William Thompson International.
The Cabinet of Dr. Caligari. 1920. Germany.
Coming Home. 1978. U.S.A. United Artists.
Deathdream. 1972. Canada. Alpha.
First Blood. 1982. U.S.A. Orion.
From Here to Eternity. 1953. U.S.A. Columbia.
FTA. 1972. U.S.A. Free Theater Associates/Indochina Peace Campaign.
Full Metal Jacket. 1987. U.S.A. Warner Brothers.
Getting Straight. 1970. Columbia
The Green Berets. 1968. U.S.A. Werner Brothers-Seven Arts.

Greetings. 1968. U.S.A. West End Films.

Hamburger Hill. 1987. U.S.A. RKO Pictures.

Jarhead. 2005. U.S.A. Universal.

Johnny Got His Gun. 1971. U.S.A. Cinemation.

Lions for Lambs. 2007. U.S.A. MGM.

The Lively Set. 1964. U.S.A. Universal.

Motor Psycho. 1965. U.S.A. Eve Productions.

Platoon. 1986. U.S.A. Hemdale.

The Revolutionary. 1970. U.S.A. United Artists.

Sands of Iwo Jima. 1949. U.S.A. Republic Pictures.

Science Odyssey: In Search of Ourselves. U.S.A. Public Broadcasting System.

Sir! No Sir! 2005. U.S.A. Displaced Films.

Stop Loss. 2008. Paramount.

Three Kings. 1999. U.S.A.

In the Valley of Elah. 2007. U.S.A. Warner.

The Visitors. 1972. U.S.A. United Artists.

Witness to War. 1985 U.S.A.

Index

Abu Ghraib, 56–58; narcissism revealed at, 57; trophy photographs taken at, 57–58; women in photographs at, 58–59
age of soldiers: British WWI myth and, 124–125; "kids"-at-war and societal image, 202; myth of "nineteen years old", 131–133; nineteen an unlikely average, 123–124; pissing on dead Taliban and, 133–134; soldiers as "kids" otherizes, 125

Babinski, Joseph: shell shock treated by, 78
Barton, Thomas: anti-war efforts impaired by public fixations on PTSD, 24
Beasts: PTSD staged as play, 185–188
Blumenthal, Senator Richard: falsely claims Vietnam veteran status, 45
Boston Globe: series on Iraq War PTSD, 22–24

Cabinet of Dr. Caligari: metaphor for German national trauma in, 84; Zombie veteran of WWI in, 84
Charcot, Jean-Martine, 72; art and photographs used by, 72–75; brain lesions and flashbacks, 121; brain lesions theory of hysteria, 73; model for Dr. Caligari, 84. *See also* railway spine; hysteria

Clements, Charlie, 29, 129; dissent pathologized, 97
Cline, David: anti-war Vietnam veteran, 26
Clinton, Hillary: combat credential claimed by, 46
coffee-house movement: Coffee Strong at Fort Lewis, 25; Different Drummer at Fort Drum, 22; Shelter Half at Fort Lewis, 25; Under the Hood at Fort Hood, 24; Vietnam Era, 22
combat in American imagination, 43; atrocities used to credential combat, 54, 56–59; combat used to credential authority, 45; definitions of combat, 47, 49; false claims of combat, 46, 116–117; image diminished in modern warfare, 59–64; index of, 46–48; Jerry Lembcke and, 46–48; PTSD and combat mutually defined, 49; societal expectations for combat, 50, 63–64; valorization of combat, 44–45

Diagnostic and Statistical Manual (DSM): "flashback" added to, 104; Freudian tradition purged from, 104–105; "gross stress reaction" dropped from, 103; PTSD added to, 103
Doonsbury. See Trudeau
Dozier, Kimberly, 160; anti-Woodruff figure, 163–165; C-SPAN *Book TV* response to Woodruff, 165–169; media

About the Author

Jerry Lembcke authored six books including *The Spitting Image: Myth, Memory, and the Legacy of Vietnam*, *CNN's Tailwind: Inside Vietnam's Last Great Myth* and the most recent, *Hanoi Jane: War, Sex, and Fantasies of Betrayal*. His opinion pieces have appeared in the *Boston Globe*, *San Francisco Chronicle*, *The Chronicle of Higher Education*, and the *National Catholic Reporter*. Jerry has been on several NPR programs including *On the Media*. The 2006 film *Sir! No Sir!* featured his book *The Spitting Image*.

Jerry grew up in Northwest Iowa and received degrees from Augustana College, the University of Northern Colorado, and the University of Oregon.

Jerry was drafted in 1968 and served as a Chaplain's Assistant with the 41st Artillery Group in Vietnam. He is presently Associate Professor of Sociology Emeritus at Holy Cross College in Worcester, Massachusetts.

CPSIA information can be obtained at www.ICGtesting.com
Printed in the USA
BVOW07*1841090814

362100BV00002B/5/P